"Let It Burn!"
The Philadelphia Tragedy

"Let It Burn!"
The Philadelphia Tragedy

MICHAEL BOYETTE
with Randi Boyette

CB
CONTEMPORARY
BOOKS
CHICAGO · NEW YORK

Library of Congress Cataloging-in-Publication Data

Boyette, Michael.
  "Let it burn!"

    Includes index.
    1. MOVE (Organization)   2. Black nationalism—
Pennsylvania—Philadelphia.   3. Afro-Americans—
Pennsylvania—Philadelphia.   4. Philadelphia (Pa.)—
Race relations.   I. Boyette, Randi.   II. Title.
F158.9.N4B69   1989   974.8'1100496073   89-9844
ISBN 0-8092-4543-4

Published by Contemporary Books, Inc.
180 North Michigan Avenue, Chicago, Illinois 60601
Manufactured in the United States of America
Library of Congress Catalog Card Number: 89-9844
International Standard Book Number: 0-8092-4543-4

Published simultaneously in Canada by Beaverbooks, Ltd.
195 Allstate Parkway, Valleywood Business Park
Markham, Ontario L3R 4T8 Canada

This book is dedicated to the memory of Reuben Pearl,
whom we honor as a writer and as our zayda.
The world is less without him.

Contents

Acknowledgments

WE ARE DEEPLY GRATEFUL to the many people who have helped us write this book. They are far too numerous to name, but we would like to take special note of those who shared their thoughts, insights, and experiences with us, especially Alberta Africa, Jerry Africa, Jim Berghaier, Tommy Mellor, Russ Johnson, and Mark Gottlieb. We also acknowledge David Weinberg of Temple University's Urban Archives Center for his help in tracking down photos and guiding us through the vast MOVE Commission files, and Wayne Bush of the *Philadelphia Daily News* for his assistance in helping us find the photographs we needed. Also, we thank our family and friends for their support and interest, especially those who baby-sat while we worked: Miriam and Fred Mayberry, Bea and Paul Boyette, Karen and Michael Joseph, Mark Chilnick, and Toby Mosko. We are grateful to Joel Ostroff for serving as photographer and sounding board; to G. C. Skipper for his understanding and patience; to Herb Chilnick for leading us to Larry; to Larry Chilnick for taking a chance on an unknown writer; to our agent, Ned Leavitt, for insisting that we rewrite the proposal three times, for his skills as an editor, and for his persistence in finding a home for this book; and to our editor, Bernard Shir-Cliff, whose enthusiasm kept us going during the long months when it seemed the book would never be done. And most of all, we thank our children: Joshua and Sarah, who good-naturedly accepted the postponement of vacations and outings, and our youngest son, Daniel, who assisted immeasurably by sleeping through the night.

Author's Note

IN THE SUMMER OF 1986 I was chosen to serve on a Philadelphia grand jury investigating the worst fire in the city's history. What I saw and heard during my two-year service on the grand jury prompted me to investigate as fully as I could the circumstances that are related in this book.

In the interests of fairness—and to avoid going to jail—I must, however, explain how this book was written. The grand jury met in secret, and the jurors are under an oath to keep the proceedings secret. This book does not violate that oath. Virtually all of the evidence we heard and saw—the transcripts of the months of testimony and the dozens of pieces of physical evidence that were presented to us—is sealed by the court. The only public statement of the grand jury consists of a 279-page report issued in May 1988.

Because I am bound by the grand jury's oath of secrecy, I have taken special pains to report only those facts that have become available from public sources. The most important of these sources are the files of the MOVE Commission, and I have relied on them extensively—though sometimes with a grain of salt.

In addition to the reports of the grand jury and the MOVE Commission, my coauthor and I have consulted countless newspaper and magazine articles. We also conducted our own independent interviews with key figures in this story who were willing to talk to us.

Finally, I wish to point out that though this story is reconstructed, it is not a dramatization or an embellishment. Every event related here actually happened or reasonably can be inferred from the evidence we collected. The dialogue is based on the actual recollections of those involved and is taken verbatim from public testimony, police reports, and other documented sources. I have tried to point out those parts of the story that are open to dispute and to present conflicting interpretations fairly.

—Michael Boyette
March 1989

Overview of Neighborhood

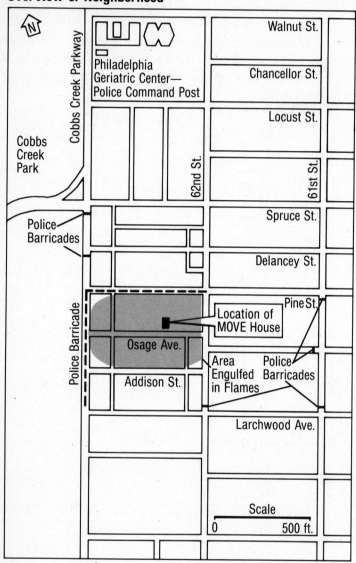

Enlargement of Screened Area

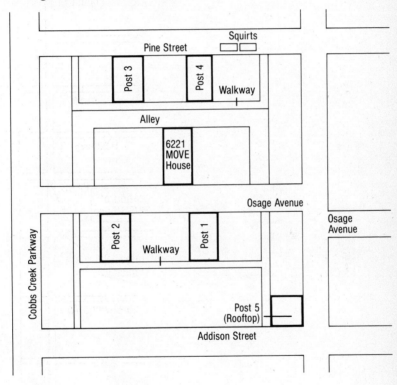

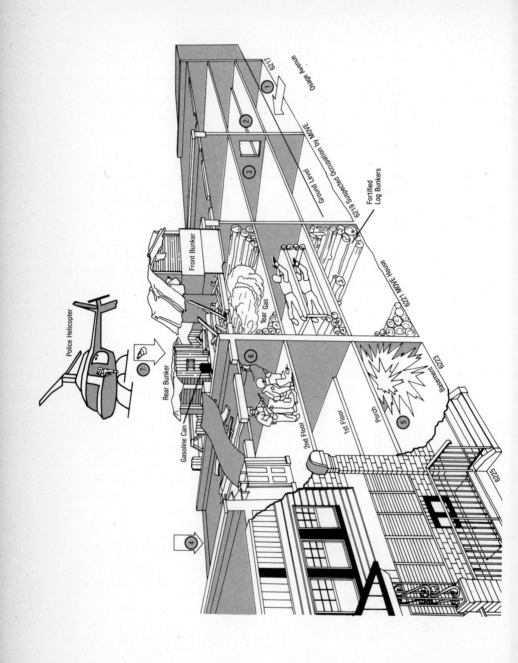

The MOVE confrontation

1—Police enter 6217 Osage Avenue on the morning of May 13. Team B planned to enter 6219 and pump tear gas through the wall into the MOVE house (6221 Osage).

2—Inside 6217, Team B sets off a hatch charge through the wall of the sun porch.

3—Sergeant Ed Connor tries to enter 6219 Osage and is hit by a hail of gunfire from the fortified bunker within the front porch of the MOVE house.

4—At the same time, Team A entered the rear of 6223 Osage.

5—Team A first tried to blow a hole through the cellar wall but was unsuccessful.

6—The team then made its way to the second floor. After several attempts, the police were able to pump tear gas into the MOVE house. After gunfire exploded through the walls, the police took cover in a closet in the upstairs bedroom.

7—In the evening, after the first assaults failed to drive MOVE members out of the house, Lieutenant Frank Powell dropped an explosive charge from a state police helicopter, intending to knock down the front bunker and blow a hole in the roof through which an assault team could insert tear gas into the house. The explosion touched off the fire that destroyed the MOVE house and the surrounding neighborhood.

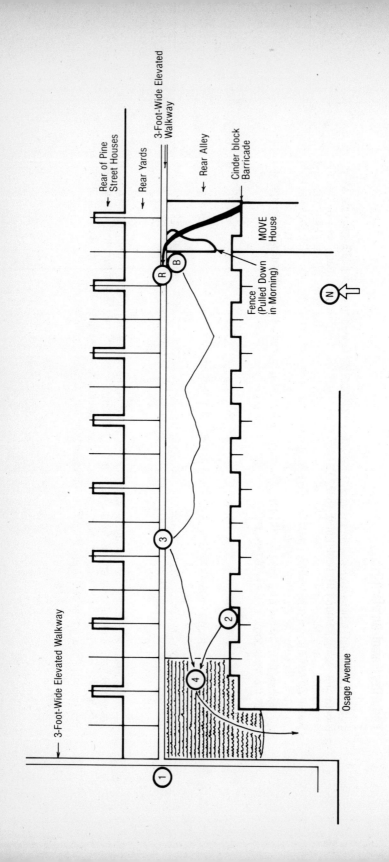

Rear of Pine Street Houses

Rear Yards

3-Foot-Wide Elevated Walkway

Rear Alley

Cinder block Barricade

MOVE House

Fence (Pulled Down in Morning)

3-Foot-Wide Elevated Walkway

Osage Avenue

N

R

B

1

2

3

4

The Rescue of Birdie Africa

Birdie, Ramona, other MOVE children, and at least one other adult emerged into the alley behind the MOVE house (far right). Ramona (R) began to walk down the elevated walkway as Birdie (B) made his way through the flames in the alley. As Officer Mellor (1) took up a position at the end of the alley, Officers Berghaier and Tursi moved into the alley (2) and waited for Birdie to reach them. Halfway down the alley (3), Ramona tried to lift Birdie onto the elevated walkway, but he fell back, striking his head on the concrete. Dazed, he stumbled past Tursi and Berghaier and began to fall into the chest-deep pool of water that had collected at the low end of the alley (4). Mellor and Tursi watched for snipers from their positions as Berghaier ran into the pool of water and pulled him around the corner and out of the alley.

Cast of Characters

THE 1978 CONFRONTATION

Frank L. Rizzo, mayor of Philadelphia.
Joseph F. O'Neill, police commissioner.
George Fencl, inspector, police department.
James J. Ramp, member of the stakeout unit; killed August 8, 1978.

THE 1985 CONFRONTATION

The City

W. Wilson Goode, mayor of Philadelphia. Elected 1983; reelected in narrow victory over former mayor Frank Rizzo in 1987.
Leo A. Brooks, retired U.S. Army general, managing director of the city of Philadelphia, 1983–1985.
Gregore J. Sambor, Philadelphia police commissioner, 1983–1985.
William C. Richmond, Philadelphia fire commissioner, 1979–1988.
Frank J. Scipione, deputy fire commissioner.
Lucien Blackwell, city commissioner.

The Cops

Sergeant Donald Griffiths, commander of Post 4. The MOVE Commission hinted—erroneously—that Griffiths may have fired on people who were trying to escape the burning house.

1

Markus Barianna, stakeout officer assigned, with Griffiths, to Post 4.

William Trudel, stakeout officer assigned, with Griffiths, to Post 4.

John LaCon, stakeout officer assigned to Post 2. Narrowly missed being killed by a bullet that cracked his riot helmet and grazed his neck.

Detective William Stephenson, self-appointed observer of the May 13 confrontation; his testimony was key to the MOVE Commission's findings that police gunfire drove MOVE members back into the burning house.

Michael Tursi, stakeout officer. Principal author of the assault plan used on May 13.

Sergeant Albert Revel, coauthor of the assault plan.

Captain Richard Kirchner, commander of the stakeout unit, who favored a frontal assault on the house.

Herbert Kirk, retired police sergeant who developed the original assault plan in 1984, on which the final plan was based.

Lieutenant Frank Powell, acting commander of the bomb squad; coauthor of the assault plan and commander of Insertion Team A.

James Berghaier, member of stakeout unit; assigned to Team A.

Lawrence D'Ulisse, member of stakeout unit; assigned to Team A.

Raymond Graham, member of the stakeout unit; assigned to Team A.

William Klein, member of the bomb squad; assigned to Team A.

James Laarkamp, member of bomb squad; assigned to Team A.

Charles ("Tommy") Mellor, member of stakeout unit; assigned to Team A.

Terrence Patrick Mulvihill, member of stakeout unit; assigned to Team A. One of the officers identified by witnesses in the beating of Delbert Africa during the 1978 confrontation; acquitted during a jury trial.

John Reiber, member of stakeout unit; assigned to Team A.

Sergeant Ed Connor, member of the bomb squad;
    commander of Insertion Team B.
Daniel Angelucci, member of the bomb squad; assigned to
    Team B.
Alexander Draft, member of the stakeout unit; assigned to
    Team B.
Marshall ("Jesse") Freer, member of the stakeout unit;
    assigned to Team B.
Salvatore Marsalo, member of the stakeout unit; assigned to
    Team B.
James Muldowney, member of the bomb squad; assigned to
    Team B.
Michael Ryan, member of the stakeout unit; assigned to
    Team B.

Others

Michael Macy, FBI agent and liaison with the Philadelphia
    bomb squad; delivered a large quantity of C-4 plastic
    explosives to the bomb squad in December 1984.
Clifford Bond, leader of the neighbors' delegation to the city.

MOVE Members
Died May 13, 1985

Vincent Leaphart Africa. Died at age fifty-four. Nearly
    everyone agrees that he was John Africa, the founder of
    MOVE, but the organization will not say whether they
    were the same man.
Raymond Foster Africa. Died at age fifty. MOVE member
    since the early 1970s.
Conrad Hampton Africa. Died at age thirty-six. An early
    MOVE member.
Frank James Africa. Died at age twenty-six. Nephew of
    Vincent Leaphart Africa and son of Louise James, he was
    acknowledged to be the man closest to Vincent.
Rhonda Harris Ward Africa. Died at age thirty. The mother
    of Birdie Africa (Michael Moses Ward), one of the two
    survivors of the fire.
Theresa Brooks Africa. Died at age twenty-six. Joined
    MOVE in approximately 1980.

Katricia Dotson Africa ("Tree"). Died at age fifteen.
Daughter of Consuella Dotson Africa.
Zanetta Dotson Africa. Died at age thirteen. Katricia's
younger sister.
Phil Phillips Africa. Died at age twelve. Son of Janine
Phillips Africa and William Phillips Africa.
Delitia Orr Africa. Died at age twelve. Daughter of Delbert
Orr Africa and Janet Holloway Africa.
Tomaso Levino Africa. Died at age nine. Son of Sue Levino
Africa.

Survivors of the Fire

Ramona Johnson Africa. MOVE member since approximately
1980.
Birdie Africa, age thirteen in 1985. Now known as Michael
Moses Ward, he lives with his father and stepmother in a
suburb of Philadelphia.

Imprisoned for the Murder of Officer James Ramp

Delbert Orr Africa
Janet Holloway Africa
Edward Goodman Africa
Cassandra Davis Africa
Michael Davis Africa
Debbie Sims Africa
Janine Phillips Africa
William Phillips Africa
Charles Sims Africa ("Chuckie")
Consuella Dotson Africa
Merle Austin Africa

Imprisoned on Other Charges

Alphonso Robbins Africa
Sue Levino Africa
Carlos Perez Africa
Dennis Sims (no longer a MOVE member)

Other MOVE Members

Gerald Ford Africa, minister of information.

Alberta Wicker Africa, practicing naturalist, widow of Vincent Leaphart Africa; in prison on the day of the fire in 1985.

MOVE Supporters, Sympathizers, and Former Members

Donald Glassey, cofounder of MOVE. Became an FBI informant in the early days of MOVE in exchange for dismissal of charges against him.

Louise James, older sister of Vincent Leaphart Africa and mother of Frank James Africa; former MOVE member; owner of the MOVE house, 6221 Osage Avenue.

LaVerne Sims, younger sister of Louise James and Vincent Leaphart Africa; mother of Debbie Sims Africa, Charles Sims Africa, Dennis Sims, Gail Sims, and Sharon Sims Cox. Ex-MOVE member.

Sharon Sims Cox, ex-MOVE member, daughter of LaVerne.

Gail Sims, Sharon's sister; ex-MOVE member.

Jeanne Champagne, ex-MOVE member; testified against Vincent Leaphart at his trial.

The MOVE Commission

William H. Brown III, Chairman
Henry S. Ruth, Jr.
Charles W. Bowser
Rev. Msgr. Edward P. Cullen
Neil J. Welch
M. Todd Cooke
Bruce W. Kauffman
Julia M. Chinn
Rev. Paul M. Washington
Charisse Ranielle Lillie
Rev. Audrey F. Bronson

The Prosecutors

Ron Castille, Philadelphia district attorney, 1986–present.
Edward Rendell, Philadelphia district attorney, 1975–1986.
Mark Gottlieb, chief prosecutor for the special investigating grand jury.

Prologue
The Sierra Club with Guns

IN THE WINTER OF 1978, after a roundabout series of events and false starts that had left me wondering whether there was life after college, I found myself living in Philadelphia. I was there simply because I had some friends who were there and because my summer job was over and I didn't want to move back home.

After a number of brief housing adventures I took a room in a heavy-gabled Victorian row house in west Philadelphia. More than one person had suggested that it would be a good place for a guy like me to live—a remark that may have been prompted by the length of my hair, my employment status, or perhaps just my general air of confusion.

Whatever the reason, it seemed they were right. West Philadelphia was then—and is today—a vast, loosely knit collection of old neighborhoods, full of beat-up cars, shaded streets, graffiti-covered buildings, and old houses in various states of disrepair.

A hundred years ago it was the most fashionable part of the city—an early suburb, a tranquil place on the outskirts of town where the well-to-do could raise their families away from the noise and crowds of downtown Philadelphia.

Although the rambling houses are still there, the genteel suburbs have long ago moved beyond west Philadelphia, and it has become a place where Ivy League students from the University of Pennsylvania and clean-cut engineering majors from Drexel University rub shoulders with blacks, Indians, Orientals, and other ethnic peoples. It is a place in perpetual ferment, an oddball version of the American melting pot.

The house I shared, for example, still had the wine cellar, butler's pantry, and carved black-walnut mantelpiece. A psychology professor had bought it and lived on the first floor. On the third floor was a sweet-tempered young woman who would disappear for days at a time, leaving her pregnant poodle unfed and unwalked. I lived on the second floor, as did a severe-looking German graduate student who had spent time in a number of communes out west, who hated the dog, and who communicated with the rest of us through ill-tempered Teutonic notes posted on doorways and kitchen appliances: "Who took my milk????" "Dog must go!"

The house next door was boarded up, and beyond that were several where young men of the neighborhood seemed to spend a lot of time. Around the corner my friends lived in a house of college kids who billed themselves as "leftists, artists, and liberals" and who could never agree whether a guy and girl who lived in one room should count as one share or two shares when it came time to divide up the rent.

It was a part of the city where those of us who didn't quite fit in somehow managed to find one another. The Moonies had a house nearby—a fact that I learned the hard way. Buckminster Fuller's office was a few blocks away, on the edge of the Penn campus. There was the New Solidarity Book Store, where you could buy the Socialist Worker party's *Militant* (but not the Socialist Labor party's *Weekly People*).

But of all the curiosities that I found among my new neighbors that winter, one was so strange that even in west Philadelphia it verged on the unbelievable. For in the neighborhood called Powelton Village, just a dozen blocks from the newsroom of the venerable *Philadelphia Bulletin* and within earshot of the classrooms of Drexel University, the Philadelphia Police Department had placed a house under siege.

The siege was the first time I had ever heard of MOVE. I didn't know then that the conflict had already been going on for nearly a year. What I read in the paper was that a group of armed black radicals had refused to vacate their headquarters and that Mayor Frank Rizzo had responded by cutting off all food, water, and utilities to the house—and had vowed to starve them out. The police, I learned, were already cordoning off the entire block.

I was, of course, outraged. But I was also curious. So, on a harsh, clear winter night, my future wife, Randi, and I walked to Powelton to see for ourselves what a siege looks like. We moved through dark streets that the biting wind had emptied of people, heads down, our frozen feet shuffling forward through the dozen or so blocks between my house and the MOVE house.

Finally we saw icy blue light at the end of the street, with dark silhouettes moving to and fro. As we got nearer it was as if we'd entered a Nazi nightmare: we saw harsh bright klieg lights, glittering concertina wire etched against the blackness, and cops in high boots, heavy leather jackets, and black peaked caps, some on horseback, some simply leaning against telephone poles, trading gossip and smoking cigarettes.

We could not see the house in the darkness beyond the lights, but we knew it was back there, in the middle of the block, surrounded by a garrison of police and completely cut off from the outside world. We could almost sense eyes in the night, watching everything from the house.

Randi and I stood huddled together in the cold for a time, until a cop broke away from his buddies and came over to hustle us along. As we walked back home I had the sense that what we had seen—the rifles and the riot helmets and horses and barbed wire—was somehow not real. It all seemed staged. The cops had been too relaxed, the night too quiet. It was as if everyone knew that sooner or later someone would get tired of the game or cooler heads would prevail.

In the days that followed, MOVE was in the news and on our minds. I began to learn more about them. They were a group of mostly black radicals, armed with automatic rifles and threatening to kill any cop who came into the house. But their agenda didn't seem political; their rhetoric seemed to have more in common with the Sierra Club than the Black Panthers. They were, a newspaper reported, a "back-to-nature" group. They did not use heat or electricity. They did not eat cooked or processed foods. They did not cut their hair. They believed in "natural law" and rejected technology. They all took the last name "Africa."

All of that was familiar enough to me. In those days you could find just about any brand of prophecy or protest that suited your fancy: Hare Krishna, Jesus freaks, the Guru Maharaj Ji, Moonies, the Christ Amen people (an itinerant band of mystics who dressed in biblical robes and rejected "killing, sex, and materialism"—though not tobacco); doomsayers and soothsayers of every persuasion. Often their ideas had a certain appeal, though you couldn't always say the same about their cooking.

In many ways MOVE sounded like just another band of dreamy-eyed people who had come together around a leader with a good rap and plenty of answers. But as I heard more about them I learned that there were some big differences.

First, of course, there were the guns. For most of these groups the battle against evil was waged with words and the warriors seemed gentle—defenseless, in fact. To them there were no enemies, only people who hadn't seen the light. Even the skinny young men and women of the radical left, for all their talk of revolution, never seemed very threatening to the system. And the system, in turn, mostly ignored them.

But MOVE had guns. Before the blockade went up, there were news photos showing MOVE members on the platform in front of their home and on the streets with rifles in hand. That was a confrontation that the system could not ignore.

There were other strange things I heard, too. There was talk of their having a dead baby in the house, which they refused to bury. It was said that they threw raw meat out of the house to feed the rats and stray dogs. The people in the house, it was said, scattered their waste in the yard.

All of that left me with mixed emotions. On the one hand I admired their commitment. It was a refreshing contrast to my own halfhearted radicalism, which was compromised by my dependence on food stamps and an affection for such benefits of the modern military industrial state as air-conditioning and good electronic equipment. On the other hand I was troubled by people who believe in *anything* too strongly; history is full of lessons about the dangers of excess enthusiasm.

At the time all of that was overshadowed by the simple facts that the mayor of an American city had publicly stated his intention to deny food and water to a group of people—

including children—until they submitted to his authority and
that the courts and the citizens were permitting him to do so.

The siege went on, but after a few weeks it had faded into
the background. Occasionally a news story or a picture would
appear in the paper, but usually on an inside page. Like what I
had felt outside the house, there was a sense in Philadelphia
that sooner or later the city or MOVE would grow tired of the
game and quit.

The killing winter of 1978 finally, grudgingly, yielded to
spring. Randi finished her semester at school, and we started
growing restless for new scenery. We sold most of what we
owned and took a bus to California. I found a job. We rented a
little apartment in Oakland, and Randi enrolled in school. Life
settled down a little.

One morning in August, on my way to catch the bus, I saw a
front-page story about MOVE in the *San Francisco Chronicle*.
In the grainy news photo I could see riot-helmeted police
officers scrambling for cover on a west Philadelphia street.
One had been killed and several others injured, I read. The
city had assaulted the house in the early morning hours, and
gunfire had erupted. The MOVE people were in jail on murder
charges; the house had been razed.

The following year Randi and I moved back to Philadelphia.
By then the furor over MOVE had died down almost completely. I didn't think much about it except when I read an
occasional news report about their trials. Years passed, and
when I thought of them at all I assumed they had ended up
like the Weathermen or the Symbionese Liberation Army,
disbanded except for a stubborn few who wouldn't give up the
ghost.

By 1985 things had changed considerably for me since my
days in west Philadelphia. Randi was pregnant with our second
child. We were trying to put away money for a house. When
the television stations started reporting that MOVE was building a fortified bunker on a rooftop in west Philadelphia, I was
surprised to hear the group was still around.

On May 13 of that year, my first full day back at work after
my daughter was born, I half-listened to the intermittent
reports about the police assault on the MOVE house at 6221

Osage Avenue. None of it seemed to be making much sense—there had been shooting early in the morning, and a number of explosions, and then, toward afternoon, the news just dried up, and no one seemed to know just what was going on.

When I got home, sometime close to six o'clock, Randi was watching the television. "You won't believe what's happening out there," she said. "They dropped a bomb on the house, and now it's on fire."

I looked at the television with the same feeling I'd had at the blockade in 1978—that feeling of unreality, the sense that events such as these could not happen on a warm spring day in Philadelphia.

All that night the bulletins continued to come in from Osage Avenue. The fire had spread to the other houses on the block. It had jumped to neighboring blocks. A woman and a child had escaped the house. The others—nobody knew how many—were still inside, surely dead. By the time we went to bed, around midnight, the houses were still on fire.

The next morning, the block was gone—utterly and totally annihilated. On television we could see weary reporters standing in the early morning sunlight before the remains of scorched and blackened walls and piles of smoldering rubble.

Sixty-one families had been left homeless. Everything they owned—every graduation picture, every family heirloom, every piece of clothing except for what they were wearing had been incinerated. Somewhere within lay those who had not escaped the fire. Already police crews were sifting through the still-hot embers, looking for bodies. The fire had destroyed everything so thoroughly that we wondered whether it would be possible to find any remains at all.

That day, gray and overcast, seemed as endless as it was senseless. City officials appearing on television said little. Slack-jawed, they seemed stunned by the enormity of what they had done and offered halting and contradictory explanations of what had gone wrong the day before on Osage Avenue.

Over the months that followed, the events of May 13 dominated the Philadelphia media. Piece by piece the story of what had happened and how it had managed to go so wrong began to emerge. Before it was over the police commissioner and managing director of the city would resign and the mayor would appoint a special commission to examine the entire incident—including the role of the mayor himself. A police cover-up related to the incident was suggested, and theories about what had happened ranged from incompetence to outright murder.

Eventually the commission issued a report that criticized the mayor and his subordinates, charged that police gunfire had prevented people from escaping the house, and recommended that a grand jury be convened to look into criminal charges against police officers and city officials.

Not long afterward a stranger stopped me as I walked out my front door and served me with a summons. That was the beginning of my reacquaintance with the MOVE organization. Out of three hundred potential jurors who had received summonses, I was chosen along with twenty-nine other Philadelphia citizens to sit on the grand jury. Over the next two years the jury sat for two days a week as the district attorney's office brought dozens of witnesses before us.

And so I became a part of this story in a way that I never would have expected. I had begun as a witness. In the end I was chosen to sit in judgment.

This story has moved in and out of my life for ten years now. Like a stray dog, it has somehow cut me out of the herd and attached itself to me, insisting almost against my will that I listen.

The people of MOVE would probably say that this is not a coincidence, that it is part of a larger purpose that governs all events. As for myself, I am struck by the fact that my relationship with this story seems to be tied up with beginnings and endings. The time I spent in west Philadelphia was a turning point in my own life, an interlude between school and life when I was desperately trying to figure out where I was headed. Years later my daughter was born a week before the 1985 assault. My wife went into labor with my younger son, Daniel, during the final deliberations of the grand jury.

During our research for this book Randi and I arranged to meet with Alberta Wicker Africa, the woman who some say is now the leader of the MOVE organization. We agreed to rendezvous in a small park in west Philadelphia.

When we arrived there, Randi and I realized that we had been in the park once before, when we were still living in west Philadelphia. It had been the first warm day of spring, and we'd sat on the hillside, watching neighborhood dogs run around in a large, exuberant pack. We were already making plans to leave, to start a new chapter in our lives.

The park had not changed at all. As we sat there, talking with Alberta, I felt as if I'd picked up a book that I had once started and then put away. In the ten years that had passed, so much had happened to us, to MOVE, and to Philadelphia. We had our three kids and our house and careers. Alberta had spent most of those ten years in prison. Her husband and many of her closest friends had died in the fire of May 13. Most of the others were still behind bars. And yet somehow fate had brought us back to this tiny, tree-filled park—almost as if by design, to tie up some loose ends.

Alberta spoke of life and death as cycles, revolving in half-seen rhythms. This story, it seems, moves in long cycles of its own. Its origins are fuzzy—almost mythical. Its ending is still unclear. It is an odd story, and I am not sure at all what the moral is. It is a story that revolved around the events of May 13, 1985, and an act that would destroy a neighborhood and sear a city.

That is a good place to begin.

1
The Bomb

THERE ARE NIGHTS WHEN Frank Powell still sees the bomb drop, when he watches it plummet past his feet and through the warm spring air. Sometimes it hits the bunker and explodes; sometimes it lands on the roof. Occasionally it misses the roof entirely and is swept off into oblivion. Some nights it contains two pounds of explosives; other nights there are ten pounds or a hundred. And when he wakes up, he realizes that it was just the dream coming back again.

But it was more than a dream. When it was all over, Lieutenant Frank Powell, the acting commander of the police bomb squad, a supervisor who was known for always doing things by the book, would be remembered for this single desperate act. He would be remembered as the man who dropped the bomb.

The scene would be replayed again and again, on television sets in Philadelphia and throughout the world: the helicopter hovering forty-five feet above the tiny row house, the lone figure of Powell leaning out of its open hatch; the bag dropping toward the roof; the long seconds of silence followed by the explosion—a bright orange ball of flame, a hailstorm of lumber and debris, a slowly clearing cloud of dust.

And then wisps of white smoke, wafting silently into the blue afternoon sky.

When the explosion came, Philadelphia Fire Commissioner William Richmond was crouching beside his second-in-command in a doorway half a block east of the bunker. Though it seemed as if half the fire department was out here in west Philadelphia, he really hadn't had much to do all day. This

14

was a police operation, and his men were taking their orders directly from the cops on the scene. At this very moment he could have been finishing up at the office and preparing to brave the evening rush hour—except for the fact that he had a promise to keep.

When the first rumors of a police operation against MOVE had begun to circulate the week before, the head of the fire fighters' union had stopped by Richmond's office. He reminded Richmond of what had happened in 1978, when two fire fighters had been shot during a similar confrontation. A lot of people had felt that fire fighters had been doing police work in 1978, that they never should have been in the line of fire. He wanted to make sure the same thing didn't happen this time.

Bill Richmond agreed with him a hundred percent. He'd watched his men risk their lives virtually every day. He'd once seen a fireman jump into a tree from a second-story window, clutching a screaming baby under one arm. He'd visited his men lying in hospitals, their lungs ravaged by smoke and heat. And more than once he'd seen the black bunting hanging from fire stations throughout the city, mourning men who'd died on duty.

That was part of a fireman's job. But it wasn't part of the job to be ducking bullets. Richmond wasn't about to have his men risk their lives in a fight that wasn't their own. And so when the union man came to see him, Richmond made him a promise. As long as there were firemen out at Osage Avenue, he'd be there, too, seeing to their safety.

Now, as he peered through the dust and saw to his utter amazement that the bunker was intact, he knew that he and his men still had a very long day ahead of them. And as if that wasn't enough, he now heard the deputy commissioner's voice in his ear, saying, "Chief, it looks like we've got a fire up there."

The time was approximately 5:45 P.M., May 13, 1985.

For nearly twenty-four hours Clifford Bond had been standing with his neighbors at a police barricade three blocks north of Osage Avenue. The night before—the evening of Mother's

Day—policemen in blue fatigues had knocked on his door and
herded him and his family down their narrow street and
beyond the police barricades. The Bonds had taken literally
nothing with them but the clothes on their backs. There wasn't
time, the police had said—and besides, they'd promised, everyone would be back in their homes by late morning.

But morning had come and gone. And as the day wore on
and the sounds of explosions and gunfire clattered through the
air, the neighbors had instinctively pressed around Bond,
asking for news, suggesting that he try to meet with the mayor.

In the months before the confrontation, as the neighbors
had tried to get the city to do something about the rotten meat
strewn in the alley behind their homes, about the rats and stray
dogs that congregated around the MOVE house, Bond had
reluctantly emerged as their spokesman and leader. In the last
year he'd led a delegation of neighbors to half a dozen meetings in City Hall, only to be told by the mayor that the city had
no legal basis on which to take action against MOVE.

It had been his idea in late April to hold a news conference,
publicly calling on Governor Dick Thornburgh to help them
where the city had not. Before MOVE had invaded his neighborhood, Bond had never known or cared much about politics.
But after months of getting nowhere with the city he'd begun
to learn, and he figured that the Republican governor wouldn't
pass up the chance to score some public relations points at the
expense of Philadelphia's Democratic mayor.

The news conference, which the neighbors had held just two
weeks ago, had been a success. People learned that armed men
were building a fortress in a quiet working-class neighborhood
in Philadelphia. One photo appeared in the *Philadelphia Inquirer* and in newspapers around the world. It showed a
MOVE member, his muscular body naked to the waist and his
face hidden by dreadlocks, using a rope to haul a can of
gasoline onto the roof of 6221 Osage Avenue.

The news reports had accomplished what the neighbors'
delegations to City Hall had not. The city had moved with a
swiftness that had astonished Bond, as the mayor sought to
prove that he was still in charge. Bond had met with the mayor

just days before, and yet he'd learned nothing of the city's plans until the knock had come on his door the night before. Even now he had no idea what was happening on Osage Avenue. But as he saw the smoke begin to rise from the street, he felt the knot in his belly twist even tighter, and he began to wonder—not for the first time—whether the city knew what it was doing.

At nearly the same instant, Police Commissioner Gregore Sambor was moving closer to the sandbags inside 6218 Osage Avenue, keeping his head low. It was an uncharacteristic pose for Sambor; he was the sort of man who always seemed to be standing at attention, even when he was sitting down. But by now his formal manner was gone and his mind was focused entirely on getting a better view of the smoke rising from the house across the street.

Here in his command post, he was just fifty feet from the MOVE house—close enough that he could have carried on a conversation with someone in the bunker. But Commissioner Sambor wasn't there to talk. He'd made his speech early that morning. It hadn't been a fancy piece of talking, but then he'd never claimed to be a politician. He was just a cop, and ever since he'd started as a foot patrolman in north Philadelphia thirty-seven years ago that was all he'd been.

Of course being police commissioner wasn't just an ordinary job. It put you in the public eye—and in the hot seat from time to time. In just this last year Sambor had already had to deal with a few scandals in the department. First the FBI had uncovered a bribery and shakedown operation involving dozens of cops and sent a top-ranking member of his administration to jail. Then the papers had run a series of articles about K-9 dogs attacking innocent citizens.

Throughout those difficult times no one had questioned Sambor's personal reputation for honesty and decency. As a young man he'd studied for the priesthood, and people still called him Father Gregory. Every Sunday he helped give Communion at St. Timothy's Church, in the blue-collar district of the city called Wissinoming.

Though the commissioner's integrity was never called into

question during the scandals, his ability to lead the department was. People said that he wasn't one to stick his neck out by trying anything new. Others, less charitable, said the problem wasn't with his neck; it was a little farther up.

Not that he wasn't book-smart. Over the years he'd passed the advancement exams and risen steadily through the ranks. Along the way he'd gone to night school, earning first a bachelor's degree, then a master's. He'd even completed the coursework for a Ph.D. in police administration, though he hadn't written his dissertation.

Despite the academic credentials, Sambor never seemed to have the street savvy that others would bring to the commissioner's job. There was a story in the department that in the early 1970s, when Frank Rizzo was still police commissioner, Rizzo had permanently assigned Sambor to night patrol—a graveyard-shift detail with little authority—because he didn't think Sambor could handle making real decisions. That, some said, was how Sambor managed to get all those degrees—by studying all night while he was working.

But even those who didn't like Sambor granted him a certain dogged persistence. The oldest of eight children, he'd been orphaned as a child and had managed to keep his brothers and sisters together, working to keep them fed and housed. He'd been a bookkeeper before he joined the force in 1947. Over the next thirty years he'd scored well enough on police examinations to advance through the ranks; by the late 1970s he headed the police academy—an assignment that also put him in charge of the pistol range and the bomb squad. In 1981 the new mayor had named him to succeed departing Police Commissioner Morton Solomon.

Perhaps because of his background in the seminary, Sambor had a love for tradition and authority. The department had an official police commissioner's uniform—a comical-looking anachronism that resembled the uniform of a Paris traffic cop—but before Sambor became commissioner no one had worn the costume for thirty or forty years, preferring business suits and ties. But Sambor wore it every chance he got—never realizing, apparently, that people would snicker whenever he entered a room.

More than anything else, though, Greg Sambor was a world-class bureaucrat. He'd survived more than three decades of department politics and infighting, and in the end it wasn't easy to say whether it had been Sambor or the bureaucracy that had emerged the victor. Nobody expected him to shake up the department; they'd figured he would simply let things go along as they always had.

And so there was an irony in the fact that when the Philadelphia Police Department faced its most difficult crisis, a crisis that could be found in no textbook or manual, Gregore Sambor was the man in charge. Today Sambor was up against something that he'd never encountered before. Three of his men had already been wounded by bullets—none seriously, thank God. The houses on either side of the MOVE compound had been destroyed by explosions and gunfire. There were rumors that MOVE had tunnels running under the streets and into the sewers. Night would fall in another hour or so. And that goddamned bunker still sat on top of the house, commanding the high ground and paralyzing the Philadelphia Police Department.

Now, as the flames burned down through the splintered debris and began to lick at the black tar paper of the MOVE house's roof, the smoke turned black and thick. In the bedroom of a house on Sixty-second Street, just above the doorway where Commissioner Richmond had been crouching when the bomb exploded, Channel 10 news cameraman Pete Kane was watching the rising flames with disbelief. Unknown to the cops on the street below, he'd been hiding in the house for more than twenty-four hours, filming the confrontation. The night before, he'd captured images of the police quietly moving into rooftop positions. Later he'd filmed the confrontation at dawn—the thick screen of smoke that obscured the street, the first rounds of gunfire, the return bursts of automatic gunfire from the police positions—and all through the long, still afternoon, when the only sound was the steady hum of compressors from the fire engines, he'd filmed the scene intermittently.

Philadelphia had seen none of this footage, for Kane had no

way of getting his tapes out of the house without revealing himself to the police. But he had phoned in live reports during the day. Now, as the smoke obscured the setting sun, he picked up the phone and dialed the newsroom of Channel 10. An engineer flipped a switch, and Pete Kane was on the air.

"I see a lot of black smoke," he reported. "It's very thick, and there are flames shooting from the roof area of either the neighbor's house or the MOVE house. . . . It's spreading, Larry. Several of the houses are on fire right now."

It was 5:50 P.M.

Across town, in a complex of offices on the second floor of City Hall, Mayor Wilson Goode was watching the Channel 10 news. He was quiet—"pensive," his press secretary would say later—as he often was when he was away from the glaring television lights and rapid-fire questioning of reporters.

At this moment he'd reached a crossroads in a political career that had seemed charmed. In 1983 he'd defeated former mayor Frank Rizzo in a bitter primary election and then won a three-way race to become Philadelphia's first black mayor. That triumph, along with the self-assured style he'd shown as he took charge of the city government, made him a man to be watched, not only in Philadelphia but on the national scene as well. The year before, Walter Mondale had even invited him to Washington to talk about being his running mate.

The mayoral primary that had propelled Goode into the political spotlight had been a study in contrasts. His opponent, Frank Rizzo, stood for old-style Philadelphia politics; he was the kind of glad-handing, deal-making, podium-pounding populist that seemed embarrassing in these modern times. His years as mayor from 1971 to 1979 had been tumultuous, seasoned with scandal and charges of police brutality and racism.

Goode's style was one of cool efficiency. As managing director he'd overseen the city's day-to-day operations for four quiet years. His campaign for mayor had been flawless, and his support was widespread among whites as well as blacks.

He was born the son of a North Carolina sharecropper. In

the 1950s he worked his way through college, earning a degree in business administration. Afterward he came to Philadelphia, a young man looking for "opportunity," as he liked to tell it.

He found his opportunity in the public housing field, where he made a name for himself as a man who could get the job done. In 1979 Mayor-elect Bill Green had tapped him to serve as the city's chief operating officer. Once again he'd done his job quietly and well.

First as managing director and then as mayor, Wilson Goode had been running the city of Philadelphia for nearly six years. He'd had to contend with the usual assortment of big-city problems—transit strikes, budget deficits, incompetence, and corruption. But now, as the growing flames flickered across his television screen, Goode found himself moving into uncharted territory. What was going on in west Philadelphia was beyond all his experience.

The word that came to his mind was *war*.

At 6:18 P.M., the twelve-foot by eight-foot bunker, its wooden sides blazing, plunged through the roof and disappeared into the second floor. Now the fire was inside the house, and putting water on the roof would only drive the flames downward through the house, spreading it among the adjoining sun porches all up and down the block. It would be the worst thing the fire fighters could do. Without going inside the house with hoses and axes, there was nothing the fire department could do now to put the fire out.

Six blocks north, on a ninth-floor escape landing, the general watched through his field glasses as the bunker collapsed. Leo Brooks had been a civilian for less than eighteen months, and he still had the bearing of an officer. He had retired from the army, where he'd supervised the vast Defense Logistics Agency headquartered in Philadelphia to run the city for Wilson Goode. He brought to the job of managing director some of the same qualities that Goode himself had shown: a low profile and a mechanic's aptitude for keeping the bloated and unwieldy city bureaucracy in some semblance of working order.

Soft-spoken, with a bit of the lilt of his native Virginia still in his voice, Brooks was a gentleman as well as an officer—an "honorable man," in the mayor's estimation, and a good man to work for as well. His years in the army had taught him to make a virtue of the need to delegate, and he usually gave his subordinates plenty of elbow room.

But now, as he watched the rooftops in flames below him, as he waited for the water to come on, he grew more and more alarmed. Already he had grabbed a walkie-talkie from his aide to report that he could see flames. Now he used that radio to try to raise Sambor. For long minutes—critical minutes—he and his aide tried again and again to reach Commissioner Sambor. He could not understand why nobody was fighting the fire.

At 6:22 P.M., Pete Kane phoned in another report. "The house is fully involved in flames," he announced. "The roof just collapsed and several houses are burning right now along with the MOVE house.

"They have not taken a hose into Osage. They are just waiting."

Fifty-five minutes after the explosion, the flames on the roof were as tall as a man. In the dark cellar three stories below, women and children lay beneath woolen blankets, not knowing whether it was night or day.

They could hear the clatter of combat boots in the kitchen above them, then the trapdoor to the cellar being pulled aside, and finally heavy footsteps coming down the stairs. The men of MOVE were gathering from their posts throughout the house, bringing with them reports of the fire.

And now, in this dark and stifling cellar, not knowing what would happen next, the family known as MOVE put its trust in the wisdom of its leader and teacher, the enigmatic figure of the Coordinator, John Africa.

Some among them had followed the teachings of John Africa for more than fifteen years now, from the earliest days of the movement. Some said he was a man; some said he was something greater. He had led his people through the wilderness—through siege and arrest and long, lonely years in jail—and his wisdom had never failed them. He had faced up to the system not once or twice, but time and again, and every time MOVE had emerged stronger. The system could not stop him, because John Africa spoke the truth and the truth is stronger than any lie.

The people who gathered now in the basement were among his most devoted followers. They had come to MOVE from a variety of backgrounds, moving ever closer to the light and warmth of John Africa's teachings. Most had come tentatively at first, attracted by the teachings but a little afraid of them, too. At first belonging to MOVE had meant changing the way they lived—eating raw foods, giving up jobs and air-conditioning. It meant strained relations with parents and friends and eventually confrontations with a system that hated them and would try to destroy them.

John Africa had told many of them long ago that they would suffer for the truth. He had predicted the confrontations, the beatings, the arrests and jail terms. He had warned them that some of them would be "cycled"—that they would be recycled back to the earth—in their fight to save the world from man's corruption.

The Coordinator, in his wisdom, had known that not everyone could make such a sacrifice. Those who could not had been given other assignments. But the people in the house on this evening had known for years that it would come to this and that when the time came they would do what they had to do.

Now that time had come. Already the second floor was ablaze. The fire was moving down through the house, closer and closer to the basement.

Soon there would be just one way out—through the two- by two-foot hatch that led from this room out into the back alley. They knew what they would find out there: the full might of the Philadelphia Police Department, countless cops with automatic rifles, machine guns, and shotguns, all trained on that tiny hatch, all waiting.

Perhaps some of them thought of the long road that had brought them here, of happier times when they had first come to know the gentle teachings of John Africa. Perhaps they recalled those long nights when they would gather together to listen to his words, when they had been like babies discovering the wonders of the world for the first time. Perhaps they thought of the future, the future they were working for, a time when man's corruption of Mom Nature, as MOVE called her, would finally cease and all people would know that man was meant to be a part of her, not to rule over her.

Perhaps they could see the forests rising again from beneath the asphalt of the cities, the cars rusting and returning to the earth, the skyscrapers crumbling into piles of stone, and the choked and polluted creeks of what was now west Philadelphia running pure and clear under canopies of virgin green. That was the vision that had brought them here. It was not for any personal glory, but for the sake of the world, that they were willing to die. The fire that was burning above them could not destroy MOVE's truths. Already it had turned on the system, spreading outward and away from MOVE. The fire that had started here tonight would grow until it had consumed the system.

It was happening just as John Africa had told them it would.

2
The Neighborhood

A DOZEN GENERATIONS BEFORE, it had all been forest. The unnamed creek ran strong and clear and full of fish; the trees had never felt the steel of an ax. Brown-skinned men and women lived as one with the land, eating what they could gather with their hands, their bodies hardened by their long and intimate acquaintance with the elements. In those days time did not march to the tyranny of the calendar; the years flowed into one another according to the long, languorous cycles of the seasons: the frozen months of winter, the softness of spring, the thick heat of summer, and the seeding of the earth and dying of autumn.

In 1643 Swedish settlers who had come to the New World built a mill alongside the creek. An Englishman, William Cobb, bought the mill soon afterward. His name survives, though his mill does not. As the white men subdued the land and cleared the forest, other mills rose alongside the dappled waters of Cobbs Creek. The first were mills in the truest sense—little more than great round stones driven by water-wheels, which would mill the farmers' grain into flour. Later came the long, low brick buildings of the Industrial Revolution—textile mills, mostly, which used the water's power to drive the great looms.

By the late nineteenth century Cobbs Creek was a mill town—a rough industrial village that was already looking over its shoulder at the rapidly advancing outskirts of Philadelphia. By the first years of this century Philadelphia had arrived, and with it the cramped gridlike pattern of streets that had first been laid out by William Penn himself.

25

The grid was Penn's contribution to urban planning. He laid
out and named the streets himself before sailing from Britain,
determined to avoid a repetition of the tragedy of the devastat-
ing London fire that he'd witnessed firsthand, in which flames
leaped across the narrow alleys and thousands died trying to
escape through the twisted streets of the city. Penn had
imagined Philadelphia as a "Greene Countrie Towne," with
blocks of well-built homes scattered among the forests and
meadows, and the grid was designed to bring order and ra-
tionality to his new city in the woods.

By the twentieth century, however, the grid had come to
serve a new and less noble purpose. The narrow streets sliced
up the city into small rectangular blocks that gave rise to a
Philadelphia institution: the row house. These were not the
fine Georgian town houses envisioned by Penn; they were
endless monotonous ranks of tiny working-class homes,
jammed shoulder to shoulder like people on a crowded bus,
with flat tar roofs and postage-stamp yards (or none at all) and
a subtle variety of facades—some with porches, some with
stoops, some with bay windows or pillars or flat brick faces. In
blocks little more than 500 feet long and 150 wide—less than
two football fields—builders managed to pack as many as sixty
tiny houses. To squeeze them all in, they had to make certain
sacrifices—things such as front and back yards and streets
wide enough for two cars to pass one another were a luxury
that few could afford.

Most of the row houses built in Cobbs Creek in the 1920s
were sold to immigrants who had come to Philadelphia during
the great migrations from eastern Europe. The neighborhood
of Cobbs Creek was mostly Jewish, a part of the city where
first-generation Americans—factory workers and small-time
businesspeople, butchers and civil servants, printers and shoe-
makers—could afford to own their own home and still ride to
downtown jobs on the new Market Street Elevated Railway.

As families moved in, the streets of the neighborhood exploded with city life. Corner stores and hangouts, gangs of
neighborhood kids, modest synagogues that reflected the dark
and brooding architecture of eastern Europe—all were
crowded on top of one another along the little streets. To the

people who lived there, a neighborhood just a few blocks square became a sort of urban version of the medieval villages in the old country, each with its own sense of self.

They were neighborhoods where people weathered the hard times of the Depression and were thankful for the roof over their heads. But when prosperity returned after World War II, the families that had lived there for twenty or more years began moving out. The houses of Cobbs Creek would never have the long green lawns and quiet streets that the new suburbs promised, and if you had done well for yourself—as many in the neighborhood had—the promise of a better life was to be found in the converted cow pastures of southern New Jersey and northeast Philadelphia.

The first black couple—a lawyer and a teacher—moved into the neighborhood in the mid-1950s. Blacks had always lived close by, but Market Street had been an unofficial boundary line. Now that it had been breached, the steady exodus of the original residents became a stampede. Blockbusting tactics would not be outlawed for another ten years, and real estate agents fanned the flames of fear in an attempt to make quick commissions. Letters appeared in mailboxes: "Your property values are declining! Sell now, before it's too late!"

Within three years the transition was complete. The synagogue on Cobbs Creek Parkway had become a Baptist church. The kosher butcher stores closed down or reopened under new ownership as corner markets. Virtually every house changed hands in the late 1950s, and Cobbs Creek became a black neighborhood.

But the worst fears of those who'd left did not materialize. The neighborhood did not deteriorate into a slum. The people who moved in were looking for the same things that the immigrants had sought thirty years before: peace and quiet and a little something to call their own.

The neighborhood would never become well-to-do; there is only so much one can do to improve eighteen- by forty-foot row houses. They are too small and too plain to invite gentrification, and the distance from downtown would deter all but the most committed urban pioneers.

Today Cobbs Creek has its share of urban problems—too

much graffiti, unswept streets, and boarded-up businesses that have been killed by the big chains—but it occupies a special niche in Philadelphia. Residents point out with pride that more blacks own their homes in Cobbs Creek than in any other neighborhood in the city. Because of its stability, it is the backbone of black political power in the city. It is also Mayor Goode's home turf.

The site of the old mills is now a swath of lush green parkland that runs all along the western border of the neighborhood, giving it a sense of openness that's unusual among the brick and concrete of west Philadelphia. Many of the people who moved in some thirty years ago are still there. Others lived there as kids and have returned to raise their own families in Cobbs Creek.

The records of the property at 6221 Osage Avenue tell the story of the neighborhood. Old deeds show that the block was subdivided in 1921. The lot for 6221 was sixty-four feet deep (including the common driveway in the rear) and eighteen feet, ten inches wide. On September 13, 1921, Samuel Cohen sold the new brick row house—containing three bedrooms, one bathroom, a sun porch in the front, and a garage in the rear—to a Mr. Philip Goldberg and his wife, Rebecca. The Goldbergs owned the house less than a year, selling it to Barnett and Rebecca Pawell. Eleven months later, on July 9, 1923, the Pawells in turn sold it to Joseph and Mary Busch for the sum of $5,886.19.

The Busches owned the house for twenty-six years, throughout the Depression and World War II. In 1949 they sold it to Louis and Yetta Brown.

The Browns sold the house in 1958 to a young black couple, Frank and Louise James, for $8,500. In 1969 the Jameses divorced. In the settlement Louise received the house, and she continued to live there with her only son, Frank Jr., until a night in 1983 when she fled, fearing for her life.

It was about the time of Louise James's divorce that the rumblings of the civil rights movement came to the streets of Cobbs Creek. The streets did not burn in waves of riots as they did in Watts and Chicago and even parts of Philadelphia, but Cobbs Creek became radicalized. New, unfamiliar words began appearing in people's conversations: they spoke of coalitions and confrontation, rap sessions, black power. People—even the middle-class people of Cobbs Creek—began to explore unfamiliar religions and ways of life: Islam, Buddhism, the Black Panthers, and other less well-known groups.

Louise James was not unlike her neighbors in background and outlook. She had grown up in a blackened-brick and concrete neighborhood behind the vast rail yards of the Pennsylvania Railroad, a single generation removed from the soul-defeating poverty of the Old South, and had witnessed firsthand the casual violence that rained down on black people every day at the hands of police. For her the turbulent sixties were a time to finally stand up and fight back. Many years later she would testify to one of the incidents that gave birth to her own political awareness:

"A brother by the name of Larry Cross was killed. This brother was going down Vine Street one day, and a police officer had stopped, and Larry passed the police officer. When the cop stopped him, he pulled him over and gave Larry Cross a ticket. Larry tore up the ticket. That was his crime.

"Two to three hours later that brother was dead. . . . He was hung. And they said that he had committed suicide. And I was outraged.

"There was a big meeting at the White Rock Baptist Church at Fifty-third and Chestnut. . . . Big people were there and little people were there, and everybody was gathered because they wanted something done about this brother's murder. And then at some point somebody said, okay, the meeting was over.

"I remember hearing a voice scream. And I didn't even know it was my own voice until I came back to myself, and I realized it was me, and I was saying, no! This meeting is over? I said, 'I will not allow you to have me go out of this meeting as frustrated as I was when I came in.' I said, 'You're going to have to tell me *something.*'

"As I continued to be disillusioned and I continued to see nothing working in this political system for me, I continued to search."

Frank James, Jr., Louise's only son, grew up in these troubled times, but it seems that he was oblivious, as children are, to the great issues that preoccupied the world of his elders. Those who knew him as a child remember his soulful eyes and shy smile. He was a quiet boy who did well at school. Clifford Bond, who lived across the street, used to play chess with young Frank. Frank was a good opponent, he remembers, and a good student as well. Frank did well enough in school to be awarded a scholarship to attend the Mitchell Preparatory School, an exclusive private academy in the old and prestigious Main Line suburbs.

As Frank grew into adulthood, he began to accompany Louise on her search for answers to the injustices of the world. As it turned out, they were closer than they would have guessed. On the other side of west Philadelphia, not far from the neighborhood where Louise had grown up, a black man was already gathering a following of hippies and radicals around him. He had a vision of a world that was just and pure and good, and he had a plan for making that vision come true.

He called his small band of followers the Christian Movement for Life. He was known by several names: Vincent Life, Vincent Africa, John Vincent Africa.

If the deep, resonant voice and angry words of John Vincent Africa struck a special chord in Louise James's heart, it was not surprising. She had grown up hearing that voice. It belonged to her brother, Vincent Leaphart.

3
The Dog Man

STANDING AT THE WESTERN and eastern ends of west Philadelphia, Cobbs Creek and Powelton Village are as far apart in
spirit as two neighborhoods can be. Where Cobbs Creek is
stable, Powelton is transient. Where Cobbs Creek is quiet,
Powelton is noisy. Where Cobbs Creek is middle-class and
middle-of-the-road, Powelton is decidedly left of center, a
neighborhood where the telephone poles bristle with posters
proclaiming revolution.

Powelton Village crowds around the perimeter of Drexel
University and the University of Pennsylvania, filled with
large, decrepit Victorians, smaller row houses, and squat,
nondescript apartment buildings. In the early 1970s, when
Vincent Leaphart first moved there, it was a neighborhood
that prided itself on its diversity and its political correctness, a
place where fraternity kids, hippies, radicals, students, professors, and poor folks lived in rented rooms and houses.

Nobody seems to know for sure just when Vincent moved
into Powelton or what prompted him to settle there. A former
neighbor, who had a small pottery studio in Powelton Village,
remembers that Vincent seemed quite at home there—"just
one more weirdo in a neighborhood of weirdos."

Even so, if you were ranking Vincent for weirdness on a
scale of one to ten, he'd earn at least a nine. Even before he
took the name John Africa, he lived in a little rented row house
lit only by candles, because he knew the "danger" of electricity. He was in his late thirties and worked as a handyman; his
niece would later recall that "he could do anything with a
scrap of wood." His house was furnished with old furniture

31

that he'd rescued from trash heaps and had rebuilt. Vincent had even created an ornate *faux* parquet floor in his apartment, carefully drawing the grain of the wood with a pencil.

But it was Vincent's other job—walking dogs for hire—that earned him his neighborhood nickname. He was the Dog Man, and you could count on seeing him in the early morning hours, walking down the street surrounded by a happy barking pack. Dogs were drawn to him—or, perhaps, to the horse meat he sold for dog food and gave away to the strays—and he, in turn, was drawn to them.

Vincent had some definite ideas about man and nature. If he saw a fly trapped in a puddle of water, he would stop what he was doing to rescue it. To him, life was a sacred thing—no matter what, no matter how large or small. Rats and cockroaches were nature's creatures just as surely as men and women, and they deserved equal consideration. Absolutely equal—he didn't spray his house with insecticide, and he fed the neighborhood rats as well as the dogs.

Those who'd known Vincent Leaphart before he'd moved to Powelton might have judged him an unlikely candidate for philosopher-at-large. He and his sister Louise had grown up in a large family, with six boys and four girls, living in a rented row house a few blocks from Powelton Village in the neighborhood known as Mantua. His father, Frederick, had arrived with his wife, Lennie Mae, from Atlanta, one of thousands of southern black families that came north to Philadelphia during the great migrations of the 1920s.

Like most of their neighbors, the Leapharts were a poor, God-fearing Baptist family with too many mouths to feed and not enough money coming in. Frederick was a paperhanger and part-time handyman; Lennie Mae had her hands full at home raising the ten children and trying to stretch the few dollars they had through the long years of the Depression.

Vincent was born into these unpromising circumstances on July 26, 1931. It appears that he had even more obstacles than these to overcome, however. While he was still a child, Lennie Mae took sick. Admitted to the same public hospital in which she'd given birth to Vincent, she rapidly worsened and died. When he was grown, Vincent would tell people that the hospital had killed his mother.

Lennie Mae left behind a family that was ruptured and grieving. Frederick, working odd jobs and faced with the demands of ten children, simply fell apart, neighbors would later recall.

But young Vincent Leaphart's problems at home were only part of the trouble. He was having trouble in school, especially in reading. Probably dyslexic, he was judged a "slow learner." Vincent's IQ was measured first at eighty-four and then, a few years later, at seventy-nine. That earned him the label "orthogenetically backward"—mildly retarded by today's standards—and a place at a special school for those who could not keep up in regular classes.

Even in this sheltered environment, Vincent's progress was slow, with one exception: he seemed to take an interest in the workings of government and society, and he did well in his civics classes. Often, though, he didn't bother to show up at classes at all, and he dropped out altogether when he was sixteen. He had reached the third-grade level, and it was the last formal schooling he would ever have.

A year later he was arrested for armed robbery and car theft. The court records of the case have long since disappeared, and the outcome is unknown. He saw combat as a foot soldier in Korea and found himself deeply affected by the contrast between the beauty of the countryside and the ugliness of war.

When he returned home, Vincent's thoughts turned to marriage and family. He started seeing Dorothy Clark, one of five sisters who'd lived down the street from the Leapharts while they were growing up. Vincent and Dorothy married in 1961 after a long courtship.

There is only fragmentary evidence of Vincent's life after he was married. His interests seem to have been wide-ranging—especially in light of his early disadvantages—and apparently included classical music and interior design. There is evidence that the marriage was rocky. Dorothy was unable to bear children, and in the early years Vincent spent much of his time in New York City, studying and practicing interior design. Finally, at Dorothy's insistence, he returned home to Philadelphia.

In 1966 Dorothy filed charges against him for assault and battery, telling police that he had hit her across the face with his hand. The DA's office declined to prosecute the case.

Despite these problems and the ones he'd faced when he was younger, Vincent settled into a fairly ordinary life. He is remembered as a "smooth dresser," a charming, cheerful man who loved animals and children. Still, there is evidence that the ferment of the 1960s did not pass him by. Dorothy had begun to follow an apocalyptic sect based in Phoenix known as the Kingdom of Yahweh. Searching for answers, looking for the truth, she became a vegetarian, basing her diet on what the kingdom referred to as "principles of natural law."

Even in those days, Dorothy later recalled, Vincent was a leader and not a follower: "He was very dynamic. He always had a spirit of helping others. He always was a person to voice his opinion, but he tried to be just and fair to all." And, she said, he was a "very deep thinker."

Eventually Dorothy and Vincent began to follow different paths to enlightenment. Their marriage faltered, and they separated in 1967. Years later, in the only interview Dorothy would ever give about her years with Vincent, she said that they separated on friendly terms, and she hinted that the break was mostly her idea: "I had made up my mind that I had to make a new life for myself, and I gave him the same freedom." She last saw him in the spring of 1968. Today she calls herself "Princess Dottie" and lives quietly in west Philadelphia, following the teachings of the Kingdom of Yahweh.

Little is known to the outside world about the next two years of Vincent Leaphart's life, but clearly some profound changes were occurring in him. He had long been considered the eccentric member of the large Leaphart clan. He often gave away what little money he had or used it to feed the menagerie of animals that always surrounded him. He'd always had a sense that things were very wrong with the world. Now those ideas began to coalesce into the outlines of a philosophy.

Perhaps living alone gave Vincent an opportunity to reflect on ideas that had been wandering through his mind for all of his life: the insanity of a system that he believed had killed his mother and destroyed his family, that had labeled him a mental defective, that had sent him halfway around the world to kill people he did not know. Perhaps the failure of his marriage and his attempts at a career in interior design left him frustrated and empty.

For whatever reasons, Vincent now began to reach back into his past and find not only his own ideas but also others plucked from the thick ideological atmosphere of the late sixties. Like a carpenter who judges his work by eye, Vincent shaped his ideas without the benefit of paper and pencil. For a year or more, he honed them and polished them.

From his ex-wife's faith he apparently took an idea that he would make his own: the principle of natural law. As a child Vincent had learned that the God of the Baptists commanded man to subdue the earth and had given him dominion over the fish of the sea and the fowl of the heavens and every living thing that crept upon the earth. Now Vincent no longer believed that to be true. He believed that man had crowned himself emperor—and ever since had been paying the price for his arrogance. It seemed clear to him that everything wrong with the world—drug addiction, pollution, poverty, prisons— could be traced back to man's insistence that he was exempt from the laws of nature.

He concluded that the world that man had created was beyond salvation. All of it was tainted, not only the factories belching poisons into the air and water but everything man-made: arts, literature, even his beloved classical music were addictions and distortions. You could not separate the good from the bad—all of it was built on lies.

At some unknowable instant in his candlelit room, that conviction transformed Vincent. It was not enough, he resolved, simply to live according to natural law. In his mind he conceived a grand and preposterous mission for himself. He would create a revolution to destroy what man had created. All of it.

At that moment Vincent Leaphart was reborn, shedding his old identity like an outgrown skin. To the outside world he seemed to be the same man, but now "Vincent Leaphart" was just one of many costumes that could be used and cast aside as the need arose. Within that shell was a newborn innocent, a man without a past and future: the smiling, enigmatic figure of John Africa.

To this day, members of MOVE refuse to identify John

Africa as Vincent Leaphart. All they will say is that John Africa is John Africa and Vincent Leaphart was Vincent Leaphart. It seems they are right in at least one sense. John Africa may have been born in the mind of Vincent Leaphart, but he was not the unsuccessful handyman with the third-grade education that Vincent had been.

Vincent's sister Louise would later try to explain it another way. She said that John Africa was the truth and that there was no other person on earth like John Africa. Vincent Leaphart and John Africa were two different people, she said. "My blood brother, Vincent Leaphart, became John Africa, and he no longer exists."

One evening in the early seventies, the man who still called himself Vincent urged Louise and their younger sister LaVerne to attend a class at the Community College of Philadelphia. "I have somebody I want you to hear," he said.

The someone was Donald Glassey, a young white instructor at the college, and his curriculum was one that the college trustees would have been unlikely to approve had they known of it.

Glassey, who'd grown up in an upper-middle-class suburb in southern New Jersey, had struck up an unlikely friendship with Vincent more than a year before. Like the disciples who would follow later, he was searching for guidance in a time that seemed to make no sense. Vincent seemed to possess the answers that had come neither from Glassey's professors at Penn nor from within himself.

The more Don Glassey talked with Vincent, the more his enthusiasm grew. He'd just finished his master's thesis at Penn, so perhaps writing was on his mind.

"You have some fascinating ideas here," he told Vincent after one of their many talks. "You should write them down."

"That's a great idea," Vincent replied, "but I can't write very well."

"I can take care of that for you," Don replied.

Thus came about a couple that was odd even by the liberal standards of Powelton: Glassey, the white radical college teacher, knowledgeable in the politics of the civil rights and antiwar movements; and Leaphart, the black ghetto Jeremiah who could scarcely read or write. Before long Vincent's Pearl Street neighbors noticed Don coming by regularly, a stack of papers under his arm.

The two of them put in a year of solid work, with Vincent dictating and Don writing everything down, organizing it into chapters, and reading it back to Vincent to be sure it said what he wanted it to say. When they were done, they had created a three-hundred-page manuscript they called The Guidelines, or sometimes simply The Book. It would become the core of the movement they were creating.

It was from this book that Don Glassey read to his students at the community college. Not long afterward, the study sessions moved from the college to the "schoolhouse," as the dozen or so regulars began to call Vincent's apartment.

A cadre of regulars began attending the sessions. Louise came with LaVerne. So did Louise's son, Frank, now a teenager, as well as LaVerne's kids, Chuckie and Debbie.

There were others at those early meetings as well: a young black man with an angry face named Conrad Hampton, a former All-City high school football champion and occasional college student named Jerry Ford, an ex–Black Panther by the name of Delbert Orr.

News of the study sessions spread among the streets of west Philadelphia. More people came to hear Vincent—some, like Don, looking for answers, others simply out of curiosity or at the urging of a friend.

Many came away unimpressed. Others felt as if their eyes had been opened for the first time. In the midst of the rambling prose they found something that struck a chord, that had an element of rightness that was undeniable to them.

Imperceptibly visitors became followers; followers became disciples; disciples became members. The group, many of them already linked by ties of blood to Vincent, soon began to consider itself a family. Its name, the Christian Movement for Life, was later shortened to The Movement. Finally it became known simply as MOVE.

MOVE attracted searchers and seekers from throughout the city. They came from many backgrounds. Some were white; most were black. Some were veterans of leftist movements;

some were politically naive. Many had attended at least a few years of college. Some had been addicted to drugs or in trouble with the law.

Alberta Wicker was one of the many who first visited the house in Powelton out of curiosity and eventually stayed on. A soft-spoken young black woman with kind eyes and a shy smile, she was a full-time student at the Community College of Philadelphia.

Alberta had grown up believing that if you needed help you could go find a policeman. She had never been arrested, nor had she become involved in the protest movements of the sixties.

Mutual friends enthusiastically told her about John Africa and The Guidelines. They said the people of MOVE could rap on any subject and open your eyes to what was wrong with the world.

One evening they took her to MOVE headquarters and she began to read The Guidelines. She chose, almost at random, the section on animals, and reading it moved her almost to tears. Fascinated, she became a regular student of Vincent's. Before long she'd left her job and moved into the headquarters, becoming one of the most ardent and committed members of MOVE. Eventually she would spend seven years in prison rather than renounce her allegiance to MOVE and win an early parole. Though there is no hierarchy within MOVE, she would come closer than anyone to the inner essence of MOVE and mysteries of John Africa. She became Vincent's wife.

Another early member was Delbert Orr, former Black Panther captain of defense and chief of security for Chicago and northern Illinois. He had come to Philadelphia for a joint council of radical causes and stayed on to learn more about John Africa. After reading The Guidelines, he said, he realized that "the four years I'd spent with the Black Panther party, the armed confrontation with police, the attacking of the government, the deaths of comrades were all for nothing, because nothing was changed." He saw that "all that had nothing to do with true revolution, but was only the theoretical so-called revolution."

A flier from these early days brims over with the enthusiasm of the first followers of the man who would be known as John Africa. It is also one of the few pieces of MOVE literature that reveals the metamorphosis of Vincent Leaphart into John Africa. It reads, in part:

> "MOVE"—An organization that is about *just* that!
>
> MOVE is an organization of people dedicated to the principles of life, truth, as written in *THE BOOK*, a published about to be released manuscript by John Vincent Africa. *The Book* is the most powerful statement in existence, as the clarity, analytical ability of the author is unequaled, unparalleled in any of the writings of man, past or present. *THE BOOK is* THE TRUTH, and it *is* to be used against the lie, this life style of perversion, distortion, schizophrenia, indecisiveness and misdirection. The Book *completely* undercuts, disproves and substantiates that nothing in man's life style is working, or has ever worked since the imposition of violation, the invention of this unnatural style of life. You have only to look at your life style to see what it has produced, deformed babies, murder, rape, genocide, suicide, countless bombs, perpetual wars and meaningless killing, a life style that is fiction, an illusion, mystery, unreal, that you cannot relate to naturally, or sanely, a life style that has pressed you, jammed you violently into a corner, strangulating the very life from you. . . . True life has nothing to do with the theories, concepts, and ideas coming from the imagination of man, for all these things are illusions working against life, and cannot produce anything but the sickness, pain and suffering you are constantly experiencing in this life style.
>
> What MOVE is about is putting an end to *all* of the impositions on life, as you must realize that in order to solve the problems it is necessary to completely cut away from all of this life style, for to hold onto any part of a cancerous style of life will only bring about that same cancer. This is why there has never been a *true* revolution, as revolution means *total* change, a complete disassociation from everything that is causing the problems you are revolting against. . . .

This early MOVE document cited a convert, a "former actress, college student, model, follower of the arts." She testified:

> "I used to like to travel alot, very much into the New York scene, started reading *The Book*, stopped traveling, dropped out of school, gave the idea of being an actress and a model up completely, and have devoted all my time to MOVE."

From a "former writer, record producer and poet" came this:

> "I have always been searching for meaning in life, but upon reading *THE BOOK*, I realized that I had seen the first and last book that is *THE BOOK* by John V. Africa, and I disposed of all of my writing, contact with publications, as there is nothing for me to write about, there is only to read, understand, and apply the principles of life in *THE BOOK*."

The same document offers a portrait of what Vincent was becoming. Like the name John Vincent Africa, the picture that emerges is of a being in transition, half man and half god:

> John Africa is a man in the true sense of the word, a man who has never believed in any of this man-made life style, who has always rejected the imposition of other so called men, their education, science, technology, religion, government. A man who has lived his life consistent with the laws of natural manifestation, a man whose reverance, respect for life has caused him to be labeled insane by neighbors, friends, even his own family, *and* those who first get into *THE BOOK*, those who could not relate to a man living in complete harmony with his beliefs, never wavering, as he has true strength in his convictions. A man who has been tested over and over again by the imposition of this unnatural style of life, but who has always remained fixed to self, his *only* frame of reference. A man who uses no heat, no electricity, has never read a book in his life, a man who can barely read and write, knows nothing about language, but look at what he has done to the English language, as there was no research involved in putting together *THE BOOK*, for he dictated from himself *THE BOOK* to someone who consented to help him put down his message of truth.

These and other praises notwithstanding, one is left with a sense that there is something about Vincent's "message of truth" that does not survive translation to the written page. At the heart of any religion there must be one possessed of that great and dangerous gift of oratory that can move nations—the fire of a Moses or Muhammed; the radiance of a Christ or Buddha.

Vincent had that gift. He was part prophet, part Baptist preacher, a father and teacher to his followers, and words on a page would never equal the mesmerizing quality of his baritone voice when he would look someone in the eye and show just what he was talking about. Without his voice his ideas seem flat, a rambling collage of apocalyptic clichés. When spoken, they became the inspired words of a holy man.

From the beginning, what set MOVE apart from the other revolutionaries and ascetics of the neighborhood was that MOVE members practiced what they preached. The only problem was that they preached the destruction of civilization. It tended to make for poor relations with their less enlightened neighbors.

In 1971 Vincent Leaphart had been one of fourteen names attached to the charter of Community Housing, Inc. Community Housing was a co-op created to buy houses before they fell into the hands of neighboring Drexel University. Though its membership was leftist, the co-op itself was a matter of expedience more than ideology. The charter made that clear: "The collective does not claim to be a substitute for revolution in our oppressive society." Decision making in the co-op was to be "non-hierarchical, non-authoritarian, and open to the entire membership." Though Vincent had little money to contribute, other members of the co-op knew that he faced eviction from his apartment and bought the house in which he lived.

Although the other members didn't realize it at the time, their organization was at cross-purposes with Vincent. In his view you were either for life or for the "life style"—his term for the corrupt technological society. Halfway measures weren't acceptable.

The difficulties began when Don and Vincent started using the co-op meetings as a platform for expounding Vincent's beliefs—with Don doing the expounding, as Vincent sat quiet and "Buddhalike," as a former member of the co-op later recalled. A bigger problem was Vincent's refusal to spray his co-op apartment for roaches, out of concern that it would poison the dogs—and also, presumably, out of concern for the well-being of the cockroaches.

When the cockroaches began to invade the other apartments in the building, the more conventional neighbors took up the matter with the co-op, which in turn sent a delegation to talk to Vincent. When he answered the door, they were shocked at the transformation that Vincent seemed to have undergone.

They did not find the gentle, life-loving man who had joined the co-op months before. Vincent was a wild man, seething with hostility. He told them in no uncertain terms that he would not spray the apartment. As for the others in the building, well, if they didn't see things his way, that was just too bad.

In the angry exchange that followed, someone suggested that perhaps Vincent had forgotten that he was living there through the generosity of members who went to work every day while he sat at home. Vincent replied that the ones who were working should support the ones, like him, who did not.

When one of the delegation objected, Vincent turned on him. "If you're not with me, then you're against me. I view you as my enemy," he shouted.

"Well, if that's the case, Vince," the man replied, "you've been playing me for a sucker."

As MOVE gathered momentum, Don invited people to move into his house on Forty-second Street, ten blocks away from Vincent's house. By the end of 1973 tensions between MOVE and the housing co-op had reached the breaking point, and the co-op went to court to evict Vincent from his Pearl Street apartment.

By then, Don had decided that MOVE needed a place to call its own, and he bought an enormous old Victorian twin house on Thirty-third Street, directly across from Vincent's house.

Even in 1974 the $4,800 Don spent on the house was next to nothing. Before it had fallen on hard times, the house must have been splendid. By the time Don bought it, it was shabby and run-down and looked like it had come out of a Charles Addams cartoon. It was an awesome, decrepit hulk, standing three-and-a-half stories above Thirty-third Street, a steep-gabled Gothic tower of rust-brown bricks, its windows tall and set deep in their frames like the sunken eyes of an aged dowager.

It was here at 309 North Thirty-third Street that the growing band began to live the life that John Africa preached. The changes in lifestyle came slowly. At first the house had heat and electricity, furniture, even a television set. The upper floors were divided into apartments. On the first floor was MOVE's headquarters; it held an office, a desk, a radio, and a telephone. The Guidelines were kept in surprisingly humble circumstances: a set of filing cabinets.

To raise money MOVE set up a car wash on the street in front of the house. It was nothing more than a hose and bucket, manned by members and operated on a strict cash basis.

Gradually life in the house began to change in ways that reflected John Africa's ideas. The apartments gave way to common rooms, named according to their function. The exercise room became the focal point of the house, a large common area where people came together to eat, study, and rap as well as exercise.

They gave away their furniture to the poor and placed sleeping bags on the floor. They took torches and scrapers to the walls and woodwork, painstakingly removing every bit of paint from the interior of the house out of concern for the lead it contained. They removed the windows and replaced them with horizontal wooden slats that let in the outside air. The dogs—some fifty or sixty of them—had the run of the house. On cold nights they slept indoors on beds of straw.

At some point—it's not clear just when—MOVE also took over the adjoining house at 307 North Thirty-third Street. The owner transferred the house to the organization for a dollar. Some say MOVE obtained the property after the group threatened another potential buyer with knives. Another explanation is that MOVE's presence in the adjoining house made 307 worthless as a rental property, and the absentee owners decided they would do better by simply turning it over to MOVE and thus avoiding having to pay the taxes on it.

Soon life at the compound settled into an ascetic routine. Everyone would rise before dawn, pile into the old school bus that the group owned, and drive to a park to run and exercise. The men would run with knapsacks full of bricks or telephone books to build their endurance.

Back at the house by sunup, people would grab a quick snack of fruit and then go out again to run the dogs. Afterward members would work at the car wash.

At night they would have meetings. A former member recalls that the meetings were used to iron out disagreements and that they wouldn't end "until you got honest." That could take hours, and sometimes the accusations got brutal, but when it was done Vincent would have a hug for the person who'd been in the hot seat. Even the men would break down and cry—and Vincent used to say that if they didn't have so much pride, he'd have taken them on his lap.

Vincent guided his flock with a firm but gentle hand. The guiding principle was natural law. Eventually that would come to mean living with no heat, no electricity, and no running water. It would also mean eating uncooked foods—including raw meat. John Africa taught that people could eat anything they could catch in their own hands—though many members chose to stick to vegetables. He also taught them to chew garlic, believing that it protected them from illness. It was not a life for the faint of heart.

And yet Vincent seemed to know when to back off, too. If a meeting dragged, he might simply jump up in the middle of it and turn on the radio. "Come on, y'all, get up," he'd say and start them dancing.

Some days would be "distortion days," when he'd declare a moratorium on MOVE's raw food diet and permit—even encourage—members to eat forbidden foods. Vincent would say that people who had been addicted had to move toward natural law gradually.

Soon the house was full of children. Some of the children came to the organization with their parents; others—perhaps as many as twenty—would be born within the organization, never knowing another life.

When it came to the children of MOVE, Vincent would permit no distortions. They would be the vanguard of the revolution, he said, and before it was all over the kids would be teaching the adults how to live. He dreamed of the day when they would be grown, raised in a life free of "distortion," unfettered by "life style" addictions, powerful warriors for the coming revolution.

Among the curious who came to the house was a young woman named Jeanne. Born in Providence, Rhode Island, to French Canadian parents, she had come to Philadelphia in 1968 to attend the University of Pennsylvania. Like many of her classmates, she became deeply involved in the antiwar movement and the civil rights movement. She eventually married Ishongo Africa, one of John Africa's earliest followers.

Jeanne's marriage was a stormy one. As Ishongo got more deeply involved in MOVE he became more and more critical of Jeanne. She was a "prostitute," he said, because she continued to work in her "life style" job. Her education was an "addiction," a worthless "distortion" that prevented her from seeing her own corruption.

Ishongo carried within him the zeal of a fanatic, and often his attacks would spill over from words to acts. Finally, she would later say, desperate from the beatings but determined to save her marriage, Jeanne decided to confront her problems at the source. She went looking for John Africa.

She came to the headquarters unannounced, she says, demanding to talk to the man known as John Africa. She wanted to know what he was telling Ishongo that enraged him so. She wanted to know whether John Africa was telling her husband to beat his wife.

MOVE members asked her into the house and led her to a barren, unfurnished room. Soon she was joined there by a man who introduced himself as Charlie. He seemed older than most MOVE members, with flecks of gray in his beard, but he looked to be very fit. Like the other members, he wore his hair in long, thick, matted dreadlocks.

Jeanne says that Charlie explained that he was a longtime MOVE member. It was his job to explain MOVE philosophy to people who were interested in the organization and its goals.

Jeanne told Charlie about the arguments with Ishongo, the insults and beatings. Was this, she wanted to know, what the organization was teaching?

Charlie became upset, she said. He explained that Ishongo still had a lot of work to do. He might be talking MOVE, Charlie said, but he wasn't living MOVE. MOVE wasn't about violence. It was about life. John Africa's principles were very clear: respect for life in *all* its forms.

Charlie then explained some of the MOVE doctrine that Ishongo had been misrepresenting. John Africa believed that the life style—the way of living that people outside MOVE followed—was corrupt, that no matter how good your intentions, you couldn't reform the system from the inside out. Surely Jeanne, as a social worker, could see that was true. How much good was she really able to do for her clients from within the system? She couldn't get at the roots of their problems. All the social workers in the world couldn't wipe out poverty and hunger or change the fact that the poor were suffering and dying off the crumbs of the rich.

When she left that day, Jeanne had to agree that what Charlie had been saying made sense. Soon she was back at the house again, eager to hear more.

As the lessons continued, as Charlie came to trust her, she later said, she learned more and more about the inner secrets of MOVE. There was more going on than most people knew, Charlie told her. The roots of the tree that John Africa had planted were already extending throughout the system. The car wash, the demonstrations, even the house they were sitting in—these were only one part of MOVE. John Africa had also created an underground network—MOVE members who looked, talked, and acted as though they belonged to the life style. Some held nine-to-five jobs; some, in fact, worked for the Philadelphia Police Department.

As time went on, she later testified, Charlie revealed even more. He told Jeanne that he was John Africa himself. As she entered into the inner circle of MOVE, she says, his lessons became more strident, his logic more convoluted. MOVE's nonviolence, John Africa told her, was simply a facade, and it would fall away when the time was right.

MOVE's strategy against civilization was simple: "Put your fist out there with the intention of him hitting back so you can get an opening. Hit him knowing he's gonna come back, so wait and get your mark. A lot of punches aren't necessary. As soon as you see you ain't getting in, stop. . . . Counterpunch. MOVE are counterpunchers."

There would be a conflagration, he foretold; a time would soon come when people—life style people and MOVE people, adults and children—would die in the conflict. But he didn't use the word *die*; he said that they would be *cycled* back to the earth. Cycling was a fact of nature, he said; there was nothing evil about it. For example, he said, it would be better for a mother to cycle her child and herself than to let the child fall into the hands of life style officials and permit its body and mind to be polluted.

Anything that helps destroy the life style world is good, John Africa taught. He told Jeanne that MOVE was secretly selling drugs to raise money. Despite its rejection of technology, it was acquiring high-tech automatic weapons.

But there was no contradiction here, no hypocrisy, John Africa explained. It was simply a case of evil being turned back upon itself. It was a counterpunch.

(Jeanne's account of her involvement in MOVE is angrily contradicted by Vincent's widow, Alberta Africa. Alberta was living in the Powelton headquarters at the time, and she says that most of the events that Jeanne described never occurred. In fact, she says, Jeanne was never inside the Powelton house and certainly never gained access to MOVE's inner circle as she claimed. Jeanne was considered a MOVE supporter, not a member, Alberta says, and she has either distorted or misunderstood MOVE's aims and philosophy. There is little, if any, direct evidence to support either claim. It is clear that soon after these events Jeanne helped acquire arms for MOVE and set up "safe houses" for MOVE members who were fugitives, but she was not directly involved in the armed confrontations, and MOVE never publicly identified her as a member.)

Even those who were inclined to be sympathetic toward
MOVE questioned why a group that rejected technology chose
to live in the heart of a city. But to the people of MOVE,
running away was no solution; sooner or later the pollution and
destruction would catch up with you wherever you were. They
said that their interest was not in escaping from the problems
of the world but in solving them, and to solve them you had to
strike at their roots.

Studying The Guidelines was only the first step. The people
of MOVE were a chosen people. They were the advance troops
of John Africa's campaign to free nature from the bondage of
modern man. John Africa wanted to use his small band of
followers to show just how big a difference a few determined
people could make. MOVE was ready to take its message to the
streets, and John Africa was prepared to show himself as an
adept manipulator of the media—including the print media he
could not read—and of the system he loathed.

MOVE's first protests came at the Philadelphia Zoo and at
pet stores, where they demanded that the animals be set free.
Don Glassey handled media relations at those early demonstrations, explaining to baffled reporters that "we don't see any
difference between putting Jews in Auschwitz, napalming
Vietnam, or enslaving black people and enslaving puppies."

The issue might have seemed ludicrous, but John Africa was
no fool. With all the savvy of a seasoned publicity agent, he
selected high-visibility public events as a forum for MOVE's
protests. Before long MOVE protestors became a regular sight
at events around the city. Their trademarks were their loud,
nonstop obscenity-laden speeches and their seeming opposi-
tion to everything. They protested Jane Fonda and Buckminster Fuller. They denounced Dick Gregory, charging that he
had stolen some of their literature, and Jesse Jackson, claiming
that he was ripping off poor people. They invaded the studio
where the "Mike Douglas Show" was taped and handcuffed
the host to protest an incident in which a runaway chimpanzee
had been shot with a tranquilizer gun and taken away in
handcuffs. Meetings of the board of education became a
regular target—apparently as much for the fact that they were
televised as for MOVE's ideological differences with the school
board.

Members of the Philadelphia Police Department's civil affairs division who monitored these and other protests had received a lot of training about the boundaries of free speech. Good-naturedly they explained the limits of the law to MOVE protesters. MOVE members were free to demonstrate, the plainclothes cops would explain, but the law said they had to follow certain rules. MOVE members listened politely and used the information in ways that surprised the cops. They weren't really interested in avoiding arrest; in fact, John Africa's plans called for them to *be* arrested. So once they knew exactly where the line was, they boldly stepped across it.

A summary of police reports prepared years later clearly showed the pattern of escalation that John Africa was engineering. In 1973 police logged ten MOVE demonstrations on causes ranging from animal rights to an appearance by Dick Gregory. There were no arrests.

The following year the demonstrations had increased to ninety-three, protesting animal rights abuses, police harassment, city policies, and the actions of the board of education. Police made thirty-seven arrests that year, on charges ranging from assault and terroristic threats to contempt of court and disorderly conduct. Members made twenty-two court appearances.

In 1975 police counted thirty-eight demonstrations. They made 142 arrests, which resulted in sixty-one court appearances.

Eventually a regular corps of civil affairs officers was assigned to cover MOVE protests, and despite the arrests relations between the two sides grew casual, even friendly. The MOVE people would rap to the cops, explaining what they were about and why they were doing what they were doing. Some of the cops, in turn, were intrigued. They even asked questions.

"Hey, Delbert," one cop asked at one of the countless demonstrations in front of City Hall, "why do you guys use such bad language all the time? Why are you always calling me a motherfucker?"

Delbert, the former Black Panther who'd come to MOVE from Chicago, explained that to MOVE anyone who violated the ways of nature—anyone who raped Mom Nature—was called a motherfucker. Besides, he added with a smile, cursing gets people's attention.

At the same time, MOVE was having more and more trouble with its neighbors. MOVE members today discount those early conflicts. They say there were a few minor disagreements but that by and large they got along with the neighbors.

Those who lived near them at the time, however, tell a very different story. They say—and documents support their claims—that Vincent and his followers subjected people to an escalating campaign of intimidation, threats, and, finally, violence.

Powelton resident Russ Johnson recalls that MOVE members would deliver papers to the neighbors, whether they wanted them or not, and then come around to collect. "I remember even at the beginning that there was something a little terrifying about them," he says.

Neighbor Ken Moberg told a reporter that after he testified about the group's dogs at a hearing of the zoning board MOVE members "harangued me, threatened to castrate me, and said they would wipe me out." Another neighbor was told that he "better move with MOVE or be wiped out."

What infuriated those who knew this darker side of MOVE and its founder was the apparent willingness of so many to take MOVE at face value. In January 1974, for example, Delbert Africa showed up at a meeting between the city redevelopment authority and the East Powelton Concerned Residents, a neighborhood group that was fighting to keep houses owned by the authority from being razed.

Delbert, announcing that he represented "MOVE, Inc.," argued that the area should be reserved for poor blacks rather than the mostly white professors and students that made up the East Powelton group. MOVE's presence gave the redevelopment authority a political out for responding to EPCR's demands. "Here's another community group with another point of view," the authority's executive director told them with a smile. "Why should we negotiate with you?"

The *Philadelphia Daily News*, reporting the meeting the next day, identified "Move, Inc." simply as a "citizens' group."

It would be none of Philadelphia's three large daily papers—not even the Pulitzer prize-winning *Philadelphia Inquirer*—that first challenged the label that MOVE itself claimed. It was an article in *The Drummer*—a short-lived underground paper—that offered readers the first glimpse of the growing contradictions of MOVE.

Writer Ken Kilimnik went to the Powelton Village house and interviewed many of the people living there. He also interviewed the neighbors and compiled a list of public demonstrations that MOVE had put on. He noted an interesting pattern: apart from a demonstration against the board of education and the protests at the zoo and circus, "every other demonstration . . . has been directed against grass-roots community groups . . . or socialist, radical, or liberal speakers."

Kilimnik concluded that MOVE was a larger danger to the left than it was to the right. Within its beliefs, he wrote, lay the "seeds of fascism"; MOVE members professed that "anything is unreal or bad if it is based on an idea: 'Government is nothing but a theory, an idea from someone's imagination, an abortion of reality.' "

He wrote, "What socialist, liberal, or conservative would deny the value of human life or ideas? What political movement, outside of the Nazis' and Mussolini's blood-soaked followers, have considered anything man-made to be worthless and evil?"

MOVE's dual personality—on the one hand affirming life and professing nonviolence, while on the other hoarding guns and threatening the neighbors like a gang of street toughs—divided the leftist community of Powelton. One side saw MOVE as one of their own, an angry voice that had been raised against social corruption, oppression, and injustice. MOVE's rhetoric had a familiar ring, and if its agenda didn't always match their own, at least MOVE seemed to be on the side of right.

Those who lived closest to MOVE had a very different view. They saw the harassment of neighbors and the disruption of the neighborhoods. They began to live in fear of their wild-eyed new neighbors.

One neighbor, a member of the housing co-op and professor

at Penn named Gerry Goldin, began to compile a list of conflicts between neighbors and MOVE. Eventually it ran to seven single-spaced typewritten pages—and even this, Goldin said, was only a partial list. Among the incidents Goldin reported are these:

> Winter 1973: Chris Peterson . . . was threatened with knives by several unidentified members of MOVE. . . . Mr. Peterson was told that he must give up an option he held to purchase 309 N. 33 Street. . . .

> Spring 1973: Jack Wright, a house repairman, was assaulted by Donald Glassey Africa in the presence of Mr. Wright's two small children. The assault resulted in a black eye and bruises. It was witnessed by another community resident, Kenneth Moberg, who testified at the ensuing trial. At the hearing Mr. Glassey was joined by other MOVE members, who called the beating "political." Mr. Wright was an active member of a community organization, the East Powelton Concerned Residents, which was presumably Mr. Glassey's reference.

> Summer 1973: The technical director of the WXPN radio station [the University of Pennsylvania–owned station that had briefly permitted MOVE to broadcast a radio show] was beaten up by MOVE members.

> January 1974 [shortly after Vincent and Don were evicted from the co-op house on Pearl Street]: Amy Boss, a member of Community Housing, was picketed by MOVE members who encircled her home . . . after dark. About 60 MOVE members shouted threats and obscenities at her over a loudspeaker, making her fear for her life. She called the police, who told her that as long as they just shouted, they could remain. . . .

> January 1974: Edith Parent, a friend of Jack Wright, but having no connection with the housing cooperative, was picketed at her home. . . . MOVE members used obscenities and made threats, calling her a Jew money lender and a Jew capitalist. . . . She called the police, who told her that as

long as MOVE did not force their way in, they could remain.

January 1974: The home of Jack Wright was picketed after dark. . . . MOVE members again used obscenities and made threats. . . .

Not all the neighbors were hostile to MOVE, however. Even today, several of them recall that they were good neighbors. Pamela Parsons, for example, lived nearby, and her children played with the MOVE children. She had some philosophical differences with them—especially about educating the children—but she remembers them as friendly and helpful. They once fixed her car, she says, and in general they were "excellent neighbors."

"The complaints in the neighborhood were based on racism," she contends. "Goldin was a nasty person, and he wanted the neighborhood to be run his way."

On April 8, 1974, Goldin says, a band of MOVE members led by Conrad Hampton Africa attacked Monty Lis, another member of the co-op. Monty lived at 310 North Thirty-third Street, directly across from the MOVE house. At sixty-two, he was called the "oldest hippie in Powelton," and neighbors said he was a fragile and gentle soul. In 1973 he filed a complaint with the district attorney's office about threats he'd received from MOVE. Neighbors say that as a result he was singled out for a particularly hateful dose of harassment, with MOVE members surrounding him in the street and shouting anti-Semitic insults at him.

Eventually Monty Lis began to fear for his health and his life, and he started staying at a neighbor's home. On April 8, 1974, he filed a charge of harassment against Conrad.

On April 21, 1974, he suffered a heart attack.

As he lay in the hospital the nurses reached Gerry Goldin and asked him to bring some things from Monty's apartment that he might need in the hospital. On his way to the apartment, Goldin says, he was accosted by a dozen MOVE members. They began shoving him and shouting at him: "You gonna be dead! Your wife is gonna be dead! You better move

out of this neighborhood and never show up on this street
again! We'll break your legs!"

The next day, April 22, Monty died, and two days later his
complaint against Conrad was dismissed.

The day after that, Goldin and Edith Parent took Monty's
brother Bernard to the apartment to collect Monty's effects.
While they were inside, they began to hear catcalls from
MOVE members out on the street. They claimed credit for
Monty's death, Goldin said, and said that Bernard would end
up like his brother. Conrad and another MOVE member
encountered Goldin on the street three weeks later and repeated the boast—and the threat—to him as well.

All the rest of that year, Goldin said, MOVE members
would repeat the threats whenever they saw him. One October
evening they surrounded his house, shouting threats and
obscenities through a loudspeaker. They made noises like a
man having a heart attack.

Goldin and the neighbors were beginning to realize just how
little the police and the courts could help them. At the earliest
incidents police had told them they were powerless to act
against the assaults unless a private criminal complaint was
filed. If they didn't know the names of their assailants, the
police said, they could file a complaint based on physical
descriptions. Goldin had filed a complaint against Delbert for
assault, but nothing had come of it.

In August 1974 Goldin and Bruce Grant, another neighbor,
wrote to the district attorney's office asking for an investigation
into the pattern of threats and violence that the neighbors were
enduring at the hands of MOVE.

They received a form letter in reply. The proper procedure,
it said, was for them to file a private criminal complaint.

Still looking for help, Goldin and Grant arranged to meet
with an assistant district attorney. He told them that they had
even fewer options than they'd thought. He was sorry, but the
cops had been wrong; they couldn't file a criminal complaint
on the basis of description alone. In fact, he said, the surname
Africa wouldn't be enough; the neighbors would need to find
out the actual legal names before they could swear out a
complaint.

And just how would they do that? "Go see the police captain at the 16th Precinct," the attorney told them. "Their pictures are on file there.

"By the way," he added as the two men prepared to leave, "I wonder if you could write to the papers and indicate how cooperative this office has been. We've been getting a lot of criticism in the press lately."

A few weeks later Goldin and his wife met with the captain of Precinct 16. To begin with, they wanted to know why Delbert Orr hadn't been arrested, since a warrant had been issued when he'd failed to appear for his initial hearing on Goldin's complaint.

That was as far as they got before the captain cut them off. "I know who you are," he said. "You belong to that East Powelton group that's had all those demonstrations. If you people in the community want to fight among yourselves, that's your business. The police will not become involved."

When they tried to protest, he told them that the matter was closed. He would not permit them to review the mug shots of MOVE members, and he had no intention of arresting Delbert Orr Africa.

Finally the DA's office and police department had a change of heart—not because of neighbors' complaints but because they learned that MOVE members had threatened a judge and an assistant district attorney. Now the DA's office was willing to let Goldin and other neighbors identify from police photographs the people who had threatened them. Assistant District Attorney William Stephens made it clear that his interest lay in the threats against the judge and assistant district attorney. He told Goldin that he was willing to prosecute the case despite the fact that Goldin had belonged to the East Powelton group and had been involved in several demonstrations.

Goldin and the other neighbors were subpoenaed to appear in court on six different days. Each time, Goldin says, the case was postponed either because of MOVE's disruptions or because the DA's office wasn't prepared.

The DA's office lost the case—because of the DA's lack of preparation, Goldin would say later. In an interview with the *Bulletin,* however, Stephens blamed the failure on the reluctance of the witnesses—he named Goldin in particular—to testify.

"One of the real problems in this case," he said, "is getting people to come forward."

Ken Moberg tried a different approach: the media. Angered by a column in the *Philadelphia Daily News* by black columnist Chuck Stone that cited "a few" neighbors who "deeply resent what they feel has been abuse by MOVE members," Moberg wrote a long, accusatory letter to Stone. He wrote:

> You do us a great injustice as well as an offense when you make such a distorted statement as to the nature of MOVE's behavior toward *many* of their neighbors over the past two years of their existence. This is all the more so distorting and offensive when we know you have made no effort whatsoever to contact us about our experiences with MOVE.

Acknowledging that MOVE was entitled to free speech and free assembly under the law, Moberg asked Stone to consider the neighbors' rights as well:

> . . . Such as the legal right to protection under the law, and to bring legal charges against MOVE when their lives and the lives of their wives and children are publicly threatened, when they are physically assaulted in public, when they are viciously abused with anti-Semitic harassment in the best of Nazi stormtrooper style, when public laws and ordinances concerning garbage, trash, public burning, appropriate use of residential property, public nuisance [are ignored], and when people who have a long tradition of tolerance and good neighborliness are simply pressed to the wall by a group which has publicly stated it intended to force anyone and everyone out of Powelton who did not agree with and join them, i.e. MOVE, then that is just pushing the situation too far.

Stone wrote back:

> The purpose of my column was to point out that MOVE, despite whatever one feels about them, was being subjected

to an organized pattern of official harassment and abuse.

I doubt if you would maintain that you and your neighbors are being officially abused by the police and the criminal justice system.

Until my column appeared, MOVE's position on police brutality had not been published. Yet, by your own admission, your charges against MOVE were amply reported by John T. Gillespie [of the *Inquirer*]. You also included a column from the "Drummer" calling MOVE "the seeds of fascism."

I don't think I was supposed to join that club.

Everything you say about MOVE's offensive denial of civil and human liberties is correct. Their excesses should be legally curbed. But that in no way excuses what is happening to them with the official destruction of their rights.

I talked with Dr. Gerald Goldin and told him I would be delighted to do another column citing in detail the specific and documented cases of MOVE members' harassments, threats and denial of civil rights.

I appreciated your letter and am forwarding it to the editor. I'm urging that it be considered as a possible Op-Ed piece. You might contact Rolfe Neill directly to help persuade him to this decision.

> Cordially,
> Chuck Stone
> Editorial Department

Editor Rolfe Neill declined to print Moberg's letter, saying it was too long. Nor did anything come of Chuck Stone's promise to balance the picture with a column about MOVE's "excesses." A similar plea for coverage by the *Philadelphia Tribune*, the city's largest-circulation black weekly newspaper, and by radio station WFLN, also went unanswered.

Ken Moberg wasn't the only one to recognize the power of the press. About the same time, Louise James Africa—Vincent's sister—had emerged as a spokeswoman for the organization. She began to write a column, "On the MOVE," that appeared sporadically in the opinion section of the *Philadelphia Tribune*. The earliest columns, which were based on The Guidelines, offered John Africa's perspectives on politics, injustice, and other social issues. Later columns took on a more conversational tone, as Louise brought readers up to date on recent demonstrations and discussion sessions. The column ran perhaps once a month for about a year.

In its earliest days—in 1972—MOVE also had a radio program on WXPN, the University of Pennsylvania's FM station. It ran only briefly, and it is not clear whether MOVE or the station decided to cancel it. Alberta Africa says that the Coordinator canceled the show and column because The Guidelines were too powerful to put out without preparing people to understand them. Whatever the reasons for those decisions, they seemed to reflect a basic outlook of the organization, for MOVE has always seemed more interested in living its beliefs than in talking about them.

By the beginning of 1976, serious trouble was brewing in Powelton, but it seemed to the people in the neighborhood that they were powerless to do anything about it.

Everything, it seemed, had been turned upside down since MOVE had arrived. Charged as racists and elitists, it was the leftists of Powelton who were being demonstrated against. It was they who were filing criminal complaints and seeking police protection from radicals. The diversity of the neighborhood had descended into disunity; people were already taking sides, and it was beginning to get ugly.

During this time, as MOVE courted confrontation on an ever-grander scale, the man now known as John Africa became less and less visible. Gone were the early morning walks through the neighborhood with the dogs. Vincent moved in the shadows within the old house in Powelton Village, hiding behind a web of aliases and identities: "Charlie," "Bill," "Vincent Africa," or simply "the Coordinator." He was destined to become a mystery figure, a perfect mystical being who spoke only the truth and could never die.

By 1974 the reporter for *The Drummer* was confused enough by MOVE to write: "John Africa is missing. When asked of his whereabouts and whether he is alive, 'Move' members uniformly smile or laugh, deny knowledge of the matter, or refuse to answer."

One of those doing the denying, the reporter wrote, was a member who called himself Vince.

During those tumultuous times, Vincent never appeared at the public protests. He was never arrested. But he was never far away. In all the early years of MOVE one civil affairs cop recalls seeing him only once. A buddy nudged him one day and pointed to a solitary black man half a block away, quietly watching the noisy protest. "That's him," his friend said. "That's the guy who's behind all of this."

4
The Guns on
the Porch

IT MIGHT HAVE GONE on like this forever—the raucous protests, the scuffles with police, the arguments with the neighbors, the nickel-and-dime theatrics and confrontations. The early active days seemed to have given over to a kind of boredom. The radio show was off the air, the column in the *Tribune* had been canceled. MOVE was still recruiting members, and its members were still shuttling in and out of jail as a result of their protests and demonstrations, but the revolution looked far away indeed.

It was not a problem isolated to MOVE. There was a sense, in Powelton, in Philadelphia, in the world beyond, that an era had ended. More than that, there was a feeling that most of the great ideas of those naive times hadn't worked. Love hadn't saved the world; the revolution had not come. Prices were going up, you couldn't get a raise—and were lucky to find a job—and you had to sit in line for half an hour to buy gas that had probably gone up a nickel a gallon just while you were waiting. The communes had all disbanded, and the guys who had been burning flags were now rushing to sign up for law school. Earth Day—that grand, glorious act of faith, that perfect first spring day just five years before when it appeared as if all of the world, young and old, straights and freaks, could join together and save the world—seemed as if it had happened in a forgotten time.

Outwardly the house on Thirty-third Street had not changed much since MOVE had first slatted over the windows. The followers of John Africa—perhaps as many as several dozen—still held to their faith and their way of life, with occasional lapses into the addictions of their former lives. New people were still coming to MOVE, but now they were a little older, a little wiser.

On Sunday, March 28, 1975, something happened. Exactly what is still open to dispute.

There was a party on that Sunday afternoon. Seven MOVE members came home after serving time in jail on disorderly conduct and contempt-of-court charges, arriving in the dilapidated school bus that the group had bought with a donation from Richard Pryor. The homecoming was noisy, and it went on well into the evening. Someone—probably a neighbor—called the police.

The request for an officer at 309 North Thirty-third Street was an almost daily routine within the police department's civil affairs unit. But this time things started to get out of hand almost as soon as the cruisers pulled up to the curb.

Chuckie Africa—Vincent's nephew, who had been one of the first to join MOVE—began shouting at the cops: "We're sick and tired of you people! Leave us the fuck alone!"

One of the officers at the scene later told reporters that he was walking back to the car when a brick caught him on the back of his head. MOVE said that the police attacked them first. Within seconds bricks were flying and nightsticks were swinging. When the dust had settled, six cops were on their way to the hospital; just as many MOVE members were on their way back to jail, charged with aggravated assault, rioting, resisting arrest, and other offenses. The cops took only the men, leaving dazed and injured women behind them.

The next day Merle Austin Africa held an impromptu news conference on the steps of the house. It was covered by reporters from the major Philadelphia papers. She announced to reporters that a murder had been committed in the street. Janine Phillips Africa told how the police had shoved her roughly to the ground on top of her infant son, Life. The cops, she said, had stomped her mercilessly, crushing Life as he lay beneath her.

Where was the evidence? reporters asked. Where was the body?

The baby's body had been "taken care of," Merle added. "He didn't have no fancy clothes. He didn't have no embalming. He was taken out in the country, put in a blanket, and left."

Four days later the phone rang at the desk of *Inquirer* photographer James Link, Jr. MOVE member Robert Africa was on the line with an invitation for dinner that evening at the MOVE house. "Bring your camera," he said. "There's going to be an announcement."

Link knew that a request like this was unprecedented for MOVE. He pressed for more details. "What sort of an announcement?"

"We don't want to discuss it on the phone. But it will be worth your while to come."

The weather was cold and rainy when Link and reporter Ellen Karasik arrived at five o'clock. It was Karasik's first visit to the MOVE complex, and she was astonished by what she saw and heard—the dozens of howling dogs, their muzzles pressed against the windows of the house, the children dressed in light shirts and shorts despite the cold and rain, the yard littered with debris.

Link and Karasik were told to wait outside. They waited—and waited. An hour went by, and finally Link announced that they'd had enough. "We're leaving unless you tell us why you called us here."

Their host, Robert Africa, simply repeated what he'd said on the phone: "It will be worth your while to stay." He also made them promise not to tell anyone what they were about to see until MOVE told them they could.

The cold and damp were cutting through them like a blade, but still they stayed. At six o'clock things took an even stranger turn, as the other guests arrived. They included city council members Lucien Blackwell and Joseph Coleman, along with Blackwell's wife and Reverend Wrennie Morgan of the city's Human Relations Commission. They seemed just as perplexed as the *Inquirer* people.

Still they were not invited in. They stood outside for another half hour and finally were ushered inside. Darkness had nearly filled the street.

Inside, MOVE members escorted them down a flight of stairs and into the basement. The only light came from candles suspended from the ceiling.

If the guests had worried about the food, the table in the middle of the cellar reassured them. In the glow of the candlelight they could see white plates, with forks, knives, and spoons arranged in a way that Emily Post would have found acceptable. On the table reserved for the guests were platters piled full of fried chicken and corn on the cob and bowls of potato salad, rice, and spinach.

On another table, for MOVE members and children, was a plate full of raw chicken legs.

"You see," Robert said, "we don't live badly. We have all the comforts we need." Even so, the dinner was tense and quiet as the guests tried to puzzle out why MOVE had gone to all this trouble.

Dinner was over, and Lucien Blackwell had just taken a bite of watermelon for dessert, when three men stood up from the other table. They walked over to the *Inquirer* photographer and tapped him on the shoulder. "Come with us."

"Should I bring my camera?"

"Yes."

As the four disappeared up the darkened stairs, Robert Africa passed around a note. It read: "The baby is here. You'll see it after dinner."

Reverend Morgan got the note first, and he simply stared at it. Jane Blackwell took one look and elbowed her husband. "Read this!" she said.

The room was silent as the note continued around from Blackwell to Coleman and finally to the *Inquirer* reporter. Karasik read it and ran up the stairs after Link.

She stumbled through the hallway and into the front room, where she could see Link's flash firing in the candlelit gloom. He was taking pictures of a cardboard box that lay in the middle of the floor, surrounded by candles.

As she bent over the box a rotten stench filled her nostrils. Inside the box a small black baby lay curled on its side on a bed of grass and dirt. In the dim light she could make out eggshells and fruit and what seemed to be garbage. She jotted some notes and moved away, her stomach churning.

By now the others had arrived in the room. They stood in a semicircle around the box. All of them seemed to be in shock.

Robert Africa stood beside the box. "Let all here be satisfied once and for all that the baby does exist."

The guests stood uncertainly. Lucien Blackwell averted his eyes toward the window, watching the rats in the gloom of the yard. When he spoke, his voice sounded distant, detached. "It looks like you have a lot of rats there," he said.

"Yeah," said one of the MOVE members who had followed them into the room, "but they don't harm anything."

Reverend Morgan said, "I've seen rats bite babies, and the babies become sick and die."

"No," said Jerry Africa. "That's an old wives' tale. That's not true at all."

The conversation lapsed into stunned silence. Finally some of the MOVE members carried the box out of the room. Before the guests left the room a MOVE member asked them once again to promise that they would not talk about what they'd seen until MOVE released the information themselves.

The visitors left, shocked and silent. Outside the rain had stopped and a fresh breeze had come up, carrying with it a hint of spring.

The visitors, by all indications, kept their promises. For a week they kept the story to themselves. A week later an item appeared in a *Daily News* column citing unconfirmed rumors that certain city officials had viewed a dead infant at the MOVE house. With the silence broken the *Inquirer* ran a long story and photograph the following day.

However, the display of the body didn't settle the matter. MOVE members said they had returned the body to its resting place after the meeting. There had been no autopsy, no determination of time and cause of death, not even a positive identification of the body. Today people in MOVE say that it would have violated their principles to turn the body over to the medical examiner. They believe that death is simply another level of life, and in that view an autopsy would have inflicted more suffering on the life that remained within the child's body.

Others claim that less spiritual motives were involved. A former member later said that Janine's baby had died earlier of natural causes and that MOVE blamed the death on the police raid to score some publicity points. The police denied that they had injured a baby during the arrests—and still do.

Was it a case of police brutality or a carefully calculated hoax? In either event the death of Life Africa marked a turning point for MOVE. With it the focus shifted away from the abstract and on to the immediate. The destruction of nature was no longer the central topic of the militant rhetoric; MOVE's main issue was now MOVE itself and its persecution by the city and the police.

During the same months the city's cumbersome licenses and inspections machinery was moving toward a showdown with MOVE. Responding to the incessant stream of neighbors' complaints, the Department of Licenses and Inspections had filed suit in November 1975 to force MOVE to permit an inspection of the house. L&I violations, in turn, would serve as the basis for condemnation of the house and eviction of the residents.

The battle dragged on in the courts until it reached the Pennsylvania Supreme Court in the middle of July 1976. The state supreme court authorized the inspection, and the city was at last poised to meet the demands of the neighbors of Powelton Village.

MOVE responded to the court order by building an eight-foot-high fence around the house.

In the months that followed, life at the Powelton headquarters took on an ominous tone. The MOVE people began drilling like a military platoon, practicing "self-defense" techniques for the confrontation that John Africa said was inevitable. Donald Glassey and others began acquiring guns and explosives: rifles, shotguns, explosives—MOVE had even approached a National Guard atomic demolition specialist with the idea of stealing an atomic bomb. Now more than the city was involved; the FBI and agents of the Bureau of Alcohol, Tobacco and Firearms—ATF—were watching the comings

and goings on North Thirty-third Street with intense interest.
Vincent had succeeded in making his complaints against the
system a federal case.

An uneasy stalemate developed. Despite the state supreme
court order, no L&I inspection took place. Mayor Rizzo stated
publicly that the only way to enforce the order was with police
and that he wasn't going to send police in for L&I violations.
The weeks dragged into months.

On May 20, 1977, sheriff's deputies arrived at 3301 Powelton Avenue, around the corner from the main MOVE compound, to evict a MOVE member who lived in an apartment
there. MOVE members thought that they had come to evict
the group from the Thirty-third Street headquarters.

Almost immediately more than a dozen people stormed out
of the MOVE house nearby and onto the platform they had
built extending back from the eight-foot-high barricade in the
front yard. Gone were the familiar cutoffs and T-shirts that
they usually favored; this time they were dressed in khaki
coveralls and berets. And they were armed.

Delbert wore a .45 pistol in a holster strapped to his waist.
Others brought out more rifles, sawed-off shotguns, clubs, and
carbines, stacking them on the porch like soldiers setting up an
armed camp.

The demonstration lasted for nine long hours, all of it filled
with harsh, metallic obscenities shouted through the portable
megaphone. The crowd swelled to close to three hundred, and
before long reporters and photographers had arrived.

The police were not far behind. Two hundred heavily armed
cops hit the streets, surrounding the house while the harangue
went on. Others, less conspicuous, were taking notes. They
were able to identify most of the MOVE members by sight, and
they carefully noted which ones were bearing arms.

MOVE demanded an apology from Mayor Rizzo. They
wanted a guarantee, in writing, from the president of the
United States that the cops would leave them alone.

It was a virtuoso performance and clearly one that had been
rehearsed. The uniforms and guns made it the guaranteed lead
story on the local news that evening. In a pattern that would
become almost routine, MOVE paraded before the assembled

firepower of the Philadelphia Police Department, defiant and fearless.

Finally, at 10:30 in the evening, they simply took their weapons and went back inside the house, leaving two hundred perplexed cops training their guns on an empty porch. Commissioner O'Neill, just as bemused, finally ordered his men to evacuate.

Later MOVE contended that the guns brandished on the porch that day were, as they put it, "inoperable." They were presented as a "deterrent," they said. Their aim was defensive, not offensive; they were simply reacting to the police actions against MOVE.

The police kept a wary eye on the house in Powelton Village, and they obtained warrants for weapons violations against MOVE members whom they'd identified on the porch. Still they did not move in on the house. Inside the compound MOVE members kept a low profile, mostly staying out of sight. For two days the city and the revolutionaries circled around one another like boxers looking for an opening.

It became, for the moment, a war of words. On Monday the city of Philadelphia weighed in with heavy artillery, the legendary mouth of Mayor Frank L. Rizzo. This was the man who just the year before had announced that he would call out the National Guard during the city's bicentennial celebration—a statement that was reported throughout the country and that helped keep tourists away in droves. He was the man who, when he was running for reelection as mayor, promised to "make Attila the Hun look like a faggot after this election's over." If a bunch of left-wing goofballs thought they were going to pull anything in his city, well, they had better think again.

Rizzo had been mayor for only four years, but it seemed as if he'd been in charge forever. A street cop from south Philadelphia, he'd stomped through the department for more than twenty-five years, finally ending up as the police commissioner. He'd won the mayoral election in 1971 on a hard-nosed law-and-order platform. Though he was a Democrat in a Democratic town, his political hero was Richard Nixon—both before and after Watergate.

Like Nixon, Rizzo was a man that people loved to hate.
Some called him a Nazi; others saw him as an uneducated,
racist buffoon. He believed in taking care of his own—it hadn't
taken him long to appoint his brother fire commissioner—and
to hell with anybody who didn't like it.

Above all Frank Rizzo loved being mayor of Philadelphia. It
is the only elected office he has ever held. It is the only one he
has ever run for. Already in 1976 he was campaigning to
change the city charter—and in particular the provision that
required the mayor to step down after two consecutive terms.
It was a campaign that would eventually fail, and in 1979 he
was forced to watch from the sidelines as one of his old political
enemies, William Green, took his job away from him.

When he stepped down, even those who hated him most
would say Philadelphia would never be the same after Frank
L. Rizzo.

Rizzo had a reputation for coming out of his corner swinging. At a news conference he announced that he'd met with the
neighbors of Powelton Village and he was very concerned
about the situation that was developing out there. He didn't
want to start anything. He didn't want anyone hurt or killed.
"If there is any violence, they"—that is, MOVE—"will start it."

But, he said, "if they start it, I guarantee you we'll finish it.

"MOVE," he concluded, "has had its day. They're going to
be removed from the community for a long time."

There is, if you look closely at the words and career of Frank
Rizzo, a paradox. Beneath the hard-edged talk he is not the
one-dimensional trigger-happy ideologue that he seems to be.
You get the sense that there is a man who knows how to cut a
deal even as he talks tough.

So it was on this day. For when all the noise and fury were
stripped away, Rizzo actually announced that the city was
going to "sit and wait it out."

Those who heard him could be forgiven for wondering if
Attila the Hun would have done the same.

One day during a lull in the standoff, MOVE members
received instructions from the Coordinator for a new "activ-

ity." Several members, including Chuckie Africa, were told to take their guns and come down from the platform onto the streets. They fanned out to neighborhood street corners and took up positions, their weapons pointed into the air. It's not clear whether John Africa's aim was to stir up the confrontation or simply to see what the city's response would be.

The response was, for the most part, restrained. Of the people who went onto the streets that day, only Chuckie was arrested, and he was released the same night. The police did confiscate his shotgun, however, and began tracing its history through the serial number.

The standoff continued for ten months. Meanwhile, federal agents were busy building a case against MOVE for violations of weapons and explosives statutes. The shotgun that had been seized from Chuckie was traced to a suburban gun shop. The man who bought it had used a stolen driver's license. The fingerprints and handwriting were Donald Glassey's.

On June 3 agents of the federal Bureau of Alcohol, Tobacco and Firearms arrested Glassey, charging him with falsifying firearms information. The district attorney's office also charged him with possession of marijuana. Bail was set at $25,000.

The feds offered Glassey a deal: a reduced sentence, early parole, and relocation through the Federal Witness Protection Program. But he had to become an informant. His attorney advised him to take the deal.

Sitting in jail, unable to make bail, Don Glassey quickly realized the error of his ways. Later he would say that he had become disenchanted with MOVE because John Africa—whom he identified as Vincent Leaphart—had abandoned his early nonviolent ways. His reasoning is difficult to accept in light of the fact that Glassey himself had purchased at least two of the shotguns and two hundred rounds of ammunition.

In any case Glassey seemed to approach his new duties with the same enthusiasm he'd once shown for The Guidelines. ATF documents show that, once released from custody, Glassey continued to stay in contact with MOVE, meeting with Vincent on July 14. At a meeting with ATF agents on July 18, those documents reveal, Glassey announced that he "wanted

to give information which would help in making further arrests on MOVE members." Glassey said he believed John
Africa was living in Chester, Pennsylvania—about twenty
miles south of Philadelphia—but that he was directing
MOVE's activities by telephone. He told them that John Africa
"had become unstable, vicious and is the total leader of the
group, ordering every activity and operation of MOVE." John
Africa, Glassey said, had ordered LaVerne Africa—his sister—
to set up a shoot-out at the MOVE compound, shooting as
many police as possible and then committing suicide, and had
ordered Janine to slash her wrists to protest police brutality.
Glassey also told them that MOVE had hidden a large arsenal
at a location he wasn't aware of.

The federal agents encouraged Glassey to stay involved in
MOVE's efforts to acquire guns and explosives. They were
trying to build a conspiracy case, and the more people they
showed were involved, the stronger the case against all of
them.

After the meeting Glassey kept in almost constant contact
with the ATF agents. The same evening he phoned them at
eleven to tell them that there would be a meeting in the
Germantown section of the city and that Vincent was expected
to attend. They told him to attend the meeting and report
afterward.

The next evening Glassey called again. The meeting had
been canceled, but it seemed that Vincent was now planning to
move to Germantown.

The next day, July 20, Glassey had a lead on where the
explosives arsenal was being kept. He believed that a MOVE
member named Witt knew its whereabouts. Glassey had several conversations with Witt that day, and he reported that
Witt was also upset about MOVE's turn toward violence.
Glassey promised the agents that he would try to find out
where the explosives were hidden.

The following day, July 21, Glassey reported that he had
"convinced Witt that John Africa had betrayed the true mission of MOVE by becoming violent and that it was their
obligation to take the explosives and hide them at a different

location so that John Africa or any members loyal to him would not be able to use them." The ATF agents prepared to make a raid.

Just after noon on July 22 Glassey called again. Witt had decided to collect the explosives—which were hidden in an old gray Lincoln parked in Alphonso Robbins Africa's sister's garage—and bury them in the wilderness of Fairmount Park, the immense wooded tract that borders west Philadelphia and the Schuylkill River. Convince him to wait until nightfall, the agents said.

Half an hour later Glassey called back. Everything was set; he and Witt would be at a corner in north Philadelphia in ten minutes. ATF agents and Philadelphia police moved into position.

For the next three hours the police kept the pair under surveillance as they shuttled around the city in Glassey's Toyota, collecting weapons and explosives. Finally, at four, they returned to Alphonso's sister's house. As Witt backed the Lincoln out of the garage and into the alley behind the house, the ATF agents pulled their cars into each end of the alley, blocking their escape. They arrested Witt and, to preserve his cover, Glassey as well.

The two cars contained an almost incredible array of explosives. The trunk of the Lincoln contained five jars of gunpowder; a gallon of denatured alcohol; a box containing fifteen pounds of gunpowder, a scoop, and a wooden mixing spoon; supplies of mercury and sulfur; a homemade time bomb; two clock mechanisms and batteries; a remote-control unit for model airplanes; timers, fuses, batteries, beakers, vials, jars, and other scientific equipment; and an assortment of books and manuals, including something called the *Silencer, Snipers and Assassins Manual, OSS Sabotage and Demolition Manual,* and the *Encyclopedia of Chemical Technology.* Glassey's car contained a timer and battery, jars of sulfuric acid, nitric acid, ammonium hydroxide, and toluene; an electric chemistry burner; and eight rifles and a shotgun, all of them apparently stolen.

Meanwhile agents had established that the gray Lincoln was Alphonso's, and they found more explosives in a footlocker that he kept at his sister's home.

At his bail hearing the following day Glassey was released on his own recognizance. At 7:30 that evening he called an ATF agent. He'd wasted little time getting back to work. He'd been in touch with Greg, another MOVE member, who brought him up to date. As a result of the arrest and confiscation of the weapons, Greg told him, they were now trying to raise money to get John Africa, Alphonso, and another MOVE member, Beowolf, out of the area. At the same time they were trying to obtain more explosives.

The next day Jeanne called Glassey. She told him that Delbert wanted to know if Glassey would be willing to pick up some "pineapples"—hand grenades. Glassey agreed, arranging to meet Jeanne at a nearby gas station.

At the meeting Jeanne told him there'd been a change of plans. There was some confusion about the "pineapples," so that was on hold for the moment. But she gave him a list of other contacts who had weapons available for MOVE. Glassey should get in touch with them and obtain the guns.

That afternoon Glassey called Greg from the ATF office as agents recorded the conversation.

Glassey told Greg that he'd received an "activity" from Delbert but that he'd been instructed to call Greg first.

"I've got other orders from Charlie," Greg replied, using one of Vincent's aliases. "Don't do anything until I talk to Charlie. Call me back at ten tonight."

Glassey called at ten, but Greg wasn't there. He tried several times the next morning, Sunday, finally reaching him a little before noon. Greg told him that all further contact from Charlie would come through Alphonso's wife. He also said that Charlie was trying to raise money so that he could rent another place in the city.

On Monday they spoke again. Glassey was still confused about what Charlie wanted him to do. Greg hadn't heard from Charlie.

"The way things were mapped out, they'll continue that way," Greg added, according to a surveillance report by the

Bureau of Alcohol, Tobacco and Firearms. The raid was only a problem because of the explosives that were seized, he said; they'd have no problem replacing the guns.

Until he heard from Charlie, they should all sit tight, Greg said. They all had the feeling that the cops were watching them, he added.

Over the next several days Glassey seemed to grow more impatient. He called Greg back and said that Jeanne had been pressing him about getting the guns.

"I told her to forget it for now," Greg said. "I still haven't heard from our friends yet."

Next Glassey called Jeanne and asked if she'd spoken to Delbert.

"It was nixed" for the time being, she replied.

That evening Glassey called Greg back and arranged a meeting in Fairmount Park. They agreed to meet at the old waterworks, a secluded spot on the bank of the Schuylkill River.

The following day, July 27, Glassey and Greg met at the waterworks. Glassey wore a hidden microphone, and an ATF agent crouched in the foliage nearby with a camera and high-powered lens.

"I've got a friend who can probably get us some C-4 [a military plastic explosive]," Glassey said. "I think it might be as much as twenty-five pounds."

Greg was excited by the news. Comparing that much plastic to what had been seized in the raid was like comparing a hand grenade to a firecracker, he said. "We'll definitely take it if you can arrange it," Greg said.

"Don't you have to check with Charlie first?" Glassey asked.

"No, not if it's a donation."

"How about Delbert or Phil?" Phil, another MOVE member, was married to Janine.

"No. Things like this are my activity. Theirs is guns."

Greg talked some more about stealing cars to get money for Charlie.

Glassey interrupted. "What should we do if my guy wants to do the transaction in New Jersey?"

"I'll go to New Jersey if I need to," Greg answered.

They talked some more about the possibility of police surveillance. They would need to be careful, they agreed. Greg then said he expected to hear from Charlie soon and would get his approval. But he was sure he didn't need the approval beforehand.

Then Greg talked about the "proposal"—a "master plan" that was the "final solution" to MOVE's problems. The plan included an extortion plot against the government and outlined the use of the explosives as a threat.

"We even thought about getting a nuclear bomb," he said. Seeing Glassey's face, he went on. "It's not that farfetched. Sometimes they're accidentally dropped at sea, and they never find them. If they lose one anytime soon, we could say that we recovered it."

"Can I get a copy of the proposal?" Glassey asked.

"I'll give you a copy when I get one," Greg told him.

Now the sting was moving into high gear. The ATF agents and Glassey set up a meeting in a restaurant parking lot in New Jersey, with imitation C-4 as a sample for Greg.

That night Glassey called Greg and told him the meeting was set for midnight.

"Meet me at Thirteenth and Pine at eleven," Greg said.

At twenty minutes past midnight a Chevrolet station wagon carrying Greg and Glassey pulled into the restaurant parking lot in New Jersey. Glassey's "friend" was waiting for them.

Glassey made the introductions, and the "friend" handed them two pounds of what looked like plastic explosive.

"Is there anything else you and your . . . associates need?" the man asked Greg.

Greg wrote out a list and handed it to him. It read:

    plastic, any amount
    grenades
    detonators
    caps
    bazookas
    mortars
    auto rifles

At the bottom were two phone numbers. He could reach

Greg at the first one; the second was only for messages. "I don't do business over that phone," Greg said. "I can't trust it. The second number's cool, though."

On the way back from New Jersey Greg got the impression he was being followed. As soon as he had crossed the Ben Franklin Bridge and arrived back in the city he began taking evasive action—running red lights, making sudden lane changes, circling around, and doubling back.

Greg's instincts were correct; the ATF agents were right behind him. But they weren't interested in arresting him just yet; they were simply keeping an eye on him.

Greg dropped off Glassey at the same corner where he'd picked him up and then continued to duck and dodge through the city. At the railway station on Thirtieth Street—just a few blocks from the MOVE house—he got out and disappeared on foot to hide what he thought were explosives. Back in the car fifteen minutes later, he continued doubling through the streets of Philadelphia until almost 2:00 A.M., when the ATF agents, dogging him to the end, watched him disappear into a bar in north Philadelphia.

Over the next several days Glassey tried several times to reach Greg on the phone—and to find out the whereabouts of Charlie—that is, Vincent—and Beowolf. But he was already too late. Vincent had left town back in June—at almost precisely the same time that Glassey had sat in jail and made up his mind to cooperate with the federal agents.

Jeanne would later tell the story of their flight. She was living with her husband, Ishongo Africa, in a downtown apartment at the time, one of the "safe houses" that MOVE had established around the city. Their relationship continued to be a stormy one, and in May 1977, she says, Ishongo held her hostage in the apartment for a day and a half. Finally she escaped and, desperate, called Vincent. He told her to come to the headquarters in Powelton Village.

The next morning she attended a meeting in the apartment that MOVE members had rented around the corner from the main headquarters. There were fifteen or twenty people in the apartment that morning, the most committed core of the organization. They were planning a confrontation with the police for the following Friday—May 20.

Before the planning began, however, Jeanne later said, Vincent had something to say, and he wanted everyone to listen. Looking at Jeanne, he began to talk about the principles of marriage.

"Marriage," he said, "is two people moving in the same direction to be right. And I've been watching you and Eddie"—Edward Goodman Africa—"moving in the same direction. He's your coordinator; you're his student. You should be married."

And so they were, Jeanne says. Vincent performed the marriage himself as the rest looked on, and then they all got down to the business at hand.

As the planning went on through the morning, Delbert turned to Jeanne. "Do you want to go with underground or aboveground activity next Friday?"

"I'll do whatever the family needs me to do," she said.

"Okay," Delbert said. "You'll be above ground."

(Again, Alberta Africa says that Jeanne's account of these events is a "blatant lie." Jeanne never married Eddie, she said; Eddie was already married. In fact, she said, Vincent didn't "perform" marriages at all.)

As it happened, Jeanne was neither above ground nor below ground on the day of the confrontation. Instead she stood among the crowd of onlookers at the base of the platform. Her brother-in-law had died, and she'd had to leave unexpectedly that morning to attend the funeral. As she came back to the house early in the afternoon, she saw the crowd in the middle of the block. And up on the stage she saw Delbert and the others with guns, bats, and ammunition.

She was stunned, she says. She had assumed that the confrontation would be like the others—verbal but not violent. She says she had never seen MOVE members carrying firearms before.

Never, that is, except for the time she had come upon Delbert cleaning a gun inside the house. When she asked him about it, he told her that sometimes it was hard to get rid of certain life style addictions. He was, he said, a gun fanatic from his days in the Black Panthers, and that was why the gun was in the house.

She was also surprised to see Ishongo on the platform, putting out information. No true follower of John Africa would inflict the beatings he had given her. No one who truly accepted The Guidelines would poison his body with drugs the way Ishongo did. The people in MOVE knew this, so why would they permit him to stand up and put out information?

Jeanne returned to her house on Thirteenth Street, troubled and confused. On Sunday the 22nd, Vincent and Beowolf arrived. They didn't say how long they'd be there.

Over the next two weeks the neighbors must have wondered what was going on as strange men and women went in and out of Jeanne's town house. They were members of the "black guard"—the MOVE underground—Jeanne later said. They didn't usually stay long. They would come in, talk to Vincent for a while, and leave.

Vincent was upset, she said, at how the confrontation over in Powelton Village was being reported in the press. As the days went on and the stalemate continued, the story moved off the front page and onto inside pages. Some days there would be no coverage at all. Vincent told her to call the papers and television stations and complain about the "news blackout" of the confrontation.

One day, she says, she asked Vincent why Ishongo was on the platform talking MOVE principles when he didn't live by those principles.

"There's a reason he's there," Vincent told her. "There's going to be a shoot-out with the cops, and Ishongo will be taken care of then."

"Taken care of? How will he be taken care of?" Jeanne asked.

"He'll be there to protect MOVE. If he gets in a shoot-out with the cops, he might get killed." Then he went on to say that if the cops didn't get Ishongo, MOVE would—and they'd set it up to look like the cops had done it.

Jeanne says she felt herself recoil. Using weapons for defense was one thing, but this was cold-blooded murder.

Still, she would say later, she said nothing. And her belief in the principles of John Africa was still strong enough that she did not abandon MOVE at this time.

Some two weeks after he arrived, Vincent abruptly announced that he was leaving. As he burned papers in a pot on the stove, he told Jeanne to wipe down everything in the house so that no fingerprints would be left behind.

When she was done, he instructed her to scout around outside for police or any undercover people she might recognize. As soon as she returned with an all-clear, members of the MOVE underground showed up in a car to pick up Vincent and Beowolf.

It was the last time she would see them for nearly three years.

Half an hour later the phone rang. It was Beowolf. He'd forgotten some socks down in the basement; he asked Jeanne to bring them upstairs.

In the basement she found the package, but it was obvious that it didn't contain socks. Back upstairs, she opened it and found a contraption made of two pipes, a plastic pill bottle containing black powder, and putty. It was, she knew, a bomb. She was almost beside herself with anger.

The phone rang. It was Beowolf again.

"Why did you leave a bomb in the basement?" she demanded.

"Be careful with that stuff," Beowolf snapped. "It's expensive." *Expensive* was a code word; it meant that it was something they needed and didn't want to lose. "Bury it in the backyard. We'll be using it later."

Jeanne took the bomb outside to the backyard. It was a common yard, used by people in the two adjoining houses as well as her. Children and dogs played back there.

She couldn't bury it in the backyard. What if the dogs dug it up? She took it back inside and waited for Beowolf to call again.

When he called, she told him she couldn't bury it in the yard. Beowolf paused, then told her to get rid of it—to take it somewhere, take it apart, and scatter the pieces. After he hung up, she walked north and east for several blocks to a deserted area and quickly, furtively, dispersed the pieces.

Despite her growing reservations, Jeanne still visited the MOVE house during the confrontation and performed the duties she was given. In addition to her meetings with Glassey to pass on information about weapons, she called the papers and television stations to bring attention to the confrontation.

As the days grew into months, she couldn't forget what Vincent had said about Ishongo. Despite the beatings she'd received from him, she still loved him, and she knew what Vincent had said was wrong. She had learned, too, that she was carrying Ishongo's child. And yet she couldn't betray her family, the family of MOVE.

In December of that year, as the standoff continued between MOVE and the police, Jeanne Africa went into a difficult labor. She tried to follow the teachings of John Africa, to deliver the child without the interference of doctors and hospitals, but her body would not cooperate. On December 16, after nineteen hours of labor, she began to hemorrhage, and despite The Guidelines and the outrage of Ishongo, she went to a hospital. Her son was born by cesarean section. She felt like a failure.

While she was in the hospital she had some time to think. She thought about the guns and about the things Vincent had said. She recalled some conversations she'd had with Don Glassey about how the organization had changed, about its inexorable drift toward violence. She thought about her newborn son and asked herself why a mother's instinct to save her child had seemed so wrong. It *wasn't* wrong, she decided. MOVE was wrong. John Africa was wrong.

When she left the hospital with her newborn son in her arms, she no longer considered herself a member of MOVE.

When he left Jeanne's house, Vincent disappeared into the underground that MOVE had carefully built over the years.

Some weeks earlier—in fact, just before the May 20 confrontation—two black men had appeared in a real estate agent's office in Rochester, New York. One had the improbable name of Jimmie Lee Phart; the other was called Ernie. They were looking for cheap property for their uncle, a real estate investor.

They found a decrepit house in a run-down part of the city. The price was less than $500, and it did not take the men long to strike a deal. They signed the papers on behalf of their uncle, whom they said was on his way to Rochester. The uncle's name was Vincent Lee Phart.

Lee Phart—Leaphart. Nobody could say Vincent didn't have a sense of humor.

Jimmie Lee was Alphonso Africa; Ernie was Gerald Ford Africa. They were two of MOVE's earliest and most trusted members. As events moved toward confrontation in west Philadelphia, they prepared the house for the imminent arrival of "Uncle" Vincent. More members of the family arrived soon, including Vincent's wife, Alberta.

Eventually MOVE bought seven houses in the Rochester area and dispatched several of the women and children to another house in Richmond, Virginia, where they established a group known as the "Seed of Wisdom."

MOVE apparently had its eye on some rural property as well. It entered into negotiations for a farm in Virginia. It was about this time that the group also entered into discussions about a farm in a rural part of southern New Jersey—an effort for which city commissioner Lucien Blackwell, perhaps seeing an easy way out of the confrontation that had dominated his district, wrote a glowing letter of reference.

When Vincent and Beowolf left Jeanne's house in downtown Philadelphia, they headed for Rochester and the house that was already waiting for them.

During his stay in Rochester, Vincent Leaphart would be presented to the neighbors and curious people who began to drop by as "Bill." Soon he would become a fixture in the neighborhood, a man known for his passion for early morning runs, when he could be seen in a blue jogging suit, running barefoot through the broken and battered streets of Rochester, trailed by a pack of barking dogs.

The other members of the clan lived under a variety of aliases, but they took no pains to disguise their lifestyle. Before long the upper windows of the old frame house were covered over with slats. They began feeding the neighborhood strays and putting out birdseed—pounds at a time—in the backyard.

Despite the way they lived, Rochester seemed a safe haven for the MOVE leadership. There in upstate New York, on the shore of Lake Ontario, they were far away from the crisis that was building in Philadelphia throughout the summer.

Far away, but not out of touch. Evidence suggests that Vincent kept in touch with the Philadelphia contingent by telephone, guiding the confrontation. It is likely that he used the people of the MOVE underground as intermediaries to take messages and instructions to the group in the house. Among his instructions, says the former Jeanne Africa, was a detailed plan for armed resistance should the police seize the house by force. He had named a select cadre of people to stay and defend the house in that case. The others—including the children and many of the women—should leave the house before any armed confrontation took place.

There is a document from this time that provides an insight into MOVE's methods, its expectations, and its perception of itself. It is a grant proposal written by someone who had an obvious familiarity with social science jargon. It is not known to whom the proposal was submitted—if, indeed, it was ever submitted anywhere. A copy of it ended up in the Philadelphia Police Department's background files on MOVE; it bears the handwritten date July 10, 1978, the very height of the police siege. It is impossible to tell whether that is when it was created or submitted or whether it is simply the date that the police obtained a copy. Certain items mentioned in passing suggest that it was written about 1976 or early 1977, but the thinking it reflects seems consistent with MOVE's activities during the time of the siege itself. Entitled "Proposal for Funding of the MOVE Organization," it describes MOVE as a "community-based, grass-roots movement dedicated to the teaching of our founder, JOHN AFRICA." It continues:

> This teaching has enabled people of many diverse backgrounds and social experiences to diagnose the problems with which they were faced in their previous existences and work collectively toward positive personal and social change. MOVE members have now begun to manifest the principle of Natural Law, the Law of *Form*, the teaching of JOHN AFRICA, as the only viable alternative to our former frustrations, anxieties and tensions.

The proposal continued in the same vein for several pages, in the tone of someone who has reluctantly donned an ill-fitting suit to borrow money:

> . . . We are taught that society imposes these addictions on children from birth and that a child's unnatural dependence on a rattle or a bottle of soda pop is not unlike his later cravings for the contents of a hypodermic needle, a stick of marijuana or a quart of wine. All MOVE members now understand and readily distinguish between wants and needs, discouraging the former in favor of the latter. . . .

On page 3, MOVE laid out its wants and needs in precise detail:

> . . . a parcel of land in a rural . . . [as well as] a number of [inner city] properties that would be conducive to the maintenance of our programs . . . large enough to house several families, preferably with a large open area that could be utilized for lectures or spontaneous discussion sessions [and] a yard of an area sufficient to provide for a few animals and the physical fitness needs of the residents . . . a large garage with running water [for the car wash].

Because of the distorted picture of MOVE in the media, the organization also wished to

> establish a communications media of our own to serve as a forum to clarify our beliefs, objectives, programs, and services. Toward this end, we have been trying to obtain a small printing press, new or used, that would serve to produce a bi-weekly newspaper or newsletter [with the costs offset by] a few advertisements and a small donation requested of its readers.

In a section entitled "Funding History" the anonymous proposal writer explained that hard times had fallen on the group since the city shut down the car wash and towed away trucks used in the handyman and moving services that the group had also provided. But, the proposal said, "even if we did have access to the vehicles, it would be difficult to expend a large labor force on these activities, as it is currently necessary to maintain a sizable presence of MOVE members at our house to discourage the police from provoking any further confrontations."

Finally, there is a carefully prepared "Line Item Budget per Month" for this wish list, coming to a total of $2,995 plus initial or down payments on the rural and urban properties and printing press amounting to $16,000.

Presumably the request for funding went unfulfilled. But it raises an intriguing question: during the siege, where did MOVE find the money not only for food and other necessities, but for the guns and explosives, the seven properties in Rochester, and the safe houses scattered throughout the city? Jeanne Africa would say later that most of the money came from drugs sold by the MOVE underground—the "black guard" that she and others say was far larger than the above-ground activities would suggest. She says that the fact that MOVE itself was adamantly opposed to "addictions" of any kind, including drugs, was explained by Vincent as an instance of evil being turned back on itself for the greater good.

If MOVE was having trouble making ends meet, things weren't going so well for the city either. As MOVE held out through the summer and fall of 1977 and on into the coldest winter that Philadelphia had seen in a century, the bills were beginning to pile up—and with them the frustration of the taxpayers. The neighbors were angry and frustrated. A news report showed that the standoff had already cost the city at least a quarter of a million dollars in police overtime and other expenses and that more than 250 MOVE-related trials had clogged the courts, delaying another two thousand criminal cases.

Finally, on March 1, Mayor Rizzo made his first move. One senses that he was reluctant—not out of fear or sympathy, but simply because he knew that he was being pushed into a corner that would be difficult to get out of. For ten months MOVE had taunted him, provoked him, and embarrassed him, and he'd refused to play the game. But now, like it or not, he was being drawn into that game. And if he had to play, he was going to play to win.

Going before Judge G. Fred diBona, the city asked for—and received—permission to build a blockade around the MOVE house. Rizzo announced that the city would no longer permit people to approach the house with food or other supplies. City water—which had been kept on out of concern for the welfare of the children—was to be shut off. The mayor announced his intentions in the most unmistakable terms: if MOVE wouldn't leave voluntarily, he was going to starve them out.

The press went wild. "Get Out or Die, Mayor Says," screamed a tabloid headline. The reporters and photographers descended on the scene in a fury, and the drama on Thirty-third Street became a daily staple of the news. Over the next several weeks, as the last furies of winter piled snow on the city, the police put up chain-link fencing around four blocks and cleared the streets inside of people. They established a tight cordon of police officers around the house. Mounted patrols stood outside the barricade, granting passage only to residents on the block and the seemingly endless procession of police detectives and civil affairs officers.

The crowds did not go away, of course. Kept back behind the barricades, they grew larger and louder. The confrontation that had been seething for almost ten months now seemed ready to ignite. MOVE had stockpiled food and water, anticipating Rizzo's move, but everyone knew that sooner or later something would have to happen. The deathwatch had begun.

As the snows of winter melted into the first rainy days of May, Frank Rizzo did something extraordinary for a man who was known as the toughest mayor in America: he agreed to a compromise. Attorney Oscar Gaskins, who represented MOVE in legal proceedings from time to time, and the city solicitor's office worked out a ten-point agreement that looked as if it would sidestep the confrontation that so many had seen as inevitable. MOVE agreed to turn over its weapons to the police and permit a search of the house. In addition it would permit the police to arrest each person in the house for whom warrants were outstanding.

The city, in turn, agreed to release immediately on their own recognizance those taken into custody. The district attorney pledged to expedite proceedings against MOVE members who were already in jail and to recommend that they too be released on their own recognizance.

And finally, MOVE agreed to vacate the Powelton headquarters within ninety days—by August 1, 1978.

The first part of the agreement went off without a hitch. Police confiscated a number of weapons from the house—all of them inoperable—and the MOVE members in the house politely stepped into the waiting police wagon for the trip to police headquarters downtown. They went one at a time, with the others remaining in the house; after booking, fingerprinting, and photographing them, the police drove each one back to the house and picked up another.

The barricades stayed up over the summer as the search began for a new headquarters for MOVE. The earlier grant proposal notwithstanding, the group now rejected the idea of a farm. They felt that they wouldn't be safe without the protection afforded by their visibility and access to the press. They deemed a run-down property in north Philadelphia as unsuitable. The August 1 deadline came and went, and MOVE announced that it wasn't going anywhere. MOVE members said they couldn't leave because they had no place to go. The next morning, Judge diBona signed arrest warrants for twenty-one MOVE members and gave the police ten days to execute the arrests.

Back in his office at City Hall, Rizzo was furious. MOVE had played him for a fool and gotten away with it. He had handled these people with a deference that didn't become him, and now his problems were worse.

On August 2 Rizzo held a tense press conference. "There will be no more bargaining, no more conversations, meetings, or agreements."

The same morning, when MOVE members failed to appear for a hearing, Judge diBona signed arrest warrants for those who had been released on their own recognizance and ordered the Philadelphia police to make the arrests within ten days.

Almost immediately after the judge issued the order Police Commissioner Joseph O'Neill called his senior people together.

There was no time to lose. The countdown had begun.

Jeanne Africa says that she went to the Powelton house for the last time in the first days of August. By then MOVE had been cut off from the world for nearly three months.

All that summer she had been troubled by what Vincent had told her about Ishongo. Just as the confrontation he had predicted seemed inevitable, she had received a call from Monsignor Charles Devlin, one of the negotiators who had been trying to work out a settlement between MOVE and the city. He asked Jeanne if she knew of anyone who was in danger inside the MOVE house. She told him about Ishongo.

Later that day the monsignor called back, urging her to go to the police. He told her to get in touch with Inspector Fencl, the man in charge of the siege.

When Fencl heard the story, he let her pass through the barricade. She does not say whether the people in the house were surprised to see her, but somehow she managed a few moments alone with Ishongo, and she told him what Vincent had said.

Several days later the police officers watching the house saw Ishongo jump off the porch and walk away from the house, never to return. Jeanne believes he is now living in France.

In the first week of August specially picked cadres of police officers met several times at a secret location. In city garages welders began attaching armor plating to heavy construction equipment. At the Philadelphia police headquarters known as the Roundhouse, a sense of urgency filled the air. Planning sessions ran late into the evenings. City spokespersons, asked about Judge diBona's order, refused to discuss timing or tactics.

Late in the afternoon of August 7 the police commissioner's office issued a confidential order. Before long the switchboard at the Roundhouse was bristling with outgoing calls. A lot of fathers and husbands would not be home for dinner that evening.

5
August 8

EVERY DAY FOR THE last twelve days the midsummer rains had fallen on the city, and life had burst forth in the lush wet heat with an almost tropical fury. On cracked sidewalks grass pushed through the pavement in thick, unruly clumps. Vacant lots had become dense green jungles. The earth that had been frozen so deeply and so long during the winter was now soft and pliable, shifting beneath the feet like something alive. Between the rains the air hung thick and blue, filled with the cries of insects and birds.

In the early morning hours of August 8 the rains stopped. A gentle breeze wafted through west Philadelphia, easing the humidity and cooling the air. Just for a few hours in the darkness it was as if the summer had lifted away from the streets, and beneath it had come just the briefest hint of fall.

Sometime after midnight cops started arriving in the vacant lot that had once been the site of the Philadelphia General Hospital—the hospital that had been the birthplace, forty-five years before, of Vincent Leaphart. They were glad for the break in the weather; it would make the job they had to do a little easier.

It was not often that you could see the police commissioner himself at a police scene at one in the morning, but Joseph O'Neill was there that night. The plan that would begin in the next few hours was unmistakably his own. Like O'Neill, it was organized and logical; there was no room in it for improvisation or indecision.

In contrast to the flamboyance that Frank Rizzo had

brought to the commissioner's job, Joseph O'Neill was a buttoned-down cop. He wasn't using the job as a stepping-stone to political office. He was a cool professional, with a reputation for being old-fashioned and at times autocratic.

O'Neill hadn't gone beyond his own expertise and that of his immediate staff to develop the plan. He saw no need to seek the advice of "experts" inside or outside the force; he knew what he was doing. He'd been personally involved in close to a hundred barricade situations. He had put together the Philadelphia stakeout squad—one of the first SWAT teams in the nation. And he'd been an engineer in the military, building bridges and roads under combat conditions.

In statements given to the media the police department later said the plan had been put together in the week since diBona had ordered MOVE's eviction. But O'Neill had actually begun thinking about the problem some six weeks earlier.

O'Neill approached the problem from an engineering point of view. He began by defining his objectives: first, to remove the children safely from the compound; second, to protect his people; third, to remove the women safely; and last of all, to remove the men.

Police knew the general arrangement of the house's interior from an interview with a jailed MOVE member. She had described the inside of 309 North Thirty-third Street to police investigators. She wasn't as familiar with 307, she said, but it was basically the same.

The house was, for all practical purposes, empty. The basement, she'd told them, was one large empty room, with a table in the center and a row of doghouses along the rear wall. The first floor—at the level of the wooden platform—had four rooms, all in a row: the living room/office in the front, a meeting room, a "dog room," and an office in the rear.

Upstairs were the sleeping areas—one room for mothers with babies, another for couples with babies, and a large room where the others slept. The third-floor attic held more sleeping areas and, in the center, the kitchen.

Armed with this description of the house's layout, O'Neill had devised a simple strategy. A bulldozer would first tear down the barricade along the sidewalk to gain access to the house itself. Then a cherry picker—a piece of construction equipment with a long hydraulic arm—would be brought into position to knock out the slats across the windows.

A key part of O'Neill's plan was its reliance on armor. To bring his people into range he devised an armored personnel carrier made out of a yellow dump truck from the department of streets. It was an ungainly rolling fortress: the front wheel had a thick steel plate almost covering the entire wheel. On the side that would face the MOVE house, sandbags were piled on the running board. More were stacked on the hood and around the window of the cab, with a tiny slit to enable the driver to see. A thick piece of steel plating some six feet high and ten feet wide was propped in the back, backed up by still more sandbags. He'd devised similar armor for the bulldozer and cherry picker, with sandbags protecting the operators, gas tanks, and other vulnerable parts.

O'Neill wanted no surprises. The police would "telegraph" their every move to the people in the house, informing them over the bullhorn what would happen next. They would use only smoke, no tear gas, both out of concern for the children and so the officers wouldn't need to use gas masks.

By the time August 8 came, O'Neill was confident—almost arrogant in his low-key way. He had devised no contingency plan; he saw no need. He was sure the plan would work.

3:00 A.M.–6:00 A.M.

Six-and-a-half blocks away from the staging area the brooding old house on Thirty-third Street was dark and silent except for the barking of dogs. But the people inside were not sleeping. A MOVE supporter had slipped through the blockade during the night to warn them that the police were assembling nearby. They knew the confrontation that had been brewing for a year and a half would come today. Earlier in the night Janine had told a reporter, "Stick around."

At three in the morning dozens of police began to arrive in trucks, methodically taking up their assigned positions. Among them were twenty-eight specially selected stakeout cops, whose job it would be to enter the house. They had been chosen because of their physical size.

Cops fanned out into the surrounding buildings to evacuate residents and set up observation posts. They sandbagged windows and rooftop positions and searched the adjacent buildings room by room. Within minutes they controlled an entire city block within the chain-link barricades.

As the press began to realize what was happening, reporters and photographers moved in closer and closer to the MOVE house. But O'Neill wasn't going to have the media getting in his people's way during the operation; he herded them into an area surrounded by chain-link fence. He would permit four reporters to move in closer, he told them. They would have to draw lots.

In an apartment building behind the police lines two officers were escorting the last of the tenants from their second-story apartment.

As they prepared to leave, one of the cops stopped at the window.

"Hey, look at this," he said to his partner. "It's a great view." The window framed the scene outside like a television screen. From this vantage point they could see everything— the cops on the street below crouching in the darkness behind their riot shields, the forbidding barricades across the street, and beyond them, the slatted windows of the MOVE house. It was a ringside seat.

As the door closed behind them on the way out, the shower curtain rustled in the bathroom, a closet door creaked open, and *Daily News* reporter Kitty Caparella and photographer Norman Lono took up positions by the window. The cop had been right. It was a great view.

The loudspeaker came on for the first time at 3:50 A.M.

"Testing, murderers. Testing."

The plan unfolded literally by the numbers. At 4:00 A.M. traffic barriers went up at Thirty-third and Powelton. At 4:20 a busload of police officers pulled up to the same intersection. Within minutes they were joined by thirty-two mounted police, all of them wearing riot helmets and flak jackets.

Inside the barricades a small group of MOVE sympathizers and supporters were already waiting, sitting on benches and milk crates along the fence. Two women—one in dreadlocks and one not—hugged each other in the middle of the street.

Charles ("Chuckie") Sims Africa came on over the loud-speaker: "Who's crazy? Tell the world Rizzo killed black babies for a health violation. You think we're crazy. We ain't crazy. Every day it's been raining. Where do you think that rain's coming from?"

Despite the months of threats coming from the house, the police did not expect trouble. In fact, the cops who'd been tapped to go into the house had been assured by their supervisors that MOVE had no guns in the house; all of them had been removed during the truce at the beginning of the blockade, and no one had been permitted to go into the house since then. They moved into position brazenly, in full view of the MOVE house. A group of them walked up the west side of Thirty-third Street, across the street from the house. The crowd of sympathizers was still at the fence. One of the women taunted the black officers: "You house niggers. You're too damn scared to tell them you don't want any part of this murder."

At 4:50 the armored bulldozer arrived on the back of a truck. A buzz went through the crowd of onlookers and reporters as they realized for the first time what O'Neill had in mind: "They're going to knock the house down!" The bulldozer sat on the back of the truck, half a block away from the MOVE house, like an actor waiting in the wings.

At 5:05, as MOVE members watched from the darkness of the porch, fire fighters in helmets and orange-and-black raincoats set up water cannons to the west and north of the MOVE house, aiming them carefully at the basement windows. Tow trucks began clearing parked cars. Two police wagons arrived, were waved through the barricade, and came to a stop directly in front of the MOVE house. Cops in riot gear emerged and began moving people away from the fence. Reluctantly the crowd retreated to barricades on Powelton Avenue to await the opening act.

Just after 5:30, as the first hints of light showed in the sky, the bulldozer rolled off the trailer and began creeping toward the fence. Above the low-pitched rumble it was possible to hear the sound of babies crying. As the bulldozer moved closer and closer, Delbert's voice thundered over the loudspeaker: "You've been killing Indian babies for two hundred years. You've been killing black babies for two hundred years. You don't give a fuck about black babies, black men, and black women."

As Delbert shouted, the bulldozer stopped in the middle of the street in front of the house. It waited, its engine idling. Two MOVE men still stood on the porch, watching.

The sun was up. The drama was about to begin.

At 6:04 Officer Benjamin Powell of the civil affairs unit strode to the middle of the street and stood beside the sand-bagged truck. Speaking through a bullhorn, he read the statement prescribed in Step 1 of the plan:

"We have in our possession writs of attachments and bench warrants for the occupants of 307–309 North Thirty-third Street. These are court orders issued by Judge G. Fred diBona on August 2, 1978, who has ordered the police to take you into custody.

"Each of you is ordered to surrender immediately. Leave your weapons and come out with your hands extended over your head. You have three minutes to walk to the street."

Delbert's voice crackled back: "You're gonna have to carry us out of this house! We're not walking out!"

Five minutes later Powell read Step 2:

"You have not surrendered. We are proceeding to tear down the fence."

The response from the house was silence.

The chugging from the bulldozer became a growl. It clanked across the sidewalk and rammed the fence.

The fence shook, but it did not fall. The bulldozer backed up and rammed it again; still it stood. Again the bulldozer advanced, and this time the fence splintered into pieces around the oncoming blade. As it crumbled and fell, rats the size of cats ran from beneath it, across the porch, and into the house.

From within the house came the sound of wailing women and crying babies. Someone shouted, "Long live John Africa!"

One of the men on the porch picked up a large dog and held it in his arms. The other bared his chest. "Come on," he cried. "Kill me! I don't have a weapon!"

When MOVE first constructed its barricade/platform, it had built it around a tree, taking care not to disturb its roots. Now the platform and tree fell with a crash as the bulldozer rolled closer to the porch.

The people on the porch ducked inside as the bulldozer crawled over the broken lumber that now littered the shallow front yard. It stopped when it reached the porch itself, but not before the falling debris had hit a corner post, knocking it to a crazy angle and threatening to collapse the entire porch.

Step 2 was complete. Now the plan called for negotiation. Monsignor Charles Devlin, the mediator who had been shuttling between MOVE and the city for months, trying to work out a solution that would prevent this confrontation, took the bullhorn from Powell. He knew the people in the house and felt he had some rapport with them. He pleaded with them to surrender.

The response from the house was swift and harsh. "You motherfucker, you ain't no priest. We'll never give up. Explain to them how you stood by and let Rizzo smash a poor black family."

The kids within took up a chant: "Baby killers! Baby killers!"

Powell announced that the police would next remove the barricades from the windows.

The bulldozer had retreated. The cherry picker moved into position, its arm extended before it like an accusing finger. Moving close to the house, it methodically punched out the slatted windows, ripping away not only the slats, but the window frames themselves and the mortar that held them in place.

When it was done, the house looked like a bombed-out shell, with gaping holes where the windows had been.

With the windows gone, it was possible for the first time to see into the house itself. It looked empty. There was no place for anyone to hide inside.

The cops began to relax a little. The operation was almost

one hour old. The police had moved against the house, and
MOVE had responded by hurling insults, threats, and debris.
But nobody had fired a shot.

At 6:55 Powell read Step 4: "Uniformed officers will enter
your house for the purpose of taking each of you into custody.
Any resistance or use of force will be met with force."

Commissioner O'Neill, standing at the corner of Thirty-
third and Pearl, raised his hand as a signal. Twenty-nine police
officers, protected by flak jackets and shields, climbed over the
rubble, onto the porch, and into the darkened house. Outside,
observers could see flashlights dancing through the upper
floors. Within minutes the cops in the house had checked the
upper floors, finding no one. All of the people were in the
basement of 309.

Suddenly, a small red van from the SPCA appeared out of
nowhere and pulled up in front of the house. There were three
of them in the van, and they either did not realize the danger
they were in or did not care. Nonchalantly they got out,
carrying their nets, and went to work. They nabbed a black-
and-white hound as he ran out of the house. Soon they disappeared into the house, looking for more dogs.

At 7:30 Walter Palmer, another negotiator, tried the bullhorn again. "If you want to come out," he told the people in
the house, "I will request that the police put their guns down."

"Leave us alone!" they shouted back.

Palmer approached the house with Powell and Police Inspector George Fencl. They walked into the house and tried
the door leading to the basement. It was bolted tight, so they
raised their voices and talked to the MOVE people through the
door.

"What do you want to do?" Palmer asked.

"Leave us alone," came the reply.

Now the dogcatchers reemerged from the house, carrying
more dogs and two orange milk crates full of puppies. Their
total catch came to twelve dogs and ten pups. They loaded
them all into the van and drove away, their day's work done.

But still MOVE had not surrendered, so the plan continued. More stakeout officers moved into position behind the barricades on Pearl Street. Powell, now back in position, read Step 5: "We are prepared to pump water into the premises which you occupy."

And they did. Fire fighters turned on the water cannons on Pearl Street, and steady streams of water began pouring through a basement window. Since the windows were only three feet above the basement floor, O'Neill was confident that MOVE members wouldn't drown, as he put it later, "unless they wanted to."

It wouldn't be long now, he guessed. Very soon MOVE would have to come out of the basement. The crisis appeared to be over.

7:55 A.M.

"They've got guns! They've got guns!"

Stakeout officer John Monahan had been looking into a basement window on the Pearl Street side of the house when he spotted a MOVE member running across the basement with a gun.

The word made its way back among the cops, but it seemed to have little effect. Perhaps it was the fact that the morning had been so uneventful and O'Neill's elaborate precautions so excessive. Or perhaps they simply found it hard to accept that these people they'd been watching for a year and a half really posed any threat. Many of the cops who'd been manning the barricades saw more of the MOVE people than they did their own kids. They knew them by their first names, had given some of them nicknames. Cops had openly walked up and down Thirty-third Street, in full view of the house, for months. If MOVE members had really meant to cause them harm, they would have had plenty of chances.

So now, despite the armored trucks and the flak jackets and the guns, many of them must have expected this long silly drama to end not with a bang but a whimper—or at worst a volley of four-letter words.

Officer James Ramp was the aide to the stakeout captain. At fifty-two he was one of the old men of the stakeout division.

People used to say that captains might come and go, but if you really wanted to know how things were done, you should go find Rampie.

Now, just after eight in the morning, Ramp was glad that this detail would soon be over. His wife had worried about his being on the barricade duty and would be relieved when he retired in a couple of months. He'd had a distinguished career—first in the Marines, where he'd seen combat in World War II and Korea, and afterward on the police force.

He was in a good mood, kidding with the other cops as he leaned against the house next to a window while a fire fighter pried the slats off. Until he'd been assigned to the MOVE detail, he'd been sitting behind a desk for a decade. Now he put his blue riot helmet on backward, going for a laugh. "Look," he joked with his friends, "I've been off the street so long I don't know what to do anymore."

Suddenly the muzzle of a gun emerged from a basement window. The cops on the roof raised their rifles to their eyes. Now nobody was joking.

Fire fighters turned on the water cannons. Four minutes later they turned them off again. Just as they did, an *Inquirer* reporter across the street heard three pops. Another reporter spotted a puff of smoke coming from a basement window. There was a brief shocked silence, and then the air was filled with gunfire as dozens of cops opened fire from the alleys and rooftops and barricades. In the midst of the firing Inspector Morton Solomon shouted an order to retreat.

Earlier in the morning the reporters, photographers, and TV cameramen had moved out of the press bullpen and gradually crept closer to the action, moving up to the very front lines. Now they were caught in the crossfire and, panicked, they tried to run for cover.

"Get down, get down!" police officers shouted. They dove back to the ground, their cameras and equipment bouncing against the pavement.

The police officers and fire fighters in front of the house scrambled for safety, scurrying on all fours like mice who've been surprised in a darkened kitchen. Jim Ramp saw Lieutenant William Krause go down. Braving the gunfire, he ran to drag him to cover.

In the apartment just above him reporter Kitty Caparella was watching the action out the window as she spoke to her editor on the phone. Suddenly she shouted, "Oh, my God! They shot a cop!"

Directly beneath the window James Ramp lay on his back, one knee bent, his riot helmet thrown to one side, his glazed eyes staring up past the reporter and photographer. Blood flowed from both corners of his mouth and pooled beneath his body.

As Krause and Ramp lay beside one another, the gunfire went on and on. It lasted a full minute, but it seemed like forever.

Then suddenly it was quiet again.

Three cops ran to Ramp and Krause. They lifted them swiftly into armor-plated trucks that took them away to area emergency rooms.

William Krause was admitted to Hahnemann Hospital in critical condition with wounds to his abdomen and arm. He would spend weeks in the hospital and lose the use of his right arm for the rest of his life.

James J. Ramp was pronounced dead on arrival at Presbyterian Hospital.

Other officers and fire fighters were also wounded during the gunfire exchange:

Police Officer Charles Stewart, with gunshot wounds to the shoulder and neck

Police Officer James Hesson, with gunshot wounds to the chest

Fireman John Welsh, with gunshot wounds to the neck and hand

Fireman Robert Snead, with shotgun pellet wounds to the forehead

Fireman Robert Lentine, with shotgun pellet wounds to the forehead

In Powelton Village, the gunfire exchange had destroyed

O'Neill's meticulous plan. Nobody knew what would happen next. They waited, watching the basement windows.

Suddenly a child appeared at the basement window. "My mommy's dead," he cried. "Help me, please." He had blood on his face as he crawled out of the window in a long, mud-soaked T-shirt.

"Come out into the street, son," a police officer yelled, but the boy just leaned against the house.

"Come into the street."

"No—you hurt my mommy."

Still the child stayed at the window, afraid to approach the police. Finally two civil affairs officers carefully climbed onto the porch and moved close to the boy.

"Come over to us."

He leaned against the house. They reached out and whisked him away from the window.

For five long minutes the police watched and waited. Then they saw a woman holding a baby in the window.

"Come on out," a civil affairs officer shouted. "No one will fire."

The woman climbed out over the wreckage, holding the infant. Then another woman came out, carrying a child in her arms as another clung to her hip.

The cops who were upstairs inside the house had dived to the floor when the gunfire started. Now they got up carefully and once again checked the upper floors for MOVE members. At the barricades a cop motioned to the front window of the cellar, and fire fighters turned on the water cannon once again. The basement filled rapidly with water. The officers who were closest to the house could see dogs inside, swimming in the deepening water.

They fired smoke grenades through the windows and into the basement. Then through the smoke came more shouts: "Help, help, I'm trying to come out." Consuella Dotson Africa emerged from the smoke with two more kids. She turned back to pull another child through the window and then spun around, raising her hands over her head. "There's more babies," she shouted. "There's one more."

Another child emerged, followed by a man holding his hands up in surrender.

At the same time Delbert was crawling out of the side cellar window, his arms spread wide. He surrendered to the same officers who, minutes before, had loaded James Ramp's body into a police van.

The cops were raging at him. One shoved the barrel of his shotgun under Delbert's chin. Another swung his helmet, hitting him in the head. As he fell to the ground a third grabbed him by his hair and dragged him across the rough concrete sidewalk. They kicked him in the face and kidneys and groin, so savagely that he could not even shield himself with his hands. He lay there, writhing, as the blows rained down. One cop was swinging so hard he split his shirt down the back.

Finally more cops came and pulled them away as Delbert was loaded into a paddy wagon. Reluctantly the cops went back to their positions.

If they had looked up at the window above their heads, they might have caught a glimpse of the *Daily News* photographer silently recording it all on film.

By 9:08—less than an hour after the shooting began—tear gas had driven out all of the people in the house. In the confusion nobody was sure how many had been taken into custody; somebody thought Chuckie might still be in the house. The police stayed in position for another half hour, shouting for him to come out. Finally they fired tear gas into the house and entered cautiously. It was empty.

One by one they began handing guns out the basement windows: two .45-caliber military-style pistols, six carbines, two twelve-gauge shotguns, and a Mauser. Forensic studies would later identify one of the carbines as the rifle that killed James Ramp.

When Judge diBona first issued the order authorizing the police to act against MOVE, O'Neill had asked him for authorization to destroy the house. He wasn't about to leave it standing to become, as he later put it, a "shrine" for MOVE. DiBona granted O'Neill's request on the legal grounds that the house had been condemned by the city. Now, with everyone removed from the house, O'Neill wasted no time putting the order into effect.

He did, however, wait long enough to permit reporters to tour the house. Those who did reported that it was filthy inside—though it was difficult to say whether that was a consequence of MOVE's ideology or the fact that it had been cut off from the rest of the world for a year and a half.

For the most part the house was barren. On the second floor was what seemed to be a gym, with a pair of boxing gloves lying on the floor. Milk crates housed a few paperback books. There was human and dog excrement throughout the house, filling several coffee cans. The reporters did not linger, and they did not descend into the basement.

It does not take long to destroy a house—even one as solid as that massive old Victorian. At noon the bulldozers—this time ordinary ones, with no armor plating—moved onto the lot and advanced toward the already-leaning porch. Their blades cut into the aged brick and gingerbread trim, breaking it into rubble and splinters. The demolition crew did its work methodically, as if it were just another lot, driving the bulldozers back and forth and tumbling the old house into its foundations.

They were finished by two in the afternoon. There was not even a hint of the house left—only the barricades still standing and, where the house had been, a field of raw red Pennsylvania clay.

The DA's office hadn't known anything about the demolition. By the time they found out, the house was gone—and they were furious. They had a murder to prosecute, and the police chief had just destroyed most of the evidence that they would need to build their case.

A few hours later a defiant Delbert Africa was brought before Judge Louis Hill on murder charges.

"When are they gonna arrest the cop who shot me in the chest and broke my jaw?" Delbert showed no signs of gunshot wounds, and if his jaw was broken it didn't seem to slow the outpouring of MOVE rhetoric.

He continued to thunder at the judge: "People come walking into a peaceful house with guns, they got what they deserved."

MOVE had murdered no one, he said. "What happened was a white racist cop shot the black cop and killed him."

In the gallery two dozen MOVE sympathizers agreed. "That's right!" "Right on!" "Racist motherfucker!" They didn't seem to realize that Ramp had been white.

The shouting from the gallery went on. "They got no right to treat Delbert that way—break his jaw."

The litany continued as one after another the MOVE members were arraigned. Janine Africa shouted at the judge: "You can't kill our babies, you asshole. You can't shoot Chuckie. You can't judge us, you ain't no fuckin' God, you ain't nothing but a stupid-ass motherfucker—"

Her voice suddenly faltered, but Merle picked up without missing a beat: "You come from the bowels of a backroom bitch." She turned to a policewoman who'd reached out to restrain her. "Don't you touch me, you bitch."

It went on like that for nearly an hour, until the exasperated judge cleared the courtroom of all spectators except the press. The litany continued in the hallway, as MOVE sympathizers talked to reporters about, as one later wrote, "police brutality and the Nazis and what the cops had done to Delbert."

To this day MOVE contends that no one in the group shot anyone that day. They cite a number of flaws in the prosecution's case: the gun that killed Ramp bore no fingerprints of MOVE members, and paraffin tests—which show the presence of gunpowder on a suspect's hands and demonstrate that he or she has recently fired a gun—proved negative. They also cited the fact that Ramp was killed by a bullet that entered the back of his head and traveled downward through his body. If he was facing the window, they ask, how could he have been hit in the back of his head by MOVE gunfire? They point to witnesses who contended that the first shots did not come from the basement but from across the street where police were positioned. And why, they ask, were the guns that were displayed that afternoon so clean when they were supposedly recovered from a basement full of muddy water?

Ramp, they contend, was killed by his fellow cops—whether by accident or design, they do not know, they say. The rifle that killed him was planted in the house to frame MOVE. The house was knocked down to destroy evidence that would implicate police.

In the trial conducted later that year prosecutors responded to all these contentions. The water in the basement made fingerprint identification and paraffin tests impossible, they say. Witnesses saw Ramp turn away from the window, exposing his back as he rushed to rescue Krause. Other witnesses reported seeing gunfire from the basement window. Fingerprints from the firearms records show that the murder weapon had been purchased by Phil Africa under an assumed name.

The case against the eleven MOVE members is largely circumstantial. Prosecutors admitted they could not prove which of the defendants fired the weapon that killed Ramp—indeed, they could not prove which of them fired a weapon at all that day. These and other questions notwithstanding, the court found all eleven of the defendants guilty of the murder of James Ramp.

At 3:00 the barricades came down. The crowd that had watched the day's events from beyond the cyclone fences now pressed forward, some angry, some curious, most simply excited at being witnesses—however far removed—to the drama of the day.

As the streets filled up and the shouting became angrier the police on the scene grew edgy. They ordered the crowd to disperse. "Go home!" they shouted.

The crowd, now numbering close to three hundred, didn't budge. "We are home!" someone cried back. "This *is* our home!"

Police Inspector George Fencl strode into the center of the street. Officers in full riot gear, mounted on horses, lined up along one side of the street. The crowd milled angrily, refusing to disperse. The cops and their horses shifted nervously. The crowd and police faced one another, hesitant, expectant.

Someone threw a cherry bomb.

One mounted officer nodded, signaling the others. He spoke calmly, almost casually: "All right."

Suddenly, in unison, the horses moved onto the sidewalks, sweeping the crowd before them. People jumped aside, falling against the parked cars. Others started throwing bottles at the cops.

The horses moved down the street as other cops, on foot, chased people onto porches and into houses. For a few frenzied minutes it looked as if a full-fledged riot would erupt.

And then it had passed with the swiftness of a summer thunderstorm. The street was empty except for the police and their horses, still twitching nervously from the unaccustomed burst of activity.

As the drama in Powelton Village began to die down, city officials were staging a show of their own across town in City Hall. Rizzo had hastily called a news conference for 4:00 P.M.—late in the day, but still early enough to make the evening news.

It had been a long day for everyone, and with the pressure of the impending deadlines tensions were high on both sides of the microphone.

A long table in the room was filled with guns, all tagged as police evidence. Flanked by Commissioner O'Neill, Monsignor Devlin, and DA Ed Rendell, Rizzo stood behind the table, looking like he hadn't slept in days. He'd spent the morning visiting the families of the dead and injured cops and fire fighters, and it had put him in a black mood.

The reporters and cameramen adjusted their equipment. It promised to be a classic Rizzo delivery, a verbal boxing match of a press conference, with MOVE as the punching bag.

Rizzo did not disappoint them. It was for people like these that they needed to restore the death penalty, he said. "Put them in the electric chair, and I'll pull the switch."

But it wasn't only MOVE he was after. He was after the reporters as well. As the mayor saw it, the entire incident,

including Ramp's death, was the fault of the press. Throughout the year-and-a-half-long siege, he said, the press had
almost openly sided with MOVE's cause, portraying the police
as killers and storm troopers: "What the press has done is
glorify a bunch of criminals, and they have put, or tried to put,
the police on the defensive."

Rizzo had a grudge against the press anyway. Over the last
several months the papers had been full of reports about police
brutality. He was especially ticked off at the *Inquirer*, which
had just won a Pulitzer for an investigative series detailing
police beatings and shootings under questionable circumstances. So if Rizzo was defensive about the performance of his
cops that day, he had his reasons. "The police showed great
restraint. The only person who died was a policeman. The
police didn't kill anybody."

Rendell added, "Throughout this entire incident the police
and the city administration has acted with extremely com-
mendable restraint—some might say there was too much
restraint." (Later, after viewing tapes and photographs, Rendell would change his mind, charging three cops with the
beating of Delbert Africa.)

After an opening salvo directed at the press Rizzo turned the
news conference over to O'Neill, but in keeping with his habits
he did not sit down. He paced off to one side, occasionally
interjecting comments.

O'Neill too was visibly angry. It was a side of him that many
of the reporters had never seen before. "The mayor's been very
kind with you," he began, as if he were lecturing children.
"I've had it up to here with individual reporters who are
constantly our adversaries—constantly."

As their deadlines approached, the reporters were busy
collecting opinions about the confrontation from people
throughout the city. At the police headquarters a cop saw an
obvious lesson to be learned from the confrontation: "This
goes to show you that you just can't negotiate with these
radicals. They don't want to listen. They don't want things
solved peacefully. You know they wanted it to end this way.
Now these animals will become martyrs, and a good policeman
is dead."

Another added, "There's no way the police can win in a thing like this. They should have killed all of them."

Lee Mathis, a black youth of nineteen who lived down the street from the MOVE house, had it figured another way. "They'd never send people like this in to kick out some white people. It's all part of the city's move to get black people out of the neighborhood."

But perhaps it was neighbor Bill Bauman, a thirty-five-year-old carpenter and former Peace Corps volunteer, who best expressed the quandary that many of the Powelton neighbors felt as their ideals clashed with the harsh reality of violent revolution. Like many of the freethinking residents of Powelton, he found himself in the unaccustomed position of defending the police's action against a group of black radicals.

"It has brought out a lot of ugliness in many of us," he told a reporter. "Liberalism was put to the test, and it often turned out to be a lot of empty slogans.

"MOVE was like a spoiled child. It acted out unless it got what it wanted, and many of us tried to understand. But you can rationalize bad behavior forever and end up feeling like a fool. I don't want to rationalize anymore.

"This kind of thing couldn't happen again here," he added. "We've learned the logic of escalation, and it stinks."

The police at the scene were finally let off duty at 8:30 that evening. Instead of going home, many of them stopped off at a meeting of the Fraternal Order of Police that was being held that night. They had plenty of complaints about O'Neill and the police brass—complaints of poor leadership, long hours, and no food, as well as some more serious charges.

One stakeout officer claimed that everything had been under control even after the shooting began, until Deputy Commissioner Solomon ordered them to retreat under fire. That was when Ramp was shot, he said. Another said the cops in the house had "relaxed" after not finding anyone on the first three floors. And, they said—perhaps in reference to the beating of Delbert—cops had been disciplined unfairly for alleged "infractions" during and after the confrontation.

The rank and file weren't the only ones upset about the plan and how it had been executed. That day police spokespersons portrayed the plan as carefully crafted and thoroughly rehearsed. It had been worked out in detail by O'Neill and his "top aides" at a meeting the previous week, they told reporters. Planning involved not only the police, but also the fire department and even the SPCA. The FBI was kept up to date as well, they said.

But behind this story of unity was the fact that some top police officials felt that the plan had been ill considered and poorly implemented. The cops who went into the house that same day had, in fact, participated in no rehearsals; they hadn't even been selected until the early morning hours of August 8. And they'd been assured that there were no guns in the MOVE house.

Two days after the assault Inspector Robert W. Martin of the pistol range—who, along with Inspector Bernard Bartley, had been second in command for the operation—drafted a memo addressed "To Whom It May Concern." In it he criticized the police operation on several grounds. Among his concerns were these: there had been too many officers inside the house, and they weren't given the right weapons (he did not elaborate) or the correct protective vests. No action was taken when the guns were first spotted, he wrote. Firemen should not have been used to open the basement windows; in fact, the bulldozer should have knocked off all the basement windows. The Uzis and Ingrams used by the stakeout officers were too inaccurate over the distances involved. The stakeout teams had poor cover in the rear, and there hadn't been enough men to keep intruders off the roofs. The water cannon should have been operated remotely so that fire fighters and police officers wouldn't be exposed to gunfire.

At the end of the memo, Martin added a terse postscript with a strong hint of anger, suggesting that O'Neill's plan did not represent a consensus among the police brass. He wrote:

> At a meeting in my office, which Chief Inspector Bridgeford, Inspector Fencl, Inspector Bartley and Captain Taylor attended, I explained to ask me no more questions about equipment to be used or Assault Tactics, because their ideas were completely opposite of mine. On that same day I

called Inspector Loftus and was told that I could not get a set of pictures of the MOVE Headquarters. I tried to reach Deputy Commissioner Solomon and was told three (3) times that he was not available.

11 P.M.–MIDNIGHT

Whatever the flaws in the plan, whatever the cost in human life and injuries, at least this terrible day was now behind the city. There would be more repercussions, of course—trials of the MOVE members, a trial of the cops who beat Delbert. Over the coming weeks there would be more questions, more news conferences, more articles, more columns and editorial cartoons. Mistakes had been made; lessons had been learned. But now it seemed that the worst was over. The long, bizarre siege had come to a close. In the end the system had prevailed. The house that John Africa built had fallen.

Late that evening Channel 6 reporter Vernon Odom stood before the empty lot on the corner of Thirty-third and Pearl, getting ready for a live report. Under the glow of the streetlights dozens of onlookers surrounded him. They were subdued, even polite.

Then, as the blinding lights for the camera pierced the darkness, the character of the crowd changed dramatically. Suddenly this restrained group was transformed into an angry mob. As if on cue, a woman began wailing: "Rizzo came down here to kill. Rizzo came down here to kill." More voices took up the chant. People crowded against the reporter. To the viewers at home it looked like a riot was about to erupt in Powelton Village.

And then Odom signed off, the lights went out, and the crowd's passion was extinguished as quickly as it had ignited. People drifted away on foot and by car. Kids rode off on their bikes. Within five minutes the crew from Channel 6 found themselves nearly alone on the dark and quiet street.

It was close to midnight by the time they finally packed up their gear and left, leaving the street empty for the first time in a year and a half. A slight glow came from a telephone booth on the corner. Inside, under the flickering fluorescent light, an unknown hand had scrawled, "MOVE 1, Police 0."

6
After the Siege

FOR A WHILE IT looked as if Mayor Rizzo's vow to put MOVE out of business for good had been fulfilled.

Eleven of those who had been in the house on August 8 were tried in 1979 on charges ranging from simple assault to murder. Nine of them were tried in a single trial. Two were tried separately at their own request.

The hundreds of earlier trials had been, in effect, a dress rehearsal for what *Newsweek* would call "the bizarre trial of the MOVE Nine." The trial looked like pandemonium to the uninitiated, but it was a well-orchestrated performance.

From MOVE's first days, Vincent had seen trials as an opportunity to "put out information," to speak the truth about The Guidelines. In the Powelton Village headquarters MOVE had held long mock trials where its members would practice and perfect their tactics and responses. Now, with a national audience, they put that training to use and transformed the proceedings into months of guerrilla theater.

The trial began in early December 1979 and lasted until May of the following year. The defendants objected to the trial, calling it "rigged." Though the court appointed "backup" attorneys, MOVE members ignored them and instead conducted the defense themselves. Their cross-examination of prosecution witnesses often descended into long, meandering harangues. The judge routinely ejected them from the courtroom.

Despite the testimony of witnesses who saw MOVE members firing carbines and other weapons that day, as well as ballistics tests linking the bullet that killed Ramp with a gun recovered in the basement of the house and a federal weapons purchase form showing that the gun and others had been purchased under a pseudonym by Phil Africa, the defendants maintained throughout the trial that MOVE gunfire hadn't killed Ramp. The evidence against them had been manufactured, they said. The police had leveled the house to destroy evidence that would have exonerated them. They produced witnesses—a neighbor, a student, three reporters, and negotiator Walter Palmer—whose testimony suggested that the first shot of the day had come not from the MOVE house but from a mysterious man in a third-story window across the street and behind the police lines.

After months of testimony the court-appointed backup attorneys for MOVE made the closing arguments. They argued the case was too circumstantial: the murder weapon bore no fingerprints, and none of the witnesses could actually link any individual MOVE member to Ramp's death. The arguments were unsuccessful; all nine were convicted of all charges and sentenced to thirty to one hundred years in prison.

In another courtroom in City Hall a related trial was also under way in early 1981. Police officers Joseph Zagame, Charles Geist, and Terrence Patrick Mulvihill were charged with aggravated and simple assault and official oppression for their beating of Delbert Africa. Newspaper reports also placed Mulvihill's partner, Lawrence D'Ulisse, at the scene, but he was not charged.

Witnesses, news photos, and videotape all documented the savage beating that Delbert had sustained on the sidewalk outside the MOVE house on August 8. The identity of the police who beat him was never in dispute. Even so, Judge Stanley Kubacki acquitted all three defendants without even permitting the case to be decided by the jury.

"Philadelphia is bleeding to death because of the MOVE tragedy," he explained. "No verdict will stanch the flow of blood. It can only be stopped by setting up a lightning rod. I will be that lightning rod."

Judge Kubacki was wrong to think his decision would end the "flow of blood." Mulvihill and D'Ulisse would be facing

MOVE again, on another day filled with death and rage. And within five years Geist would be dead, shot in the face by his wife with his own gun.

In July 1980, in the federal courthouse in downtown Philadelphia, came the most stunning trial of all: the *United States* v. *Vincent Leaphart, aka John Africa.* It had taken federal agents three long years to pick up his trail after he'd disappeared from Jeanne's house. They had finally traced him to Rochester, where they arrested him along with Alberta, Alphonso, Jerry (Gerald Ford Africa), Conrad, and others. Alphonso and Vincent were tried on conspiracy and weapons violations; the others faced a separate trial on riot and other charges related to the 1977 armed confrontation.

Federal prosecutor Marc Durant laid out the government's case against John Africa in his opening argument: he and his followers had illegally acquired explosives in a plan to terrorize several major U.S. cities. The evidence in the case, collected during the three-year investigation, was abundant. It included Glassey's testimony and taped conversations with MOVE members, the cache of explosives recovered from Witt's car in 1977, and the testimony of the federal agents on the case.

In addition to Glassey, the prosecution relied on another key witness: Jeanne Africa. By the time of the trial her view of John Africa had come full circle from the love and blind faith that she had once given him. In the intervening years she'd become a born-again Christian, and she now believed that John Africa was Satan. She believed that he "washes out your brain of the system, but he also programs you with his evilness and his witchcraft."

The prosecutors' strategy was, first, to lay out the evidence linking Vincent with the acquisition of explosives and firearms and a plan to plant bombs in major cities and, second, to show the jurors the extent to which he controlled the MOVE organization. Rejecting the services of a court-appointed attorney, Vincent and the other defendants chose to present their own cases. The defense strategy, as conducted by Alphonso, was hardly a strategy at all; it was more of an extended advertisement for John Africa's ability to cure people of drug addiction, prostitution, and other vices. He paraded MOVE members up on the stand, one after another, each testifying to the miracles that John Africa had performed in their lives.

Frank Africa told the jurors that "since being in MOVE I have seen all kinds of situations that I hadn't seen before.

". . . A good example is August 8th. That day the cops came up to kill all MOVE people. They fired point blank at MOVE people. But nobody died that day, and John Africa protected us just as he has always protected us. They came out there to kill us that day, but it didn't happen.

"Here's another example of a miracle: we ran out of water, and it started raining. It's hard for people to accept these things as miracles, because it's beyond their conception. They have to categorize it as something in this system. If you are only familiar with the system, it is hard for you to understand the power of truth. You don't know what it is when you see it."

Under Alphonso's friendly questioning MOVE member Eddie Africa testified to the perfection of John Africa: "John Africa is perfect. All perfect means is what is right. Your idea of what perfection is is mystical, because you see perfect as being impossible.

"Perfect means doing what is right all the time, and it's possible to do what is right all the time. John Africa has done that. Your courts have not—such as those cops who shot the people who were handcuffed [a reference to a controversial police brutality case in Philadelphia in the 1970s]. They were set free, innocent. When the cop that beat Delbert Orr Africa, he was set free, told he was innocent.

"These are the courts you ask us to defend, you ask us to come to for justice—all right? Same courts that order the house to be torn down, that order us to be placed in a starvation blockade. That's the courts that you tell us we've got to come to for justice. We've come to them. We've come to them not for justice, but to show them we know they're not right."

On cross-examination of Eddie the prosecutor tried to establish that John Africa and the defendant, Vincent Leaphart, were one and the same—to show, in fact, that Vincent directed all of MOVE's activities. He asked:

"Is there a man, a single individual, a man who is John

Africa who always is perfect? Or is that a spirit?"

"John Africa is a person," Eddie answered. "John Africa is a black man. John Africa is right. We are working to be like him."

"Is he one individual man who gets up in the morning and puts on his clothes, who you can see walking down the street?"

"Yes, he's a man. He's not no ghost flying around here. John Africa is a man."

"Have you ever seen him?"

"Yes, I have."

"Is he here today?"

"Yes, he is."

"Can you point to him?"

"John Africa is with Alphonso. Vincent Africa is John Africa. John Africa is in—"

"Who knows the most about The Guidelines of teachings of John Africa? What man in this courtroom?"

"Vincent Africa."

"Thank you."

It was not a defense that seemed destined to win the hearts and minds of the middle- and working-class members of the jury. When all the "evidence" was presented, Vincent himself rose to address the jury for closing arguments. It was the only time the founder of MOVE ever gave an official statement about his organization and his philosophy.

He began softly, simply. Before he was done, he'd wept nearly a dozen times.

> I'm not a guilty man. I'm an innocent man. I didn't come here to make trouble or to bring trouble, but to bring the truth. And goddamn it, that's what I'm going to do.
>
> I'm fighting for the air that you've got to breathe, and I'm fighting for water that you've got to drink. And if it gets any worse, you're not going to be drinking that water.
>
> I'm fighting for food that you've got to eat. And you know you've got to eat it, and if it gets any worse, you're not going to be eating that food.
>
> Don't you see, if you took this thing all the way—all the way—you would have clean air, clean water, clean soil and

be quenched of industry! But you see, they don't want that. They can't have that.

I've been a revolutionary all my life. Since I could understand the word *revolution*, I have been a revolutionary. And I remain a revolutionary, because, don't you see, *revolutionary* simply means to turn, to generate, to activate. It don't mean it should be evil and kill people and bomb people. It simply means to be right. If this world didn't revolutionize, everything would stop. If your heart didn't revolutionize, you would stop. If your lungs don't revolutionize, you would stop.

He paused and then began another train of thought: "Deer don't run down people—but people run down deer. Monkeys don't shoot people—but people shoot monkeys. Yet monkeys are seen as unclean and people as intelligent.

"You can go as far as you want in the forest, and you won't find no jails. Because the animals of the forest don't believe in jail. But come to civilization, that's all you see."

That was the entire defense—days of testimonials and a sermon about clean air and water. It stood against a case that federal agents had spent three years building, a case the prosecutor later called his strongest ever. But when the jury returned after five-and-a-half days of deliberations, the courtroom was stunned. By unanimous vote it had found Vincent and Alphonso innocent of all charges.

Vincent left the courthouse carrying a box of fresh fruit, exchanged a few words with reporters, and climbed into a waiting car surrounded by ecstatic supporters. As the car sped away it was the last time he would face reporters and television cameras.

By the time Vincent's trial started most of MOVE's far-flung members had come back to Philadelphia. The arrests in Rochester closed down the operation in that city. The house in Richmond closed halfway through his trial.

Vincent had originally set up the Richmond "Seed of Wisdom" chapter to be nonconfrontational, a place where the children could stay during the confrontation in 1978. But trouble had started within days after the women and children arrived. Prompted by reports that children were being abused, welfare officials in Richmond demanded to have a doctor examine them and asked to see birth certificates.

Sharon Sims Africa and her sister Valerie, the two adults who had stayed on in the house with the kids, refused. When the officials threatened to return with a court order, the two women prepared for a siege. They boarded up the doors and windows and mounted a loudspeaker in the front window.

The scene that was played out in Philadelphia was repeated in Richmond. By the time the police returned with the court order the house was sealed off. The police set up barricades around the house and moved into position. Mounted on horseback and carrying rifles and tear gas grenades, the Richmond police surrounded the house for two-and-a-half hours before they retreated. Major James Parks of the Richmond police told reporters they had pulled back because they didn't want a confrontation: "We respect their religious beliefs. We'll see if something can't be worked out."

Fearing the children would be taken, the adults and children stayed barricaded in the house for nine months. Money came from MOVE headquarters by way of the Western Union office. Neighbors did their shopping for them. Finally, by May of 1978, the money stopped coming, as the Philadelphia house suffered under its own siege.

For a year and a half afterward, the Seed of Wisdom house was left alone, although the Richmond police were watching it carefully and had already been in touch with the police in Philadelphia. In contrast to the violence in Philadelphia, life in Richmond settled into a quiet routine. Sharon and Valerie took jobs to bring in some money. Sharon started seeing Frank, a man in the neighborhood who had a fondness for going out in the middle of the night for coffee.

Sharon was with him one evening when a police car pulled them over just after they'd left the house. They had a warrant for Sharon's arrest for kidnapping, neglect, and other charges. At the same time they'd raided the house and picked up Valerie.

The children were placed in foster homes for three weeks

while MOVE raised money to bail out the two women. When they got the children back, they were in a "horrible state," Sharon later told a reporter. Their hair had been cut and washed; the infants were wearing diapers; they'd been exposed, for the first time in their lives, to cooked food and television. That night she and Valerie took the children back to Philadelphia.

The two women returned to Virginia for the court hearing. When the attorney for the state learned they'd taken the children away, he moved to have them held in contempt. Court-appointed attorneys for the children argued that the children should be removed from the care of the two women and made wards of the state. Although the judge did not grant the contempt order, he did give custody of the children to the state—an essentially empty act, since the children were already outside of the state's jurisdiction.

It was raining that day by the time Sharon and Valerie got back to the house after the hearing. They ate lunch, packed their belongings, and closed up the house. As they drove away from the house for the last time, the car got stuck in the muddy driveway, and they had to get out in the downpour and push it. They finally got free and drove away, headed for Philadelphia. As they left, a police cruiser turned the corner, passed them, and pulled into the driveway, bringing warrants for their arrest.

In 1981 these people of MOVE—the women and children from Richmond, the children of the jailed members, members who had been released from prison—all began to converge on Louise James's little row house on Osage Avenue. They came not as part of any grand design, but simply because they now had nowhere else to go.

Adding to those who returned were new recruits. Ramona Johnson, a black prelaw student at Philadelphia's Temple University, became interested in MOVE from the trials and soon quit school to join up.

Twenty-year-old Theresa Brooks, a black woman from an upper-middle-class family in New Jersey, also began to follow the teachings of John Africa—much to the anger and bewilderment of her family. She had dropped out of college and had been a member about six months when she wrote a long letter to her family explaining her decision:

Family:
 This letter is addressed to each of you. I'm putting what I have to say in letter form, *not out of fear to tell you face to face*, but I'm doing it this way with the hope that you'll be able to *understand* & *hear all* that I'm saying. Feel free to read it a couple of times so as not to miss a thing! Many of you have already formed your own opinion about me & my involvement with MOVE. You already have preconceived ideas about them. What you *need* to do is listen to me. 1st let me tell you *all*, I love each one of you. *Those* of you who've decided to *disown* me, *not talk* to me or whatever, it doesn't change my love for you.
 Since many of you have formed opinions about me, I've decided to write this letter with the intention of clearing up a few things. I'm a committed, uncompromising MOVE supporter. I'm *not* brainwashed, as some of you have stated. If there's been any washing being done, it's washed my brain clear!!
 Anything a MOVE member tells me or anyone else, they qualified. How much of the *stuff* Rev. ___ puts out does he qualify. He's a leader, where has he lead you? If you question anything you here come from MOVE, it can be *cleared up* & *qualified*! Can Rev. ___ make that same claim?
 ... I'm a committed MOVE supporter because MOVE is *right*. They are totally committed vanguards of revolution. They're a united organization, dedicated to speak out against *all* & *any* wrong. This includes wrongs in the courts, in the jails, in the church & on the street. .
 MOVE believes all life is important. Man, animal, marine & vegatation all are just as important. Man took it upon himself to *labal* himself as superior & animal life inferior. The *same* man who said *whites* are *superior* to *blacks*!!
 ... MOVE is sensitive and loving. Yes, sometimes they are loud and hostile when someone is trying to kill your child, you're gonna holler & yell as loud as you can so someone will hear you. This is the same thing MOVE does. They're yelling about the wrongs being done to them & all

the rest of the oppressed people. They are totally *committed* to *truth, right & justice*.

. . . Concerning the garlic—some of you have commented on that. Many of you know garlic is good for you. It's a natural medicine that kills poisons & bacteria that we breath in take in threw food & air. If anyone's noticed I didn't get the flu this year. Oh, so you didn't either. Well how many of you were out walking 1–3 miles in the rain & snow. Coming home nights cold and wet. As far as the smell goes I can deal with that. To stop eating garlic because it smells is a *pretty weak* reason to give it up & take the chance of getting sick, or even letting unwanted toxins live in my body.

. . . I'm not asking you to join MOVE. I'm asking you to *listen* to me, ask me questions, don't judge me. Not one of you is qualified to judge me on the information you've *read* in the papers or *heard* on the news, or even gotten from a Phila. cop. To *try* & judge me on that would only *allow* you to *misjudge* me.

The Family Africa is also my family. Blood don't make a family. . . . *All* my family is important to me. Think about what I'm saying. Many of you reading this letter know *darn* well there ain't that much understanding in this family.

. . . Blacks are *always* crying about the prejudice towards them. Yet the *same* blacks have ignored to hear MOVE's crys of prejudice towards them.

I'm not ignoring their crys. I hope you all don't either. MOVE isn't just fighting for themselves, they're fighting for us all.

Please give me some feedback! Makes sense, doesn't it?

The *Power of truth is final*. I'm speaking nothing but the *truth*.

To quote John Africa: A just person will ignore his pride when he hears what's right. An unjust person will ignore what is right & hold fast to his goddamn pride.

Ona move—

Despite the friction, Theresa's mother kept in touch, once sending her a parcel of clothes and occasionally visiting the house. She noticed a change come over Theresa in 1983. Theresa began to talk in what her mother called "street talk"—uneducated slang. She remembers that her daughter's demeanor changed accordingly. All of the changes, she said, coincided with the arrival at the house of Frank Africa.

After serving nearly three years in prison on riot and conspiracy charges, Frank James Africa was paroled in 1983. Parole records show that he settled into an apartment and lived quietly. Toward the end of 1983 he requested permission from his parole officer to move into his boyhood home at 6221 Osage Avenue. By the time the parole office acted on his request, Frank had already moved.

Technically it was a violation of his parole to move without permission, but the request had been a routine one and his parole officer approved it after the fact. He sent Frank's file to the west Philadelphia parole office.

After receiving the case the west Philadelphia parole officer followed standard procedure and visited the parolee's new address to determine its "suitability." When he arrived at 6221 Osage, he saw a row house in need of paint, with a vegetable cart parked on the street outside. When he knocked on the front door, a man in dreadlocks answered.

The parole officer explained who he was and why he was there. The man at the door told him that Frank wasn't home, but he invited the officer to come in and talk to the other people in the house. Later the officer filed a report stating that although the people living at 6221 Osage Avenue were engaged in an "alternative lifestyle," the house offered a "stable environment" for Frank James Africa.

Perhaps it is simply coincidence, but the return of Frank James Africa to his mother's house marked the beginning of problems with the neighbors on Osage Avenue. Until then the other neighbors had tolerated MOVE's presence in the house. Some had been more than tolerant; they respected MOVE's goals even if they didn't agree with its methods. Clifford Bond was one of them.

Bond had come to the neighborhood by a roundabout route. Born in nearby Chester, Pennsylvania, he lived in Media, Pennsylvania, and New Mexico before he married and settled with his wife into the home she'd grown up in. A schoolteacher and nutritionist, he had little active interest in politics or revolution. Even so, he agreed with a lot of what the MOVE people had to say—about injustice and how the people who were in power always seemed to get ahead at the expense of the little guy.

So despite the history of violence in Powelton, Bond wasn't too worried when MOVE came into his neighborhood. In fact, he'd often stop to buy fruit from the handcart that they kept in front of their house, and he'd occasionally take the time to stop and talk some philosophy with Conrad Africa or one of the others.

All of the neighbors prided themselves on their ability to live and let live. On that single narrow block there lived a Buddhist family, a police detective, and an elderly white man who'd stayed behind when other whites had left in the fifties. Even so, those who lived nearest the MOVE house began to experience some problems. Just as had happened with Vincent's original apartment in Powelton, adjacent houses soon became infested with roaches. People started seeing small, ill-clad children digging through their trash. At night they could hear people running across their rooftops.

During the day the MOVE adults would round up the children and lead them out the back of the house, down a gangplank that stretched across the alley and onto the narrow sidewalk that ran behind the houses, and lead them half a block to the wooded expanse of Cobbs Creek Park. There the children received an education in the skills MOVE deemed important. Instead of reading or arithmetic, they worked at calisthenics. They ran in the park and bathed in the creek. At night, when the weather was good, they slept on the rooftop.

Late in 1983 the violence that had followed MOVE from its beginnings came to Osage Avenue.

The neighbors say that it began as a fight over a parking space, though it had been preceded by increasing tensions between the neighbors and the people of MOVE. On September 4, they say, neighbor Butch Marshall parked in front of the MOVE house in the space usually occupied by MOVE's cart. In the argument that followed, Marshall was beaten and bitten in his face, back, and groin so severely that neighbors had to take him to the hospital.

MOVE member Jerry Africa says this account of the incident isn't accurate. Though he wasn't living at the house, he was there almost every day and heard the story from those who were, he says. According to him, the trouble had begun months earlier, when Marshall's kids started making fun of the MOVE children and, later, bullying them. When the adult MOVE members complained to Marshall, Jerry Africa says, Marshall threatened them with a gun.

Alberta Africa—who was in prison at the time—says that Marshall started the argument on September 4: "Conrad was standing next to the curb, and when Marshall pulled up, he bumped him with the fender—on purpose, you know. When Conrad said something to him, he said, 'Fuck you, I'll do it again.' That's how the fight started."

Like the allegations of violence in Powelton, she says that the neighbors' early complaints against MOVE are the result of prejudice, misunderstanding, and biased reporting in the press. Police and the papers routinely ignored MOVE's complaints and played up those who spoke against them, she says.

The neighbors, curiously, have a similar complaint. They say that their pleas to the police and to the city were discounted or ignored. Because of MOVE's violent history, they say, the city went to extraordinary lengths to avoid any confrontation and declared their neighborhood a no-man's-land.

After Butch Marshall was attacked, neighbors Carrie Foskey and Inez Nichols collected names for a petition to the city. They drew up a laundry list of complaints: the garbage that was left open so that animals could feed on it, the dogs and cats that ran loose through the neighborhood, the raw meat that MOVE left outside for strays and rats, the fence that MOVE members had constructed across the alley, blocking access to the neighbors' rear garages, the sale of produce in a residential neighborhood, the attack on Marshall and another that had occurred shortly afterward on another neighbor.

The neighbors, banding together into an informal alliance, also contacted their elected representatives. One, state representative Peter Truman, urged the neighbors to wait just a few months. A historic election was taking place: Philadelphia was on the verge of electing its first black mayor, and surely the neighbors didn't want to do anything that would cast him in a bad light.

Wait until after Wilson Goode is elected, Truman told the neighbors. After the election, he said, "I'll go out there and tear that fence down myself."

In the fall of 1983 the smart money in the mayor's race was on Wilson Goode. He ran a flawless campaign, defeating former mayor Frank Rizzo in the Democratic primary and going on to sweep a three-way race in the general election. A black man who had graduated from the University of Pennsylvania's Wharton School of Business, he had accomplished what many had predicted was impossible, bringing together everyone from poor blacks of north Philadelphia to the business leaders of downtown. His election signaled a new Philadelphia, one that was ready to turn its back on the old politics of division and privilege and embrace a vision of unity.

Goode didn't bring a strong political agenda with him when he became mayor. Since he had been managing the city under Mayor Bill Green for the last four years, the day-to-day direction of the city continued in much the same manner. His choices for the city's top administrative jobs, for example, were based on pragmatism and experience rather than ideology. Retired army general Leo Brooks, who had managed a sprawling defense supply center in Philadelphia, was a widely praised choice for managing director. Gregore Sambor had been next in line for the commissioner's job in the police hierarchy after the departure of Commissioner Morton Solomon, and Goode named him to that post. Fire Commissioner William Richmond continued in his job. Others in Goode's cabinet were selected from his former staff or were holdovers from the Green administration.

That promised to be the tone of Goode's administration: practical and noncontroversial. There would be no grandstanders. Goode's government promised to be just that—good government—and when he won, it seemed to be a victory that all of Philadelphia could savor—and not least of all the people living on Osage Avenue, who believed that now they had found someone who would listen to their grievances.

But things did not turn out quite that way. After the election Pete Truman did not come out and tear down the fence. Nor did anyone else from the state or city government respond to their call for action. The incidents of violence and harassment continued.

The violence on the street was matched by increasing violence within the home itself. One day in early December neighbors watched in alarm as Louise ran down the street chased by her son, an ax in his hands.

Through all the early years of MOVE, Louise's own commitment to the organization had run hot and cold. Now, it seemed, she had become the victim of a vendetta within MOVE itself. It is not clear exactly why; Alberta Africa has said that she "wasn't willing to do some of the work that needed to be done"—that she wasn't facing up to her own shortcomings and trying to overcome them. It is true that she had not abandoned the life style; despite her espousal of MOVE doctrine, she had lived a fairly ordinary life on Osage Avenue.

Whatever the reasons, Louise apparently began to be singled out for punishment. According to a police report, she said that she was forced to live in her bedroom as the members knocked out the walls of her house and boarded up the windows. They used her telephone, running up hundreds of dollars in long-distance charges. They intercepted her mail.

In a police report filed later Louise said that John Africa had once ordered Frank to beat her after Sharon Sims, her niece, refused his order to marry Jerry Africa. She told police that one day in October Frank had seen her slip a letter into her pocket and confiscated it. John Africa had called the other MOVE members into Louise's bedroom and ordered her to read the letter out loud. It was from a MOVE member in Muncy prison, and it attacked Louise virulently. After reading a few sentences of obscenities and rantings, Louise refused to go on.

Vincent, she told police, had turned to Frank and ordered him to beat her until she started to vomit. Then Frank took a pillow and put it over her face.

"Do you want her cycled?" he asked, looking at Vincent.

"No," he said. "Not this time."

It was not long after that, Louise said, that she told her brother she wanted to spend a week in Atlantic City. He told her she could pack some things into two trash bags. She did, and she left the house, never to return. She went to live with her sister LaVerne, but the harassment did not end. LaVerne had dropped out of MOVE along with her daughters Sharon and Gail. Like her sister Louise, they received dozens of poison-pen letters from jailed MOVE members. The house was besieged with phone calls—some days she received as many as sixty—as other members called her day and night and accused her of being a traitor.

There is some evidence that Frank was secretly trying to save his mother by driving her away from the house. When LaVerne left MOVE a few months before Frank's attacks on his mother, she had a long private conversation with Frank. He told her that he was concerned about his mother. Because the efforts to secure the release of the MOVE members who were still in jail hadn't succeeded, Vincent was planning yet another confrontation. Frank wanted her out of the house before it occurred, but he was worried that if he told her about the plans she would try to interfere to protect him. If the beatings and abuse were part of Frank's plan to get his mother out of the house before something happened, they accomplished his goal.

By the end of 1983 all of Vincent's energies seemed to be directed toward winning the release of the jailed MOVE members. Legal avenues had been tried and had failed, so now he was determined to provoke the city into action. And he planned to use the neighbors as his pawns in the game.

On Christmas morning Betty Mapp heard a sound outside her living room that she had never heard before. At first she thought it was Christmas carolers, but as she listened more closely she realized with a shock that no carolers would use language as vile as what she was hearing.

It was the sound of an angry, almost unintelligible voice: "Motherfucker Santa Claus!" it began, then launched into a string of obscenities and threats. MOVE had set up a loud-speaker on the front of the house.

Someone called the police. They came and then simply drove away without getting out of the car. Working in shifts, MOVE members ranted for eight hours that Christmas Day. Over and over again they called for the release of thirteen jailed MOVE members. On the day after Christmas they began again. And again on the days that followed. When neighbors went to the MOVE house to complain, members freely explained their strategy: the city wouldn't listen to MOVE's grievances, but sooner or later they'd have to do something about the neighbors' complaints. Go to City Hall, they urged the neighbors; the loudspeakers would be silenced only if the city responded to their demands.

By New Year's Eve it was clear to the neighbors that the loudspeakers—and the obscenities—were there to stay. And despite the phone calls to the police and to city officials, no one was going to lift a finger to help them. First it had been the meat and the bugs and the strays, then the attacks. Now they were being forced to live under a nonstop amplified audio assault.

The new year of 1984 did not look promising.

7
1984

LATE IN THE AFTERNOON of February 20 Louise James, LaVerne Sims, and Sharon Sims quietly entered the lobby of the Centre Hotel in downtown Philadelphia. Bypassing the front desk, they went upstairs to Room 2218.

Inside the room they met Delores Thompson, a police officer attached to the civil affairs unit. Out of sight, in an adjoining room, were four other cops from the civil affairs unit and the organized crime unit.

Louise had requested the meeting, and she did most of the talking at first. John Africa and his followers had taken over her house, she said. They'd run up monthly telephone bills as high as $400. She'd been paying the parking tickets on their van.

Ever since he'd been acquitted at his trial, Louise said, he had been "obsessed with power, telling his followers that he outsmarted the whole United States." Now she was worried that he was planning a confrontation and that he would take her son, Frank, down with him. John Africa was using Frank, she said, as his "disciple and bodyguard," and she feared he wouldn't let Frank out of the house to report to his parole officer, in an attempt to provoke a confrontation with the city. She also mentioned that her son and Theresa Brooks had gotten married according to MOVE law.

It was obvious that day that Louise feared for her life at the hands of MOVE. She said that John Africa saw her and her sister as a threat because they "knew all the principles of his teachings." If he could cycle them and get away with it, she said, he wouldn't hesitate to give the order. Witt—the man

whom Don Glassey had talked into leaving MOVE in 1977—
had been found dead, floating in the Schuylkill River. MOVE,
she said, had been responsible for his death, though she
wouldn't elaborate. (Officially, Witt's death had been ruled a
suicide, and there is no evidence linking it to MOVE.)

Louise had come to the police, she said, because John Africa
was planning a confrontation and people were going to get
hurt. Four members were due to be released from prison in a
few months, and John Africa was drawing up "plans of action."

If they should ever see John Africa leave the house, she
warned, it would mean trouble—that he'd given a specific
order and was stepping away. He would never become personally involved in the confrontation himself, she said.

Louise said the three of them—she, LaVerne, and Sharon—
would keep in daily contact with one another. If any one of the
three wasn't heard from, the others would "suspect foul play"
and notify the police.

As she left, Louise promised to get in touch with Officer
Thompson at a future date with more information. "I just
wanted you to be aware of this information in case something
happens," she said.

On February 28 the new mayor received a brief letter from
Jerry Africa. It read:

> To Wilson Goode:
> This is a short reminder to you to let you know it is no
> accident that you are having so much difficulty with your
> administration. All you need to do is look back at those
> previous mayors administration who went against whats
> right to see your future.
> We realize even you can't explain why in such a short
> time in office you have been plagued with all manner of
> controversy. And as long as you continue to allow the plight
> of innocent MOVE people to remain in prison, you and
> your administration will only suffer set back after set back.
> You saw what happened to Frank Rizzo's career after
> what he did to MOVE people. Til this very day he's hated
> for that and other violations against people. And since

you'd been in office you have yet to do anything, or speak out about those injustices so how can you expect to see your administration travel a different course for disaster, when you are following in their footsteps.

As I said earlier this is only a reminder to let you know its no accident you are having such a difficult time. You have to be right in order to expect right and as long as you allow innocent people to remain in prison, when you personally have documented proof of their innocence. Then you can expect things to continue to worsen for you and your administration. The MOVE organization doesn't have to get into nothing with you now cause you are already in alot of trouble, an you now know why.

On behalf of the MOVE Org.

JERRY AFRICA

Long live the power of freedom. Long live John Africa forever.

Two weeks later, on March 9, Police Commissioner Gregore Sambor met with Goode and brought him up to date on the situation on Osage Avenue. Sambor told Goode about the neighbors' complaints and that MOVE had blocked the alley behind the house. But that wasn't the worst of it. They were now barricading the house itself.

It was beginning to look like Powelton all over again. The heavy wooden slats, the bullhorn, the nonstop harangues—it was, unbelievably, all recurring.

But there was also a new wrinkle, Sambor explained. Lumber and other construction materials were piled on the flat, narrow roof, and wooden pallets had been arranged around the skylight that dropped into the bathroom on the second floor.

Goode, for his part, listened attentively. But he took no action, nor did he recommend any to his police commissioner. In his mind, he would later say, the problems on Osage Avenue were a "police matter."

That spring television reporter Vernon Odom found himself once again covering the story of MOVE, a story that he had followed since the days of the Powelton standoff in 1977. On May 3, with a camera crew in tow, he knocked at the fortified

door of the house on Osage Avenue, asking for an interview.
He got one.

As he spoke with Frank Africa, onlookers saw a hooded man
emerge onto the roof, wielding a shotgun. Almost immediately
dozens of stakeout cops were dispatched to the scene. They
quickly surrounded the house as the hooded figure paraded
across the rooftops. And then they waited.

Inside the Bond home Clifford's young daughter watched
the man through the living room window. She called her
father. "Daddy," she asked, "what is the man doing on top of
the roof with a gun?"

Clifford Bond had no answer for her. "Isn't that against the
law?" she persisted.

"Yes," he answered. "It's against the law."

After an hour and a half the figure on the roof disappeared
back down into the MOVE house. The police shouldered their
rifles and went away. No arrests were made; no warrants were
issued. Goode held a press conference later that afternoon at
which he explained that he did not "want to do anything that
will cause an unnecessary confrontation." When asked about
the neighbors' long list of complaints, he answered, "I prefer
to have dirt and some smell than to have bloodshed."

On May 28, 1984—Memorial Day—Clifford Bond led the
first delegation of neighbors to meet with Mayor Goode,
demanding that the city evict MOVE from the block. One at a
time they recited to Goode their list of complaints. They told
him that MOVE had threatened to have a confrontation on
August 8.

As he later testified, Goode replied that he didn't want to
"in an unprepared manner, end up with a confrontation on
that street that would cause the loss of lives, that would have
innocent people, perhaps, injured or lose their lives and property damaged unnecessarily."

He told the neighbors that over the next few days he would
research the question of whether the city had a "legal basis" on

which to act against MOVE. But he did not want to be hasty.
Any plan that he devised, he said, would be well thought out.

Despite the neighbors' frustration, their visit did have an
effect on Goode. Just two days later he visited U.S. Attorney
Ed Dennis at his office in the federal building. He had with
him a number of city officials, as well as Philadelphia district
attorney Ed Rendell.

Goode suggested to Dennis—who, as the top Justice Department official in Philadelphia, oversaw the FBI as well as
the federal prosecutors—that perhaps what they had here was
a federal problem. These people had made numerous threats
over the loudspeaker against the president. There was word
that John Africa, in whom federal agents had taken such an
interest just a few years before, was at the house and planning
another violent confrontation.

Dennis didn't buy any of it. Threats over a loudspeaker
didn't warrant federal intervention, he told Goode and the
others. And yes, there was a federal warrant outstanding on
John Africa, but he would not act on it without concrete
evidence that John Africa was at the house. Federal agencies
would not become involved.

But he did leave Goode with a promise. They would closely
monitor any confrontation that might develop between MOVE
and the city—to ensure that MOVE's civil rights weren't
violated.

May slipped into June, and the frustration of the neighbors
mounted. Police continued to monitor the house off and on.
They noted that a lot of soil was being carried out of the house
and speculated that MOVE might be constructing tunnels
under the house. MOVE members began hanging raw meat on
the back alley fence and continued to build up material on the
roof.

Holidays offered the best opportunity to get all the neighbors together. On the Fourth of July Bond led his second
delegation down to the mayor's City Hall offices.

Again Goode told them that he had "no legal basis" on

which to act. He did promise to have a blocked street drain fixed and to provide mental health services for the neighborhood children.

What Goode didn't tell them was that DA Rendell had indeed provided him with a legal justification to arrest at least some of the MOVE members at the house.

He had asked Rendell to investigate criminal charges, and Rendell's staff had responded with a lengthy legal memorandum stating that there was probable cause to obtain a search warrant to search the house for explosives and weapons and that there were several arrest warrants outstanding against MOVE members known to be living in the house. On June 22 Rendell sent the memorandum to Goode with a cover letter:

> Dear Wilson:
>
> Enclosed please find a memorandum prepared by my staff which analyzes our legal options as to actions that could be taken against the MOVE members currently residing at 6221 Osage Avenue. As you will note by reading the memorandum, none of these options are completely satisfactory, and all of them have some significant drawbacks. The memo sets forth both a legal analyses of our alternatives and a strategic look at the feasibility of all of the alternatives.
>
> I would reiterate, however, what I expressed to you at our first meeting, that I believe it is imperative to do something as quickly as possible, before the situation grows even worse and before MOVE members receive a higher profile from increased media attention. I think it would be a good idea if we all got together again to discuss these options, but I believe that a combination of some of our alternatives with arrest warrants and a search warrant might do the job. However, none of our thinking is fixed, and I would be more than interested in hearing from the Commissioner, the Managing Director, and the City Solicitor as to their appraisal of the situation.
>
> Sincerely yours,
> EDWARD G. RENDELL

Goode knew, from the DA's memo, that Frank Africa had been declared delinquent by the parole board at the beginning of May. He knew an adequate basis existed for seeking search warrants and additional arrest warrants. DA Rendell had told him his staff was standing by, ready to take statements from the neighbors and go to court for the warrants as soon as he gave the word. Why, then, did Goode tell the neighbors that he had no legal basis on which to act?

Three years later, in his testimony before the grand jury, Goode explained it this way:

"What I meant by that statement was that we did not have warrants signed by a judge that we could go into the house and, in fact, make arrests. . . ."

But, the prosecutor argued, the only reason Goode didn't have those warrants was that he himself had made the decision not to seek them. Wasn't that so? Goode replied:

"I would point out that the answer to your question is yes. . . ."

Whatever convoluted reasoning he used that day, he was hard-pressed to explain to the neighbors how a group of people could transform their quiet neighborhood into a nightmare and the authorities would be powerless to act. They knew of MOVE's violent history, of course—but did that put MOVE out of reach of the law?

Many asked themselves whether the fact that they were a tiny black neighborhood in west Philadelphia was the real reason the city saw no reason to act. If MOVE had set up housekeeping among the expensive town houses of Society Hill and a delegation of wealthy doctors and lawyers had come to Goode, would he give them the same tap dance? They left the meeting angry, frustrated, and empty-handed.

Goode didn't tell the neighbors that the police were already working on a plan for the August 8 confrontation that MOVE had promised. Late in May, after receiving the first reports that MOVE was "planning something," Commissioner Sambor had called Sergeant Herbert Kirk, an eighteen-year veteran who was an instructor at the police academy and who had worked under Sambor before he'd been named police commissioner. He asked Kirk to come down to police headquarters to see him.

"I want you to draw up a plan to assault the MOVE house,"

he told Kirk when he arrived, giving him the police intelligence files on the Osage Avenue house. Sambor told him that he should keep three things in mind: The plan should be designed, if at all possible, so that no one in the house was injured. It had to be ready in time for the August 8 confrontation. And it should be prepared in the strictest secrecy. Sambor had the uncomfortable feeling that MOVE knew a lot about what went on in the police department. Sometimes it seemed the group knew more than he did himself.

Kirk started his research by watching videotapes of the 1978 confrontation. He met with the fire commissioner, who assigned a senior fire fighter to advise him on the type of equipment the fire department could make available.

He quickly saw that the approach used in 1978—the armored battering ram and bulldozers—wouldn't work this time. The street was too narrow to maneuver the heavy equipment, and the construction of the row houses made it virtually impossible to isolate the MOVE house as the police had been able to do in 1978.

Studying the surveillance photos of the Osage Avenue house, he began to consider a rooftop assault. The best approach, it seemed, would be to insert tear gas into the house from above and flush out the occupants.

But recalling that MOVE members in 1978 had shot through the first floor from the basement, Kirk looked for a way to keep officers off the roof itself. He decided that if he could create a small hole near the parapet that divided the roof from the neighbors, police could stay on the adjacent roof while they pumped tear gas into the hole. Cops would need to be on the roof for only a few seconds, first to place an explosive charge that would create the hole and then to put the tear gas generator in position.

Kirk rounded up two other cops that he'd worked with before. He figured he'd need some advice about explosives and special tactics.

Lieutenant Frank Powell, with more than twenty years on the force, was acting commander of the bomb squad. He was friendly, down-to-earth, with a good rapport with the men who worked under him. But people said he was a straight arrow. If you tried to sneak out fifteen minutes early on Powell's shift, he'd call you on it. Though he supervised the bomb squad, it wasn't really his area of expertise; he'd spent years as a supervisor in the stakeout division.

The second cop, William Klein, on the other hand, was a true demolitions man. His familiarity with explosives went back to his days with the Marines in Vietnam. During the war Klein had gone down into Vietcong tunnels to flush out the enemy. Dark, narrow, and twisting, the tunnels were a place where every step could lead to an ambush with nowhere to hide.

After he was discharged from the Marines, Klein had joined the Philadelphia Police Department. As a patrolman in west Philadelphia he'd even had a few run-ins with MOVE at the Powelton house. Eventually he had been assigned to the bomb squad.

It took a certain type of person to be comfortable around large quantities of explosives. Most of the guys on the bomb squad, Klein included, were fascinated by the stuff. They had probably been the kind of kids who pleaded with their parents to stop at fireworks stores down south on the way to Florida or always managed to have a couple of cherry bombs squirreled inside their desks at school.

To the men of the bomb squad the nuances of various explosives—their detonation rate and temperature, their composition and applications—carried the same significance as horsepower and valve design to hot-rodders. In the hands of an expert, setting off explosions can become almost an art form, but the squad didn't actually get the chance to do much of it.

Bomb squads get their greatest publicity from defusing bombs. But to take a bomb apart you also have to know how to put one together. There were endless subtleties to this work—how to construct "countercharges" that will safely set off a terrorist's bomb after an area has been evacuated, "shaped charges" in the form of a cone that are designed to concentrate the force of the explosion into a single-directional blast, and "hatch charges" that can cut a neat hole through a solid wall or blow a door off a car while leaving the rest intact.

There were dozens of explosive products and devices on the

market, most of them developed for industrial applications and some for use by the military: "jet-tappers," a small shaped charge used to clean out blast furnaces; "det cord," which looked and felt like a bead of caulk; "deta sheet," a thin, flexible material that could be shaped into special-purpose charges. The magazine at the police academy contained supplies of all of these, as well as others. There were small but potent charges that were used to set off dynamite and other explosives; electrical and mechanical fuses that could be set with time delays; HDP boosters, which were often used in conjunction with other explosives; and Tovex, a commercial mining explosive manufactured by Du Pont that looked like a gel in sausage casings.

The best explosive of all, in the opinion of Klein and the other members of the bomb squad, was the military plastic explosive known as C-4. A milky white substance with the consistency of modeling clay, it was known as the "Cadillac" of explosives. It was versatile and easy to use. Though extremely powerful, it was also remarkably safe. You could mold it in your hands into whatever shape you wanted. You could hold a match to it, and it wouldn't even burn. Neither bullets nor shotgun pellets would set it off—only a blasting cap or another high explosive.

Unfortunately it was almost impossible for the bomb squad to get. Under federal regulations C-4 was normally made available only to the military, not to civilian police forces. But if a cop went to one of the sessions that the FBI regularly put on, he could usually manage to pick up a little of the leftover C-4 at the end of the session.

Kirk had in mind an explosive charge that would be powerful enough and concentrated enough to blow a small hole in the roof of the MOVE house without hurting anyone inside or outside the house. The best device for that would be a "water charge"—or, as it was sometimes known, a Tupperware charge. To construct one, plastic explosive is spread evenly around the outside of a lidded plastic bowl. The bowl is filled with water and sealed, and the flat lid is placed against a wall or other obstacle. The shape of the bowl concentrates the force of the explosion against the water inside, which is driven like a piston against the wall. As it passes out the far side of the wall, the water vaporizes harmlessly from the heat of the explosion.

C-4 would have been ideal for the Tupperware charge, but when Kirk approached Powell and Klein in the summer of 1984, the only C-4 that the department had was used to train dogs to sniff out explosives. It probably didn't even amount to a pound, and with the handling by dogs and trainers, it had gotten pretty funky. There might have been a little more stashed away in people's lockers, but it wouldn't have been much. Klein improvised with other materials.

Working with Klein and Powell, Kirk drew up a plan to assault the house. He called for two squirts—fire engines with nozzles that can be raised on long booms and directed by remote control—that would first sweep the roof clear of MOVE's debris and barricades. Then teams of stakeout cops would run across the adjoining roofs, use the water charge to blow a four-inch hole in the roof of the house, and pump in tear gas. It would either drive the occupants out or, if they stayed in the house, render them unconscious.

Kirk worked with Powell and Klein to devise a charge that would be just powerful enough to breach the roof without hurting anyone inside the house—even if someone happened to be standing directly beneath the blast. Kirk had managed to track down the original construction records for the houses on Osage Avenue, and he used them to build small sections of exactly the same composition to test the charges.

He tried to think of everything he could. He had mechanics build a special nozzle for the tear gas machine so that it would reach across to the adjoining roof. He read articles in scientific journals about the effects of tear gas, particularly on children.

To be sure the fire fighters would be able to train the squirts precisely where they would be needed, he had one of the squirts brought out to the fire academy training tower, where he reconstructed the physical layout of the roof of the MOVE house. He set it in place on the training tower and placed the squirt about as far away as he calculated it would be from the MOVE house on August 8. Since the operator wouldn't be able to see the MOVE house, he had the operator turn his back while he radioed instructions. It took them about ninety seconds to home in on the target.

Klein volunteered to test the effects the charge might have on the cops on the roof. Wearing a protective suit, he crouched behind a low wall that had been built to resemble the rooftop parapet while the explosive was set off. To be sure no one inside the MOVE house would be hurt, dummies were placed in a pit beneath the reconstructed rooftop. There was a lot of dust but no damage.

Kirk also devised a backup plan that called for cops to enter the houses on either side, blow small holes in the adjoining walls, and pump tear gas into the MOVE house. They would have to use this second plan if the kids were still up there when the shooting started.

When everything was finished, Kirk typed up a summary of the plan and locked it in a filing cabinet in his office. As a precaution against leaks—leaks that could get back to MOVE and lead to the death of a police officer—he made no copies.

On July 13, Louise James called Officer Delores Thompson. Frank, she said, had become a mental cripple, totally dependent on John Africa. If he walked to the supermarket eight blocks from the house, he'd stop five times on the way to call the house and speak to his uncle. Theresa, she said, would do the same.

Louise wanted the police to pick up Frank if they got the chance. "I'd rather see him serve his parole violation in jail, away from other MOVE members, to deprogram his mind," she said.

"I can deal with that," she went on. "Because if that happens, Vince will do one of two things. He'll either leave the house or order the others out front for a confrontation." Either way was fine with her, she said, as long as Frank was safe.

"I don't give a damn about the others," she said. "As much as Vincent says he loves Frank, he never visited him in jail. And he won't visit him if he goes back, so Frank won't be exposed to him and his teachings."

Thompson asked her why she didn't take legal action to have the group evicted.

"I want my house back," Louise agreed. But as long as Frank was still in the house, she said, she didn't "want to be in the position of telling the city I want MOVE out and forcing MOVE to take a stand. I don't want to be in the position of forcing the city to kill them."

She added: "I'm thoroughly convinced that Vincent Leaphart is legally insane, especially since the time when he ordered my own son to kill me." When that had happened, she said, his "whole personality changed to that of a madman. If I'd even scratched my head while they had me pinned to the floor, they would have taken it as an obnoxious gesture, and I'd have lost my life."

After the incident, she said, Vincent and the other MOVE members talked to Frank for thirty-four hours nonstop to convince him that he'd done the right thing. Vincent named him "Naturalist Minister," she said, giving him the right, like Vincent himself, to inflict punishment on the other members.

That was all she had to tell, Louise said to Thompson before she hung up. She'd continue to stay in touch.

As tensions grew on Osage Avenue, anybody who could manage to stay away did so. The parole board, after a meeting with civil affairs officers, ordered parole officers not to serve the warrant against Frank. The city Department of Licenses and Inspections issued instructions to its employees that they were to stay away from "MOVE property" unless they received approval from the L&I commissioner. The police officers on the scene kept a low profile, dressing in plain clothes and driving unmarked cars.

On July 25 Officer Thompson received another phone call from Louise. She and her sister LaVerne had to meet with the mayor, Louise said. They needed to negotiate the release of the jailed MOVE members before August 8.

"They're definitely planning a confrontation on August 8th, and the mayor better be prepared to deal with the situation. He

can't take the position that if he ignores MOVE they will go
away. My neighbor told me that all the neighbors have taken
up arms for August 8th, and MOVE is definitely ready."

"You mean they have guns?" Thompson asked.

"What do you think?"

Also, Frank seemed to be sick, Louise's neighbor had told
her. He didn't venture beyond the sidewalk or the driveway in
the back. If the neighbor was right about Frank, she said,
she'd probably go public, announcing that she was no longer a
MOVE member and explaining why.

Officer Thompson told her that police assigned to the
MOVE detail had also noticed that Frank was sick.

On the other end of the line Louise burst into tears. "I'll go
over there," she wept. "I'll go over there with a hatchet in my
hand."

On July 28 Goode met once again with the neighbors.
Under pressure to do something about MOVE, he told them
that he would "act when I feel it is appropriate."

On July 31, Louise and LaVerne finally had their meeting
with Goode. They told him that MOVE was becoming more
violent and would use its weapons against police.

Goode interrupted, looking at Louise. "You used to be a
MOVE member. You used to live in the house." He had met
Louise and LaVerne before. When he was managing director,
they'd come to him to see if he would help them find housing
for MOVE and to protest the treatment of MOVE prisoners.
He'd even intervened to ensure that MOVE prisoners in the
city's custody received a diet of fruit and raw food.

"That doesn't matter," Louise replied. "I'm concerned
about my family that's in that house. I'm concerned about my
son. I don't want anyone to be hurt."

"I need suggestions about how to resolve this," Goode said.
"Neither you nor your sister has offered any suggestions."

Louise changed the subject, now seeming to ally herself
with the MOVE people. "The problem," she said, "is with the
neighbors. They complained to the city that MOVE had its
loudspeakers on twenty-four hours a day. They only had it on
two times.

"And they never tell anyone how the MOVE people bake

bread and give it to the neighbors. They never say how MOVE shovels all the sidewalks and porches up and down the block in the winter, for no charge. They won't even take money when people tried to give it to them.

"And what about the Buddhists living next door—they burn incense and chant all night long, keep MOVE people awake. What about the neighbor who threatened the children with a gun?"

But Goode was interested in details, not an argument over who'd done what. How many people were in the house? Louise didn't know. Her concern was for her son's safety. She told Goode what she'd told Officer Thompson—that she wanted Frank picked up for a parole violation when he left the house.

"If I were to do that, would it cause a confrontation with the other MOVE members?"

Yes, Louise replied. It probably would. Goode dropped the subject.

"Do you want your house back?" Goode asked.

"Yes," she said. "But not if it means there will be a confrontation."

Before she left, she demanded that Goode secure the release of the jailed MOVE members. That was what the organization wanted, she said. They wouldn't settle for less.

"I can't live through another August 8," she said, referring to the Powelton Village shootout.

"There's nothing I can do to get those people out of jail," Goode said.

"You could look into it and get a pardon from the governor."

"You know he's not going to do that."

"But you haven't tried, have you?" Louise said.

"No," Goode answered. "Do you know anything about Dick Thornburgh?" Governor Thornburgh had begun his political career as a tough district attorney in Pittsburgh.

"Yes, I know about him. But you have to make an effort."

"Okay," the mayor said. "I'll get back to you." He never did.

On the morning of August 8 Sergeant Kirk found himself in a state police helicopter circling the MOVE house. From his vantage point he could see the elements of his plan falling into place as if on a giant game board. He could see the squirts already in position and the police barricades on the surrounding streets. Four blocks north of the MOVE house he could see the large brick bulk of the Philadelphia Geriatric Center, an old-age home that was serving as impromptu headquarters for the operation. Hundreds of cops and fire fighters had gathered there that morning to receive orders. Then they'd moved quickly, evacuating the street and surrounding the house. So far everything had proceeded according to Kirk's plan.

Kirk had gone up in the helicopter to get a last look at the fortifications atop the house. His plan was designed to use the least force necessary, and any last-minute work by the MOVE people to strengthen their defenses would have changed the picture considerably.

The roof looked the same as it had in the surveillance photos. The wooden pallets still stood around the skylight in the center of the roof. That and the surrounding debris would easily be cleared away by the powerful streams of the squirts.

But as Kirk looked down at the roof he saw something that he hadn't considered in his plan: the children.

The kids sat there, apparently unaware of the threatened conflict, and as long as they were there the plan was stymied. The squirts would have swept the children right off the roof. And without the squirts the MOVE people would have a protected vantage point at the skylight to shoot at any cops who came over the roof.

Fortunately, though, the backup plan—blowing holes through the side walls—would still work. Kirk remained confident that the police would be able to introduce tear gas into the house and drive MOVE out without seriously harming the people inside and without putting cops in danger.

It will never be known if he was right. The August 8 "confrontation" ended without a shot being fired. Perhaps MOVE was waiting for the cops to try to evict them as they had in 1978. The cops, on the other hand, came with the expectation that MOVE would provoke a confrontation.

But MOVE's only assault that day was through the loudspeaker as the members vowed to stay in the house. Finally the police and fire fighters simply left. The reporters and television crews lingered a little longer, but before long the street had returned to normal—or at least what had passed for normal over the last eight months.

The neighbors returned one by one throughout the evening. As neighbor Lloyd Wilson passed the MOVE house, Frank shouted to him from the impromptu stage that they had set up in front of the porch.

"You went to the cops about this wood," he said to Wilson. In the days before, Wilson had twice asked Frank to move some wood that blocked the sidewalk in front of his house.

Wilson believed in giving people the courtesy of a reply when they spoke to him, no matter who they were. "Frank," he said, "the police were standing right there. The civil affairs unit was standing right there when I said that to you. I didn't have to go to the cops to tell them that I asked you to move the wood again."

Frank started calling Wilson a traitor, saying he would not help support their cause. He grabbed him, and they nearly came to blows. Cops at the corner made no attempt to intervene.

Wilson left his house that night, afraid that he "might have done something stupid." The next morning he went to the mayor's offices in City Hall and confronted Goode as he emerged from a conference with Sambor and Managing Director Leo A. Brooks.

"Look, this is it," he said, walking up to the mayor. "Last night I was actually attacked by Frank James. What are you people going to do?"

Goode, apologetic, explained that he was on his way to another appointment. But he turned to Brooks and Sambor and asked them to talk to Wilson. They spoke for a long time, but to little avail. Sambor and Brooks were sympathetic, but they had to tell him that the city had not figured out a way to resolve the continuing crisis. "Only an act of God," the managing director told him, "could change this."

The same day, Sergeant Kirk was wounded after surprising a burglar in his house. He never returned to active duty, and he officially retired some months later. His single existing copy of the plan, which he says was kept in a locked filing cabinet in his office, was never seen again.

During the last week of August Clifford Bond received a phone call from a man named Thomas Palmer. He was from a social service agency known as the West Philadelphia Consortium. As Goode had promised in June, a request had come down through the mayor's office asking the consortium to offer mental health counseling for the neighbors.

After a meeting with Bond and another neighbor, Palmer developed a proposal for counseling for the children. It would be scheduled to take place every Monday for three hours and would be designed to combat "fears and bad habits" that the children might be picking up from playing with the MOVE children. It included "group building skills, socialization, and counseling which would enable them to better understand and live within a system of culture clash," according to a statement later given by Palmer.

Until May 13, 1985, that once-a-week counseling program was the only official assistance provided to the neighbors in response to their demands.

With the coming of the cooler weather of fall, the bugs and the odors abated somewhat and tensions on the block seemed to ease. The incidents with the neighbors dropped off. The MOVE house itself became quiet.

Police observers and the neighbors noted, however, that there was still plenty of activity going on. They observed MOVE members carrying large sections of tree trunks into the house and carrying mounds of soil back out.

And on the rooftop they watched as two heavy timber structures rose under the saws and hammers of the MOVE members. They were rectangular, one tall enough for a man to stand inside, the other, toward the rear of the house, about half the size. Thick steel plating had been installed behind the wood, and small rectangular holes had been cut on all sides, a little lower than eye level.

There was no mistaking what they were. They were fortified bunkers. And the holes were gun ports.

The police observers duly noted their observations and filed their reports. Commissioner Sambor later said he never saw them. The reports had been lost, he said, somewhere in the trackless bureaucracy of the Philadelphia Police Department.

8
Spring 1985

THROUGH THE LAST MONTHS of 1984 and the beginning of 1985, Wilson Goode half hoped the problem of MOVE might just go away. They were talking about moving out of the city altogether; Jerry Africa had hinted that they might go to Richmond. As bad as the situation looked on Osage Avenue, Goode didn't believe it necessarily had to end in armed conflict.

The neighbors thought otherwise, and by the spring of 1985 they had decided they weren't going to take it anymore. They were sick of promises, procrastination, and the outright lies that Goode and his administration had handed them—and they were tired of the threats and intimidation that MOVE had directed at them. They had watched, incredulous and impotent, as the people of MOVE methodically built their fortified gun bunkers under the seemingly uninterested eyes of the Philadelphia Police Department.

Goode's latest pledge was that they wouldn't have to go through another summer like the one they'd had the year before. But by the middle of spring not a thing had been done. Caught between ineptitude and terror, the neighbors were ready to try some politicking of their own. And if that didn't work, if nobody at all would come to their aid, they were ready to take matters into their own hands.

TUESDAY, APRIL 30

On April 30 the neighbors held their first and only official news conference. During their long months of frustration they had learned a few things about politics and the way things worked in the real world, and they reasoned that Dick Thornburgh, the popular Republican governor of Pennsylvania, just might take the opportunity to embarrass the Democratic mayor in the state's largest city. They hoped publicity would work where their pleas had not.

Soft-spoken as always, Clifford Bond read the press statement that the neighbors had prepared.

"We are here to let the governor know about the disquietude and general state of terror we are forced to live under by the MOVE organization. We want the governor to know that regardless of whatever may have happened in its past, today MOVE is a clear and present danger to the health and safety of our entire block. We also want the governor to know that we have been to our elected representatives in city and state government, but to date nothing of any consequence has been done. We are now asking Governor Thornburgh to step in and deal with this situation."

He continued: "Four years ago, the MOVE organization moved into 6221 Osage Avenue. We welcomed them there, and many of us extended a helping hand. We gave them clothing, fed their children, purchased their fruits and vegetables, and accepted them into our block family. In return for our kindness, we have been cursed, abused, and beaten by these same MOVE members. On three separate occasions MOVE members have attacked and beaten residents of our own block, each without provocation.

"It has been evident to us that MOVE has no intention of living in harmony or even peacefully with us. As their actions have demonstrated, MOVE holds nothing for us but a vicious, vindictive, malignant contempt. This attitude, combined with their eagerness for violence, makes it imperative that MOVE be removed from our block—immediately. We cannot impress this upon you enough. If the MOVE organization is allowed to remain on Osage Avenue, and continue to abuse us, there will be blood in the street.

"Governor Thornburgh, 146 people live on our block; 78 are children. We have senior citizens, young married couples, and grandparents. We are law-abiding, taxpaying citizens. We love our block, and we will not be driven out by anyone.

"We ask you now, sir: Is there a public official in this state with the backbone to act for the public good? Is there a law enforcement agency in this state ready to enforce the law by any legal means necessary? We trust, Mr. Governor, that you are such a public official, and that you command such a law enforcement agency."

The gauntlet had been thrown down. The question now was who—Goode or Thornburgh—would pick it up.

It had taken John Africa more than a year, but he had finally succeeded in getting the media's attention. Wilson Goode had tried to wait him out, but MOVE had won—just as it always had in the past. Now it wouldn't be long before the city was forced to confront the group. And when the confrontation came, the cameras would once again show black radicals defending their home against an army of white cops.

MOVE responded to the neighbors' press conference with hours of threats over the loudspeaker. They threatened Goode, cops, and the neighbors and the neighbors' children.

In the midst of the rhetoric they also claimed that they had wired the adjoining houses and would blow them up if they were attacked.

When Police Commissioner Sambor heard about the neighbors' news conference, he decided he'd better dust off Kirk's plan from the year before. He called in the commander of the stakeout unit, Captain Richard Kirchner. Recalling that Frank Powell had been involved in the planning the previous summer, he got hold of him as well. And he brought in Sergeant Al Revel, an instructor at the police academy. Sambor had known Revel for years; both were crack shots and had competed together in many marksmanship contests. Sambor didn't have a lot of people under him whom he knew and trusted, and when it came to something as important as this, he tended to circumvent the official pecking order and go straight to the people, like Revel, who he felt could do the job.

Sambor told the three of them that they would need to put

together a plan for assaulting the MOVE house. To begin he asked Revel and Powell to take a look at the old plan and see whether it could be updated.

WEDNESDAY, MAY 1

The next day—the first of May—Revel and Powell rummaged through Kirk's old office looking for the plan, but they couldn't find it. Powell called Kirk at home and asked him if he knew where it was. Kirk didn't but said he'd give the commissioner a call.

Later Powell and Revel contacted Sambor with the news that they couldn't find the plan. Kirk had also tried to get through to Sambor but hadn't been able to reach him.

Sambor told them to talk to the others who'd helped assemble the plan. "See if you can piece it together," he told them.

Back at the police academy Revel drafted Officer Michael Tursi to help "piece together" the plan. Tursi was an experienced cop who'd worked stakeout before coming to the academy as a firearms instructor. In stakeout, he'd been known as a "thinker," the kind of cop who took a methodical, almost scientific approach to his work. Looking at the background information Revel had collected, he suggested they set up posts in houses along Osage Avenue and behind the MOVE house on Pine Street, surrounding the house, and he offered to go out to the site with Powell to scout out the best locations.

Meanwhile, on Osage Avenue, everything had changed. The news conference made both daily papers in Philadelphia and the television stations. For most Philadelphians, who had heard virtually nothing about the problems on Osage Avenue, the news that MOVE was back was shocking enough. The fact that the group had been permitted to build a gun bunker on top of its row house and that it seemed to be preparing for a confrontation verged on the incredible.

That day reporters and photographers from the *Inquirer*, *Daily News*, wire services, and out-of-town papers descended on Osage Avenue, and the story was soon making its way into papers across the country. One dramatic photo showed a

MOVE member, his body muscular and his face set in determination, standing in front of the still-unfinished bunker, hauling a can of gasoline up to the roof by a rope.

THURSDAY, MAY 2

As Frank Powell saw it, he was getting dragged into something that wasn't his job. Kirchner was the head of stakeout, and this was a stakeout operation. Let him update the plan, Powell reasoned.

But Powell didn't have much hope that Kirchner would come through. Kirchner had a reputation as a man who avoided making decisions—and nobody had heard from him since that first meeting when Sambor said they needed a plan.

In exasperation Tursi, Powell, and Revel arranged a meeting with Kirchner. They planned to use the meeting as an opportunity to put the ball firmly in his court. They also arranged for Inspector John Tiers—who was Powell's boss as well as Kirchner's—to attend. And they invited two detectives who had been collecting intelligence about the MOVE house.

Leading Kirchner and the others into an empty classroom at the police academy, Powell, Revel, and Tursi laid out the aerial photographs that detectives Benner and Boyd had collected and explained to Kirchner and Tiers that the plan Kirk had devised was obsolete. They presented the ideas they'd come up with, which involved inserting tear gas into the house from adjoining houses. Then Powell laid the whole problem at Kirchner's feet—but Kirchner wasn't about to pick it up.

"You've got to develop a new plan," Powell said. "If you need any help from the bomb squad or pistol range, let us know."

Kirchner seemed unconcerned. "Fuck it," he said. "Go in there with two stakeout units and drag them out by their hair. If they give me any shit, we'll shoot them."

Powell, Revel, and Tursi looked at one another and then at Inspector Tiers. He said nothing.

After the meeting broke up, Powell turned to Tursi and Revel. "I don't want any part of this," he said. "It's not my problem."

"Listen to me, Frank," Tursi said. "Kirchner's mentality is going to get cops killed. We've got to put together a plan."

Powell thought it over. They all had good friends in stakeout. The thought of Kirchner sending them up to the front door of the MOVE house was terrifying. Reluctantly he agreed to help.

Over the next several days the three of them worked out a plan. As they reviewed the pictures of the house and its fortifications, it seemed as if MOVE had figured out Kirk's strategy. They had used the intervening months to fortify all the vulnerable areas that Kirk had exploited. They'd laid railroad ties over the tar paper roof. They'd built the fortified bunkers, making a rooftop assault impossible.

One of them suggested that two squads could enter the adjoining houses, blow holes in the common walls, and insert tear gas. They adopted that as the basic concept and began to work on refinements.

They were especially concerned about the bunkers on top of the house—particularly the front one, which commanded a view of the entire neighborhood. In the last few days MOVE members had apparently finished it and pushed it forward so that the front of it extended past the edge of the roof by a few feet. It gave them a clean line of fire all up and down Osage Avenue.

They guessed that Kirk's idea of spraying the rooftop with water from the squirts could still dislodge the fortifications. But they did not consider that MOVE might have access to the adjoining houses, permitting members to fire on police who entered the houses.

They did, however, recognize that their plan might have shortcomings, and they tried to seek the help of experts. Powell asked a number of stakeout officers to critique the plan. He took aside an FBI agent who was visiting the academy and asked his advice. He, Revel, and Tursi discussed the plan, probing it for flaws. Everyone they talked to felt the plan was sound. Of course none of them had had any practical experience with an operation of this sort. Powell, Tursi, and Revel were in uncharted territory.

FRIDAY, MAY 3

On Friday Mayor Goode called a special meeting of his top
officials at his office in City Hall. He also asked District
Attorney Rendell to attend. They had all read the papers, so no
one was surprised when Goode announced that he was revers-
ing his hands-off policy toward MOVE.

Goode asked Rendell whether the warrants that had been
drawn up the summer before were still valid. Rendell was sure
they were but said he'd like to take additional statements from
the residents and use them to secure fresh warrants. He
volunteered to have his staff interview the neighbors and
others over the weekend and have new warrants ready for a
judge's signature by May 6, the following Monday.

MONDAY, MAY 6

Over the weekend the DA's office interviewed nineteen of the
Osage Avenue neighbors. On Monday deputy DAs Eric Han-
son and Bernard Siegel summarized the results in a memo to
Rendell. Though they were careful not to recommend any
specific course of action, it was clear where their sympathies lay:

> Any attempt to enforce the law at 6221 Osage Avenue will
> almost certainly end in armed conflict. MOVE continues to
> defy authority, to annoy its neighbors, and to commit the
> same violations of law as last year. The same, unhappy
> options for action remain; the dangers, however, are now
> even greater. . . .
>
> We do not pretend to know whether action or inaction is
> the better immediate course. There is, however, no reason
> to believe that MOVE will become more pacific or reason-
> able or that, in the end, armed conflict can be avoided. . . .
> Every approach that we can think of—even inaction—
> includes the likely necessity of confrontation *at some
> point.* . . .

TUESDAY, MAY 7

On Tuesday Powell and the others met once again with

Kirchner, Benner, and Boyd at the police academy. Tursi and Powell outlined the plan they were developing and asked for the others' reaction and feedback. Nobody had any criticisms or comments.

Later that day, in a meeting at the mayor's office, Goode held a meeting to follow up on his earlier one. Rendell first summarized his deputies' memo and reiterated that the mayor should move quickly. Goode asked him to prepare the warrants as soon as possible.

Then the mayor turned to Sambor and directed him to draw up a plan to execute the warrants. The plan should be designed to safeguard the police officers, the fire fighters, and the people in the house. The cops should be handpicked, with an eye to their coolness in difficult situations.

Almost as an aside Rendell said to Sambor, "Of course you'll keep the mayor informed on the progress of the plan."

"No," Goode injected. "You gentlemen are the experts. You don't need to keep me informed of all the details."

It was a comment that Rendell found odd in light of the subject under discussion. He left the meeting with a deep sense of foreboding.

WEDNESDAY, MAY 8

On Wednesday City Councilwoman Joan Spector announced at a City Hall news conference that MOVE currently owed more than $1,500 to the city in gas and water bills. The city, she charged, was "subsidizing those terrorists." Goode, speaking to reporters afterward, countered that turning off the water and electricity would not "solve the problem the neighbors are faced with out there."

The same day, Powell received a phone call from the commissioner's office. He was told to plan on attending a meeting at the Police Administration Building the next morning.

Almost as soon as he hung up the phone rang again. It was Tiers. The commissioner was breathing down his neck, he said. "We got to have a plan. The commissioner wants a plan. We ain't got nothing, and we're in trouble. Can we use yours?"

Tiers had never actually worked in the stakeout unit before

assuming his post as inspector, so perhaps it wasn't surprising that he was short on ideas for the operation. Powell and the others had kind of hoped that there would be at least one other plan to consider, but Tiers was Powell's boss. If he wanted the plan, it was his.

"Good," Tiers said into the phone. "Stop by my office tomorrow morning before we meet with the commissioner."

THURSDAY, MAY 9

On Thursday morning Tursi handed Tiers a copy of the plan. He barely looked at it. "Okay, that's it," he said. "We'll go with this."

At Sambor's office Tursi explained the plan to Sambor. He told him it had been "drawn up by the police academy"— which included units under the command of Powell, Tiers, and Kirchner. Like Kirchner and Tiers, Sambor had nothing to add to the plan.

Later that day Tursi presented the plan again, this time at a meeting that also included police commanders and three FBI agents, including Michael Macy.

"I want you all to play devil's advocate with this plan," Tursi said. "Help us find its weak points."

Macy suggested that the charges be placed under the stairwells, since it would be unlikely that anyone would be standing on the opposite side of the wall.

Fire Commissioner William Richmond and his deputy had been asked to attend the meeting to review the plan. Richmond did find one problem with the plan. "The squirts aren't powerful enough to push off that front bunker," he said.

Revel later said that when he heard Richmond say that, his hopes were dashed. In his mind the removal of that bunker was critical to the plan they'd created. The bunker gave MOVE the high ground and would put every officer out there at risk. On paper the plan could still work, but the risks were far greater. Sambor didn't seem to understand why Revel was concerned.

After the general meeting the planners met with the commissioner to talk about the kinds of arms they could use.

"What do we have in the armory?" Sambor asked.

They had a number of automatic weapons, including Uzis, M-16s, and .50-caliber rifles.

Powell spoke up. He knew a source of additional weapons. The owner of a gun shop in suburban Philadelphia had offered to lend the police department heavy weapons. "Should I get them?" he asked.

Sambor answered, "If you can get them and they can be transferred legally, go ahead."

Later that day, after contacting an ATF agent and arranging for official clearances, Powell sent out a crew to pick up three Browning automatic rifles—commonly known as BARs—as well as an M-60 machine gun and a 20-millimeter antitank gun.

Powell also called Sergeant Ed Connor and told him that he would head one of the "insertion" teams. Connor, a short, heavyset Irishman, was considered to be a little bit of a loose cannon in the department, but he certainly wasn't afraid to be where the action was.

"I want to pick my own team," Connor said. No problem, Powell told him. "Who's leading the other team?" he asked Powell.

"I am."

May 9 was also the day that Managing Director Leo Brooks—the number two man in the city administration—left town. He was driving to Virginia to attend his daughter's graduation. Though the timing was unfortunate, he had been left with the impression that the MOVE assault would not take place until sometime during the week of May 13. He planned to return to Philadelphia on the evening of May 12.

That afternoon, in Brooks's absence, Sambor briefed the mayor personally. "Where do you stand with the plan?" Goode asked him.

Sambor told him about the two meetings he'd held that day. He cautioned that the plan wasn't firm yet; a final planning session was scheduled for May 11. But as things stood then, May 13 was to be the day. He said the police would evacuate the neighbors on Sunday, the 12th.

"But Sunday is Mother's Day," Goode pointed out. "Don't you want to wait a few days?"

"No. The longer we wait, the more time MOVE will have to get ready."

Goode deferred to his judgment. Sambor, after all, was the professional.

Sergeant Revel was still worried about the bunkers, even if Sambor was not. Perhaps a wrecking ball could be used to destroy the bunkers. He called a contractor who did work for the city and asked whether a crane could be brought in to do the job. After visiting the site, the contractor told him that he didn't have anything big enough to do the job. He suggested that he contact another contractor by the name of Paul Geppert.

Later that afternoon Goode and Sambor met with Rendell in the mayor's conference room. Rendell told them the warrants were prepared but not signed by the judge. He also suggested that they get a court order for "spike mikes"—special listening devices that would permit the police to eavesdrop on the MOVE house—to be inserted into the adjoining wall. It was a good idea, Goode and Sambor agreed.

FRIDAY, MAY 10

On Friday, May 10, Goode met with Clifford Bond. The mayor played it cool, saying nothing about the impending action and promising to attend a community meeting on the following Saturday, May 18.

On his way home Bond probably didn't even notice yet one more stranger in his neighborhood pacing off distances and eyeing the rooftops. It was the contractor, Paul Geppert, accompanied by Revel.

After he went back to work and made some calculations, Geppert called the police academy and asked for Revel. He wasn't in, so Powell took the call.

"The reach is too far to use a bucket," he said. "How about a wrecking ball? I don't have enough room to swing it, but I can probably drop it straight down on top of the bunkers."

Geppert Company had some experience with MOVE; it had been the contractor that had razed the Powelton house. Paul Geppert didn't seem intimidated by the threat of violence on Osage Avenue. He suggested as an alternative that they put armor plating on a crane and go directly up Osage Avenue.

Powell didn't like that idea. It was too dangerous.

"Well, let me give you a price for it anyway," Geppert said. "To use the wrecking ball, we'd set up on Pine Street. We'll need a two-hour setup time, and we'll have to take out one dead tree." The price would be $6,500. To go down Osage Avenue would cost about half of that.

Powell thanked him and told him he'd get back to him. He'd have to run it by the commissioner.

"Okay," said Geppert. "I'll be here."

Powell later said that when he told Sambor about the options, the commissioner had a problem with the price. It was the end of the fiscal year, and the department was out of money. "I'll have to go to the Hall"—City Hall—Powell recalls him saying.

Sambor later called back, Powell said, and told him to forget about the crane idea; he said that the mayor would not approve the money.

Sambor has denied this version of events. He says he rejected the crane dropping a ball on the house because he was concerned about the children's safety. He feared that the ball might go through the bunkers and into the house itself. Money, he said, was never the issue. Goode later testified that Sambor never briefed him on the possibility of using a crane before the operation began. The testimony of Revel, Tursi, and Geppert, however, indicates that Powell told them at the time that the city had rejected the crane option because it cost too much money.

Without the crane, Powell wanted to call off the whole plan. Again it was Tursi who calmed him down and encouraged him to go forward. It wasn't absolutely necessary, he said, for the bunkers to be removed. The plan was still sound. After some discussion, Powell agreed.

SATURDAY, MAY 11

On Saturday, May 11, according to the grand jury's public report, Tursi presented the plan for the last time. This time the meeting room at the Police Administration Building was crowded with people. Police commanders from the commissioner down to the commanding officer of the police garage were there. So were the fire commissioner and his deputy chief, as well as a lawyer from the city solicitor's office.

Sambor called the meeting to order. "All right," he said, "somebody brief us on the plan here."

The commanders all looked like they "were trying to hide under their chairs," Tursi later recalled. Finally Sambor turned to Tursi, who was probably the lowest-ranking cop in the room.

"All right, Mike," the commissioner said. "Get up here and brief us on this thing."

Tursi laid out the plan that he and Revel and Powell had devised. It had changed little since their early planning sessions.

Two of the fire department's squirts would be positioned to throw water against the bunkers. They would either knock the bunkers off the roof or at least obstruct the vision of anyone inside.

MOVE would be issued an ultimatum and given fifteen minutes to surrender. If they did not, the squirts would be turned on and smoke grenades shot into the street. Under cover of smoke two insertion teams would move down the street and into the houses adjacent to the MOVE property. One team would go into the basement of 6223 Osage—just west of the MOVE house—and the other would go to the second floor of 6219, on the east side. They would use the jet-tappers to blow three-inch holes into the masonry walls and use a pipe and sledgehammer to open the holes all the way into the MOVE house.

Each team would carry a "pepper fogger"—a gasoline-powered tear gas generator equipped with a special metal nozzle that would fit into the hole. The nozzles had been modified so that MOVE members couldn't shoot down them and disable the pepper foggers.

At a prearranged signal each team would start the pepper foggers, filling the basement and upstairs of the MOVE house with tear gas and driving the people in the house to the first floor. As in Kirk's original plan, it was anticipated that MOVE members would then surrender. If they did not, the tear gas would disable them. Even if they had gas masks, the tear gas would eventually displace enough oxygen from the air to render them unconscious.

Again, Tursi asked everyone in the room to try to find holes in the plan; again it sailed through with barely a comment.

Fire Commissioner Richmond wanted to know about the shaped charges: would they cause a fire?

"No," Sambor replied, "they've been tested."

Richmond's other concern was the safety of his men. "I want to be sure fire fighters are out of the line of fire," he told Sambor. And he pointed out again that the squirts wouldn't be powerful enough to dislodge the bunkers.

Sambor still seemed to consider the last point a minor detail. They would use the water anyway, as a diversion and to obscure the vision of anyone firing from the bunkers.

Bringing the meeting to a close, Sambor stood for emphasis. He didn't want a free-for-all, he said. This was a carefully controlled police operation. "Anyone who doesn't adhere to this plan," he warned, "will be dismissed."

After the general meeting, the supervisors who would be directly involved remained to iron out the details. Sambor insisted that a supervisor be assigned to each post. He reiterated that cops would fire only on orders and only at visible targets.

They reviewed the latest intelligence information that had been gathered by detectives Benner and Boyd. It included the wire photo of a MOVE member hauling a gasoline can onto the roof. Other aerial photos of the rooftop showed a number of metal cans, including one on which one could read the word *gasoline*.

"What do you think they plan to do with all that gas?" someone asked. They speculated that MOVE might be planning to pour it on the heads of any cops who approached the front of the house and then set them afire.

The detectives also reported that a cache of explosives had

been stolen in Chester County and might be in the MOVE house.

"They could have the place wired," a cop said. "There might be booby traps inside."

"If they surrender, keep them right in front of the house while the dogs sniff the house," Sambor ordered. "If there are any booby traps, they'll be in danger, too."

Boyd and Benner said the latest evidence showed that four or five adults and four to eight children were possibly in the house. "There's no way to surprise them," they reported.

Every day one of the adults in the house took the MOVE children to the park, and Sambor had already given orders for the children to be picked up if possible. Though he did not know it at the time, a snafu had gone down the line, and the civil affairs officer assigned to the scene was never told how important it was—or why—that the kids be taken into custody. After he received the order, in fact, he had stood aside to let the kids pass through a police barricade. Later, after the MOVE people got wind of the coming confrontation, they'd simply kept the kids in the house.

The detectives also reported on the possibility that MOVE had dug tunnels. Neighbors had seen them carrying large wheelbarrows full of dirt out of the house.

After reviewing the intelligence and making final assignments, Sambor summed up: "They have four options," he said. "They can surrender, they can self-destruct, they can booby-trap the house and give themselves up, or they can use the children as hostages." The cops would have to be prepared for all four, he said.

Sambor issued orders for the evacuation of the neighbors on the following day. "They'll be back in their house the next day by 10:00 P.M.," he predicted. Operation MOVE had begun.

Early that afternoon Richmond held his own meeting at the Fire Administration Building. He made his own views very clear: "I do not want a repeat of 1978," he told his command personnel. "The safety of fire fighters is to be preeminent. Our role is to *support* the police department. No fire fighters on the front lines." He designated Deputy Chief Walter Miller as the on-scene commander and assigned two squirts, two pumpers, three rescue units, and a ladder company to provide ladders for police. All units were to assemble at 3:30 A.M. on May 13.

After the meeting, the president of the fire fighter's union stopped by the fire commissioner's office. The two men reviewed the plans, and Richmond reiterated his instructions from the meeting: no fire fighters would be placed in the line of fire. To make sure that order was followed, Richmond promised that he would be with his men. "My only job out there," he said, "is to make sure the fire fighters are safe."

When they reported for work on the evening of May 11, stakeout officer Jimmy Berghaier and his partner, Tommy Mellor, received orders to report to sign out Uzis and report to Sixty-second and Pine streets, just around the corner from the MOVE house.

Berghaier and Mellor had been through some rough scenes together. For years they'd worked on the "Granny Squad," an undercover operation aimed at robbers who preyed on old folks and others who were helpless. One of them would play decoy, disguised as an old lady or a drunk, while the other waited in ambush.

It was a job filled with danger, where you had to follow your gut and make split-second decisions. If your timing or instincts were off, you could die. Once, for example, Berghaier had been assigned a new partner as part of a change in department policy. They were working the subways, where there had been a rash of robberies, and Berghaier was disguised as an old man.

Somehow they'd gotten their signals crossed when the train pulled in. Berghaier stepped into a car filled with young toughs. His partner was supposed to get into the adjoining car, wait for the holdup to go down, and come in to make the arrest. But as the train pulled away, Berghaier saw his new partner standing on the platform. Alone inside the car, Berghaier couldn't defend himself, and he didn't dare let them know he was a cop. He was lucky; he wasn't robbed. But official policy or no, he never worked with his new partner again.

Not that things always worked perfectly even when you were

with your regular partner. Every situation they walked into was unpredictable. Sometimes the bust would go smoothly, but every now and then it turned violent. Berghaier had had his share of stitches and bruises and close calls.

People had a hard time understanding why he did it. His father, for example, had been upset when he'd told him he was going to be a cop. Jim was a disciplined student and did well in college, but he felt out of place on a college campus in the late sixties. Perhaps because his brother was fighting in Vietnam, he had a hard time identifying with the radical slogans and antiwar fever. On a whim he'd applied to the police academy and was quickly accepted.

He'd been with the force for nearly eighteen years, starting as a district cop and soon joining the K-9 squad and then stakeout. Other cops said he was one of the best—athletic, quick on his feet, and cool under pressure. Like Tursi, he was considered a thinker.

And he had not succumbed to that cynicism that so often plagues cops who've spent years dealing with the dregs of humanity: he still believed that what he did made the world a better place. He loved being a cop, and he loved working stakeout. It was the good guys against the bad guys, with nothing but your partner and your own instincts to rely on.

Berghaier and Mellor, as well as their partners, Jesse Freer and Danny Pharo, met their boss, stakeout lieutenant Dominick Marandola, on a narrow street near the dark mouth of an alley. The stakeout cops' instincts were already telling them something was wrong.

"The back of the MOVE house is down this alley on the left," Marandola told them. "You're going to escort a sound technician into the house next door." Inside the house at 6219 Osage Avenue, he explained, another team had already begun to drill a small hole into the common wall, using a special silenced drill. The sound technician would insert a spike mike into the hole.

Mellor and Berghaier exchanged glances. After so many years together, each could tell what the other was thinking without saying a word. And they were both thinking the same thing: this was trouble coming their way.

When the sound technician arrived, the four of them moved quietly into the alley. Marandola stayed behind.

They had gone only a few steps when Marandola signaled them to wait. The team in 6219 was coming out, he said; they'd heard people moving around on the second floor and believed that MOVE members had broken through the walls upstairs.

"Wait here," Marandola told them, disappearing to consult with someone. When he came back, he told the team waiting by the entrance to the alley, "It's still a go."

Berghaier and Mellor looked at one another again. Terrified, the four men began to make their way down the pitch-black alley. This operation didn't make any sense—and that meant it was dangerous.

Halfway into the alley, Berghaier heard quick footsteps coming up behind him. He turned—it was Marandola again. "Come on back," Marandola said. A kid on a bicycle had just dropped off a note. It was from MOVE; they knew what was going on in 6219. If the cops didn't leave the house immediately, they'd be killed, the note said.

Later that night Sergeant Connor was awakened at home by a phone call. The voice was familiar, but he couldn't quite place it. "There's a change in plans," the voice said. "Nineteen's been compromised. Go into 6217 instead."

Connor jotted down the message and turned off the light. Then he stared at the darkened ceiling of his bedroom until Mother's Day dawned.

SUNDAY, MAY 12

Early on the morning of May 12 police began knocking on the doors of the houses along Osage Avenue, Pine Street to the north, and Addison Street to the south. The mayor had ordered the houses evacuated, the police told the residents.

Most of the neighbors went willingly, taking along no more than a change of clothes. The police had told them they'd be able to return by Monday evening at the latest. The ones who didn't want to go were informed that the mayor's order authorized the arrest and removal of anyone who refused to comply.

All day MOVE members were seen doing last-minute work on the house and the front bunker. Negotiators—some sent by the city, others apparently freelance—came and went up the street. Channel 10 cameraman Pete Kane settled into a second-floor bedroom in a house on Sixty-second Street. He knew the family, and they'd permitted him to stay, hidden from the cops, when they evacuated. From his vantage point he could see west down Osage Avenue to the MOVE house and beyond.

During the night Pete Kane intermittently taped the preparations taking place on the street below. The cops worked methodically. An unarmored tow truck drove down the street and began towing away the cars. Fire engines and pumpers arrived and moved into position. Fire fighters set up ladders to the rooftops. Utility workers shut off the gas and electricity to the block.

The empty block fell silent except for the sound of the fire engine diesels. A kid on a skateboard appeared from somewhere and started to go down the street. A cop stepped out to the street and turned him back.

From the MOVE house a final tirade began over the loudspeakers. It would go on for hours into the night.

Leo Brooks was approaching the Harbor Tunnel in Baltimore when he heard a report on his car's radio that Philadelphia police were evacuating the residents on Osage Avenue. In the two-hour drive back to Philadelphia, he listened for more news but found out little. He was surprised; when he'd left just a few days before he hadn't thought that the mayor would want to move this quickly.

He drove straight to his City Hall office and called Sambor. Sambor had just finished briefing him when the phone rang. It was the mayor. Sambor had briefed him too, and the two men compared notes.

Goode was debating whether to be at the scene the following morning, but Brooks was emphatic. MOVE had threatened Goode's life, and he would make too tempting a target for them. "I strongly advise you to stay at City Hall, Mr. Mayor,"

Brooks said. "I'll be at the scene along with Sambor. You don't need to be there."

Jim Berghaier and other cops who'd been assigned to the insertion teams spent most of Mother's Day at the pistol range at the police academy, practicing their shooting. The same day the members of the insertion teams that would handle the explosives began getting their gear together. They constructed hatch charges that would be used for emergency escapes. In addition to the jet-tappers that would be used to breach the walls, each demolitions man decided what to bring according to his own experience: their supplies included deta sheet, det cord, blasting caps and boosters, and fuses. Not knowing what to expect, they also took a healthy supply of the C-4 that Mike Macy had brought them the Christmas before.

After he finished target practice, Berghaier went home, but his wife and kids had left to visit the grandparents. He took a brief nap. It wasn't turning out to be much of a Mother's Day. The following day, his son's birthday, didn't look too promising either.

After dinner the phone rang. It was his sister.

"Call Dad," she said. "He's worried about you." Berghaier called his parents' house and spoke to them for a few minutes, reassuring them that he'd be safe.

Berghaier stopped at his brother-in-law's house at around eight o'clock. They drank coffee and spoke aimlessly for a while. Then Berghaier said, "Listen, Cary, if anything should happen—take care of my family. Nothing's going to happen—but just in case." Berghaier meant it when he said nothing would happen; he always believed that as long as he stayed in control of a situation, he'd be okay.

Stopping back home again, Berghaier changed into the blue fatigues and baseball cap that were the uniform of the stakeout unit. He packed a jar of Vaseline jelly to protect his skin from the caustic effects of the tear gas. He also packed an extra jar he'd picked up in case someone on the team forgot to bring his own.

Driving down the highway to the academy, dressed in combat gear and carrying his shotgun on the seat, he couldn't shake a feeling of unreality. In a few hours he'd be making an armed assault on a house full of armed revolutionaries. This is some Third World country you see on TV, he thought to himself. This isn't America.

At 11:00 P.M., Powell, Connor, and Tursi briefed the two insertion teams at the pistol range at the police academy. They explained the plan in detail. Connor showed them homemade "flashbangs" and "stun grenades"—small nonlethal explosives designed to disorient an opponent. Most officers carried Uzi submachine guns or M-16 automatic rifles, as well as service revolvers, .357 Magnums, and shotguns.

After all the questions were answered, they climbed into the back of a police truck and set off across town for the Philadelphia Geriatric Center at Sixty-second and Walnut streets—four blocks north of Osage Avenue. From there they would receive their final briefing, move into position, and wait for dawn.

9

The Morning of May 13

ALL NIGHT, SINCE THE first word of the evacuation had gone out, the watchers had been gathering: reporters, photographers, television correspondents and cameramen, neighbors and relatives, would-be mediators, community activists, and rubberneckers. They pressed against the police barricades, hundreds of them, badgering the cops for news, any news, about what was happening on Osage Avenue.

From the darkness beyond the barricades came the sounds of activity—men moving about, trucks arriving, equipment being moved into place. As it had throughout the night, the sounds of MOVE members on the bullhorn and their monotonous litany of four-letter words droned in the background. At the barricades the onlookers peered into the gloom, waiting for dawn.

By dawn it was no longer a neighborhood.

On both sides of Osage Avenue, along Pine and Addison, up and down Sixty-second Street and Cobbs Creek Parkway, the houses stood silent.

On the corner of Sixty-second and Osage the heavy diesel engines of the fire trucks throbbed, pressurizing the water for the squirts.

In the alleyway entrances at each end of the block the insertion teams shouldered their gear and shifted uneasily.

In the five police posts surrounding the house, stakeout officers checked their weapons.

On the rooftops police spotters peered over sandbags, watching the gun ports on the MOVE bunkers.

Crouching behind his sandbags, on the sun porch of a house across the street from MOVE, at least one stakeout officer figured this was going to be 1978 all over again. When this day was over, cops would surely be dead—and as far as he was concerned, it would be the fault of the Philadelphia Police Department brass.

His mind wandered back to the early morning hours, when he and the other cops in his post had moved through the narrow walkway behind the houses. It had been barely three feet wide; even walking single file it had been a tight squeeze between the high wooden fences on either side.

That was one of only two ways out of the house he was in. The other was through the front door—out into Osage Avenue and MOVE's direct line of fire.

What would happen, he asked himself, if someone in this house took a bullet? There were no paramedics or first-aid supplies in the house—not even a stretcher. He couldn't shake the image of a screaming, bleeding cop being carried out the back door and down that long walkway, loaded like firewood on the shoulders of his buddies.

That wasn't all. Captain Kirchner told the men that there'd be sandbags. There were sandbags, all right; when he stood up they came just about to his knees. If he crouched down, he could protect himself up to his waist. As for the rest, he was exposed—and if those bastards in the front bunker could see him as well as he could see the bunker, he was going to be a perfect target.

At the west end of the alley behind Osage Avenue Bill Klein of insertion team A was thinking about real estate.

Not that he wanted to; he just couldn't get it out of his head. He'd been selling real estate on the side for some time, and he'd decided to go for his broker's license. The state exam was just five days away, and Klein had begun hitting the books pretty hard.

Now, despite the armed militants he was about to face, despite the machine guns poking from the stakeout posts, despite even the bag full of explosives that hung from his waist, he was looking at the houses on Osage Avenue with the eyes of a real estate agent.

You'd sell this kind of house as a "starter home"—show it to a young couple, probably black, no kids, a couple of civil service jobs between them. You'd call the house "solid"—with the kind of construction and attention to detail you don't see in your newer homes. The sun porch would be a big selling point—especially the fanlight glazing across the top—and it might distract them from the tiny kitchen and dining nook that were crowded side by side in the back of the house.

Upstairs you'd have a master bedroom in the front and two small bedrooms in the back. In between, in the center of the house, would be a bathroom. Closet space would be a problem.

At 6:00 A.M., the sun rose red on this warm and humid day.

In the minutes after dawn there was still no sound except the pulsing of the fire department diesels. And then, precisely at six o'clock, came a harsh, metallic call:

"Attention, MOVE! This is America! You have to abide by the laws of the United States!"

Crouching behind the sandbags on the still-dark sun porch of 6218 Osage Avenue, Commissioner Sambor read the words off a yellow tablet without a hint of irony. It sounded as though he'd had trouble getting the wording right, had worked over his opening like an amateur toastmaster preparing for a retirement party. The phrases did not flow; they lurched along in staccato bursts of police report prose:

"This is the police commissioner. We have warrants for the arrest of Frank James Africa, Ramona Johnson Africa, Theresa Brooks Africa, and Conrad Hampton Africa for various violations of the criminal statutes of Pennsylvania.

"We do not wish to harm anyone. All occupants have fifteen minutes to peaceably evacuate the premises and surrender. This is your only notice.

"The fifteen minutes start now."

From his vantage point in Post 2, Officer Ed Furlong watched through binoculars as two black men in dreadlocks scurried across the roof of 6221 and disappeared into the front bunker. They walked bent over, as if they were carrying something heavy in each hand.

Sambor had barely finished reading his statement when he was answered by the amplified voices of MOVE: "Come and get us, motherfuckers. But you better be sure your insurance is paid up! You be sure you call your wives and families, 'cause you ain't coming home! You come in this house, 'cause we got something for you!"

Another voice broke in: "You're going to be laying in the street! Come on in and get us! We'll kill you where you stay; we'll kill you where you lay! We see you on the roof. We know you're in those houses.

"You remember 1978? You ain't leaving this street alive. You gonna die out here!"

The harangue went on and on. And then, as suddenly as it had begun, it ended. Again the street was silent except for the throbbing bass of the diesels.

Sometime in the night thirteen-year-old Birdie Africa had been roused from a troubled sleep by the sound of amplified voices. He heard glass breaking and Ramona's voice over the loudspeaker: "Did you all hear that? We're putting gas in all these houses. If one house get it, all of these houses are going to get it." Eventually he'd fallen back into a doze to the sound of the other adults putting out information over the loud-speaker.

Now, at dawn, he heard Sambor's voice as the adults came to him. They gathered up Birdie and the other children from the second-floor hallway where they'd been sleeping and led them down into the cellar.

At the back of the cellar was what had originally been the house's garage. Now it had been sealed off from the alley by cinder blocks, with a single fortified hatch that was just big enough for one person to climb through. At the other end of the garage was a door leading into the rest of the basement.

The women led the children through that door and into the sealed garage. Inside it was pitch black and musty. The women and children lay down on the cool cement floor and pulled wet blankets over themselves to protect them from tear gas.

By an odd coincidence, the house at 6217 Osage Avenue belonged to a detective on the police force, and he'd given Connor a front door key earlier that morning. He'd been worried about the damage that might be done to his house, and Connor had reassured him that they'd keep it to a minimum. In fact, he'd promised to take all the pictures off the wall so they wouldn't fall and break. At least the key would help them get into the house quickly, Connor thought as he and his team waited for the signal to begin.

At 6:15 the first smoke grenades were fired. Within seconds dense white smoke filled the street and alley and thousands of gallons of water flooded across the rooftops. One stream arced south from the squirt on Pine Street, pounding against the rear bunker. The second, coming from Sixty-second Street, fell short of the bunkers by a hundred feet. Most of it rained down into the eastern alley and landed on the heads of Ed Connor and the men in insertion team B.

Soaking wet, weighted down with Uzis, explosives, and the pepper fogger, Connor's team started down Osage Avenue. In the gloom and smoke they could barely make out the steps jutting from the doorways onto the sidewalk. They stumbled past, keeping count so they would know when they reached 6217. They were halfway there when the first shot rang out.

Connor and Officer Salvatore Marsalo raced through the smoke to the stoop of 6217. As Marsalo provided cover, Connor used the key provided by the owner to unlock the door. The rest of Team B—Officers James Muldowney, Daniel Angelucci, Salvatore Marsalo, Jesse Freer, Alexander Draft, and Michael Ryan—crowded through the narrow doorway as Connor peered into the smoke, looking for the source of the gunfire. And then they were all inside and Connor was on the radio with Marandola.

"Team B to Post 1—we're inside 17."

Frank Powell and the other six men of insertion team A were moving east in the alley behind Osage Avenue. As they stepped into the mouth of the alley, it was as if they had left behind the spring morning in Philadelphia and arrived in an alien world. The houses to their left were dim in the haze and the darkness. Ahead was a sheet of roaring water from the squirts, looking as if someone had taken the alley and put it at the base of Niagara Falls.

And behind that wall of water were people who were shooting at cops. Maybe them.

In line behind Powell, Jim Berghaier could just make out the fence behind 6221. MOVE had built the fence—six feet high and solid inch-thick planks—across the width of the alley when the organization had moved in. Now, with their threats still ringing in his ears and the gunshots coming from the MOVE house, Berghaier realized that anyone on the other side of the fence had a clear shot at them—and could take Team A down like bowling pins.

"Tear gas!"

Mellor, just ahead of Berghaier, pressed his large frame against the brick rear of one of the row houses. He too had seen the fence—and like Berghaier, he realized he was at the mercy of anyone on the other side. Now, exposed and vulnerable, he had to stop, shoulder his rifle, and adjust his mask. Despite the petroleum jelly, the gas burned his hands and neck.

There wasn't supposed to be any tear gas, he thought. According to the plan, there'd be smoke but no tear gas.

Nobody was behind the fence. Team A reached the back door of 6223 Osage without incident, forced it open, and entered the basement laundry room. By now the gunfire was intense.

If anyone had still hoped that the squirts could knock the bunkers off the roof, they knew better by now. Firemen and policemen had brought the second squirt around to Pine Street. Side by side like a pair of long-necked cranes, the two of them pummeled the rooftop of 6221, blasting down tarps and pallets, sweeping loose lumber and debris onto Osage Avenue, the roar of their compressors combining with the

sound of rushing water to make a steady white noise that
carried to the streets beyond. In the last fifteen minutes they
had thrown thousands of gallons of high-pressure water
against the bunkers. The bunkers hadn't budged an inch.

In the relative safety of 6217 Osage, Ed Connor was keeping
a promise he'd made to the man who owned the house. One by
one he took the pictures off the living room wall and laid them
carefully on the floor. Muldowney and Angelucci were in the
tiny dining room preparing a charge to breach the plywood
partition that separated the sun porches of 6217 and 6219.

They worked deliberately. There was no rush. On a piece of
cardboard about three feet square they laid down a rectangular
loop of a substance that looked like a bead of caulk. It was det
cord, a high explosive contained in a plastic sheath. They
looped the det cord around twice more and attached a fuse.

Connor, done with his housekeeping, raised Post 1 on the
radio and told Marandola they were ready to proceed. Then he
carried the charge into the sun porch, taped it against the
partition, and set the fuse. He and his men crouched behind
the sofa and waited.

By now, throughout the rest of the city, another workweek
was beginning. The weather report called for sunny skies, with
highs near ninety.

The first explosion of the day came at 6:18. It rained down
plaster on the heads of Connor's men and blew the glass out of
the windows in 6217 Osage. As the plaster dust began to settle,
Connor crept onto the porch and peered through the hole into
6219.

Inside the dust filled the air so densely that he could hardly
see across the sixteen-foot-wide house. At this hour the weak
morning light barely penetrated the drapes across the sun
porch windows. On the other side of the porch the partition
adjoining the MOVE house had a hole in it that matched the
one his men had just blown. Connor figured the force of the
explosion must have blown the first partition across the porch
and into the other side.

He peered into the dark interior of 6219. It seemed to be empty. Carefully he began to climb through the hole. It did not occur to him until much later that the drapes to the sun porch had been open the night before.

The mayor stepped out from his kitchen. From his back porch he could hear gunfire and the sound of explosions. He would later say that "it sounded like a war zone out there."

In the basement of 6223 Frank Powell's team could hear the water pounding against the roof, pouring through the second-floor skylight, and raining onto the bathroom floor. They had secured the house—checked it from top to bottom—and regrouped. Klein prepared the downstairs charge.

Klein had already placed a large charge on the living room wall on the side opposite the MOVE house. If need be, they could detonate the charge and escape into 6225. Now he placed the jet-tapper high on the basement wall, just below the steps. The idea—the only part of the plan that came from the FBI agents—was to put the charge in an area where it wouldn't be likely to harm anyone on the other side.

When it was done, they waited. The plan called for them to wait until Team B had successfully breached the eastern wall of the MOVE house.

On the other side of the MOVE house Connor was stepping through the hole when MOVE opened up on him.

Later Muldowney would estimate that the gunfire came from at least three locations—from the sun porch of the MOVE house, along the baseboard where it joined 6219, and from the top of the stairs in 6219. To him it looked and sounded like buckshot and .22-caliber rifle fire.

Pinned down by the gunfire, the men saw Connor turn and dive back through the opening. The partition splintered around him as bullets ripped into it.

"I'm hit!" Connor cried as he slammed to the floor. "I can't move!"

Freer sprayed machine gun fire toward the MOVE house and dragged Connor into the living room of 6217.

"I can't move my legs!" Connor shouted. Freer looked at
Connor's back. A single bullet hole had pierced the jumpsuit,
right over his spine.

As the pain subsided, Connor found that he could indeed
move his legs. His spine—and, most likely, his life—had been
saved by his protective vest. Later that day the forensics guys
would dig a flattened .38-caliber slug out of the vest. Connor
escaped with a bruise the size of a half-dollar.

Some minutes later, after Connor was feeling better, the
assault on 6219 began again. Team B threw more flashbangs
into the hole, but the firing went on. Connor took aim with his
Uzi at the porch bunker, where the heaviest firing seemed to
be coming from, and opened fire. The other men in the team
also returned fire, taking turns to conserve their ammunition.
A woman's scream came from inside the bunker, but the firing
went on.

Connor fired at the bunker again. The screaming stopped.
But the gunfire continued.

"Get the C-4," Connor said.

The team had regrouped in the living room of 6217. The
firing from the MOVE house had stopped, but they knew it
would begin again the minute they showed themselves. Connor was ready to go to heavier ordnance.

He told Angelucci and Muldowney to rig a block of C-4—a
1¼-pound brick about the size of a quart of milk—with a six-
second fuse. They looked at one another: a pound and a
quarter was a lot of plastic. Properly placed, it was enough to
drop the whole house and bury them.

Connor didn't call Marandola. "I'll take responsibility," he
told the team. Still Angelucci and Muldowney hesitated. "I
said I'll take responsibility," he repeated.

When they were finished, Muldowney handed the charge to
Connor. "You throw it," Connor said.

"You wanted it—you throw it," Muldowney answered.

"I'm ordering you to throw it," Connor said. "I told you I'll
take responsibility."

Minutes later, despite his better judgment, Muldowney
found himself lying in the living room, his head pointed

toward the sun porch. Angelucci crouched over him, his gun aimed at the partition. As the others slid Muldowney onto the floor of the porch, Angelucci pumped cover fire into the hole.

With a sidearm toss Muldowney lobbed his homemade bomb through the hole, across the porch of 6219, and against the front-porch bunker of the MOVE house. He and Angelucci were barely inside the living room again when the blast came.

The explosion reduced the sun porch of 6219 to kindling and destroyed the thin partition between it and the porch of the MOVE house. Through the debris, one could make out half-exposed heavy structures inside the MOVE porch. They seemed unaffected by the explosives.

The firing stopped briefly after the explosion; then it began again. Connor took Muldowney and Angelucci aside. "Give me another one—a bit heavier."

Muldowney looked skeptically at Angelucci.

Despite Connor's instructions, Muldowney and Angelucci figured a pound and a quarter of C-4 was enough. When they'd finished with the charge, it was exactly the same as the first—one block of C-4. Again Muldowney held it out to the sergeant. Connor shook his head. "You throw it," he said.

This time it worked. It worked so well, in fact, that it threw half of the MOVE porch into the middle of the street.

Looking through the hole, Angelucci was shocked. He could see, in what was left of the MOVE porch, something that ·looked like a log cabin. MOVE had used heavy tree trunks to build a bunker inside the porch. There were ports cut out at the top and bottom, with long, narrow crawl spaces behind them. They were designed so a person could lie protected in the spaces and shoot through the ports.

As Angelucci looked, Freer edged up beside him.

"Look," Angelucci said to him, pointing to the upper crawl space. "Do you see it?"

Freer's eyes peered through the dust and debris, trying to make out details in the darkened space. "What?"

"Do you see something up there?" Angelucci pointed again.

"I can't tell," Freer said. "A jacket, maybe."

Angelucci didn't think it was a jacket. He was almost certain

*Vincent Leaphart, 1970—the handyman who founded the MOVE
organization.* (Photo: *Philadelphia Bulletin/*Temple University
Photojournalism Collection)

Early MOVE members, left to right: Ted Williams Africa later died in a psychiatric hospital. Conrad Hampton Africa died in the 1985 confrontation. Jerry Ford Africa is still a MOVE member. LaVerne Sims, Vincent's sister, left the organization in the early 1980s. Donald Glassey made a deal with federal agents and testified against Vincent during the 1981 trial; his whereabouts are unknown. (Photo: *Philadelphia Bulletin*/Temple University Photojournalism Collection)

Outside the Powelton Village headquarters in the early 1970s. (Photo: *Philadelphia Bulletin*/Temple University Photojournalism Collection)

Masters of publicity, MOVE members protest alleged police brutality outside the Powelton Village headquarters in March 1976. (Photo: *Philadelphia Bulletin*/Temple University Photojournalism Collection)

Frank L. Rizzo, mayor of Philadelphia from 1971 to 1979. (Photo: *Philadelphia Daily News*)

The "Guns on the Porch" day, May 20, 1977—the beginning of a fourteen-month standoff between MOVE and Philadelphia police. (Photo: *Philadelphia Bulletin/*Temple University Photojournalism Collection)

MOVE members preach to the crowds during the 1977–78 confrontation. (Photo: *Philadelphia Bulletin/*Temple University Photojournalism Collection)

Frank James Africa, Vincent Leaphart's nephew, reads accounts of Rizzo's ultimatum to MOVE, March 1978. (Photo: *Philadelphia Bulletin/* Temple University Photojournalism Collection)

A woman breaks through Rizzo's five-month blockade of the MOVE house to deliver food to the group. (Photo: Associated Press)

MOVE members during the blockade, including Alberta Wicker Africa (center, with hand on hip), Vincent's wife. (Photo: *Philadelphia Bulletin/* Temple University Photojournalism Collection)

Gunfire erupts in the early morning of August 8, 1978. (Photo: *Philadelphia Bulletin/*Temple University Photojournalism Collection)

Police officer James Hesson, wounded in the chest during the 1978 gunfire exchange, is carried to safety by other policemen. (Photo: *Philadelphia Bulletin/*Temple University Photojournalism Collection)

After half an hour of shooting, the firing stopped and a child emerged from the basement. The other MOVE members in the house followed. (Photo: *Philadelphia Bulletin/*Temple University Photojournalism Collection)

Police officer James Ramp, killed in the 1978 confrontation. (Photo: Philadelphia Daily News)

Philadelphia police officers savagely beat and kicked Delbert Africa after he emerged unarmed from the MOVE house. Three of them were later tried—and acquitted by a judge who refused to let a jury decide the case.

John Africa after his acquittal in 1981. (Photo: *Philadelphia Bulletin*/Temple University Photojournalism Collection)

Birdie Africa and Conrad Africa on the rooftop, just before the 1985 confrontation. (Photo: Philadelphia Daily News)

Louise James, Vincent Leaphart's sister and owner of the house on 6221 Osage Avenue. (Photo: Philadelphia Bulletin/Temple University Photojournalism Collection)

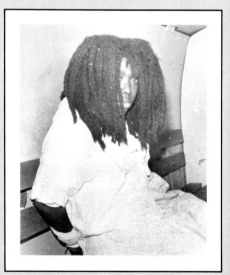

Clifford Bond and his daughter in a church shelter the day after their home was destroyed by the fire. (Photo: Wide World)

Ramona Africa, the only adult survivor of the fire, sits in a police wagon after surrendering to police. (Photo: Wide World)

Despite the publication of this photo in the days before the confrontation, Police Commissioner Sambor insisted that he had no knowledge that MOVE had gasoline on the roof before the bomb was dropped. (Photo: Wide World)

A water cannon operated by Philadelphia police fails to dislodge the rooftop bunker on the morning of May 13. (Photo: Wide World)

Police Lieutenant Frank Powell drops the explosive "satchel charge" on the roof of the MOVE house. (Photo: Wide World)

Officer James Berghaier on the day of the MOVE confrontation, May 13, 1985.

In the early evening of May 13, police and firemen watch as smoke billows from the MOVE house. (Photo: Wide World)

A police officer watches from a nearby rooftop as fire spreads uncontrolled through the MOVE compound and adjoining houses. (Photo: Wide World)

Osage Avenue after the fire. (Photo: *Philadelphia Daily News*)

The morning after. (Photo: *Philadelphia Daily News*)

The "Big Four." From left, Mayor Wilson Goode, Managing Director Leo Brooks, Fire Commissioner William Richmond, and Police Commissioner Gregore Sambor. (Photo: Philadelphia Daily News)

The rebuilt houses on Osage Avenue.

Delbert Orr Africa, in prison for the murder of Officer James Ramp. (Photo: *Philadelphia Bulletin*/Temple University Photojournalism Collection)

Sue Levino, in prison for the murder of Officer James Ramp. Her son, Tomaso, died in the fire on May 13. (Photo: *Philadelphia Bulletin*/Temple University Photojournalism Collection)

Rhonda Ward Africa, Birdie's mother; died in the fire on May 13. (Photo: *Philadelphia Bulletin*/Temple University Photojournalism Collection)

Raymond Foster Africa, died in the fire on May 13. (Photo: *Philadelphia Bulletin*, Temple University Photojournalism Collection)

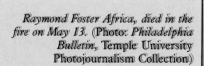

that he was looking at a body—with its decapitated head resting between the knees.

But even this blast didn't stop the shooting for long. Apparently the MOVE people had access to the second floor of 6219; the path of the bullets suggested that they were firing into 6217 from the top of the stairs. Other bullets seemed to be coming from the baseboard level, as if MOVE had cut ports between its basement and the first floor of 6219.

Connor radioed Marandola and told him they were stalemated. Marandola, in turn, raised Powell and told him they'd have to proceed without Team B.

In the basement of 6223, Klein set the fuse and took cover on the far side of the tiny cellar. The others had already gone upstairs.

The blast barely penetrated the thick stone foundation. Nearly all of the force was instead blown back into the basement, knocking down the steps. It also dislodged hundreds of cockroaches that had migrated into the joists and woodwork from the MOVE house. They rained down on Klein like a biblical plague and quickly scampered away.

After Klein propped up what was left of the steps and made his way upstairs, the team regrouped.

The charge hadn't gone through. If he put another charge down there, it would blow the joists loose.

Powell decided to try the next charge upstairs. He told Mulvihill and D'Ulisse to stay on the first floor.

In the second-floor hallway, at the top of the stairs, Klein placed his second jet-tapper while the others took cover in the front bedroom. When the blast came, it threw him through the bedroom doorway.

Klein slowly got up and dusted himself off. He seemed disoriented. The jet-tapper had once again failed to breach the walls. Though they'd tested them earlier against a cinder block wall, the solid brick walls of the row house had proved to be much stronger. Finally Powell suggested that they simply put another jet-tapper in the crater that the first had created. The second blast, he figured, should breach the wall.

Klein and the others went back to the front bedroom to get the third and final jet-tapper. As Klein bent down to prepare the fuse, the room erupted in gunfire.

The firing was coming into the bedroom—*through* the wall adjoining the MOVE house. The officers dove to the floor as chunks of brick and plaster flew across the room.

Klein felt a pain in his knee as if it had exploded; he'd been hit by a bullet or a piece of the wall. A splinter of oak flooring had ripped into his hand. Powell fired a burst toward the wall and the shooting stopped.

Instinctively they all crawled toward the closet. It was maybe four feet square. Guns and all, they scrambled in, unable to close the door. Powell had dragged Klein toward the closet, but he couldn't fit inside. He sat outside, bleeding from his knee and his hand.

"I'm going to die," he said out loud. "I'm going to die before I get my broker's license." Klein could still hear blasts of gunfire from the first floor and Powell frantically calling for help on the radio, but suddenly everything seemed hushed. Expectant, almost. Right near his ear he could hear rapid, shallow breathing—his own? No, it was Officer James Laarkamp.

Klein imagined dark eyes peering through a peephole in the common wall. MOVE was waiting for them. The MOVE people would hold their fire, wait for them all to come out of the closet, and then cut them to pieces. Everyone in this closet was a dead man.

And the only thing he could think of was that he'd never get his broker's license.

On a rooftop diagonally across from the bunkers two cops lay on their bellies, trapped by an avalanche of gunfire. When the shooting started, they'd tried to evacuate the roof but couldn't move from behind the low brick parapet in front of them. They'd set off smoke grenades, but it seemed someone had taken a good bead on them, for the bullets still zinged inches above their heads. Finally the firing eased off, and the two escaped down ladders held in position by fire fighters.

In Post 4, on Pine Street behind the bunkers, Sergeant Don

Griffiths crouched in a bedroom window and watched bullets
rip into the sandbags and splinter the wooden frame. In Post 1
a sharpshooter heard a bullet zing past his shoulder and strike
a sandbag. Bullets ricocheted up and down and across Osage
Avenue and beyond. One hit a car parked half a block away on
Cobbs Creek Parkway.

Officer John LaCon, stationed on the front porch in Post 2,
stopped firing for a moment and bent down to examine his
rifle. As he did, a bullet passed through the screen door and
the space where his head had been only seconds before. It split
his riot helmet in two like an oyster, seared across the skin of
his neck, and buried itself in the woodwork of the porch
behind him.

How much time had they spent in the closet? Klein wondered. Maybe minutes; maybe hours.

He studied the bullet holes in the common wall. They were
arranged in a circle, slanting away from the center as if someone had stood on the other side and swung a machine gun
around in an arc.

What was happening on the other side of that wall? Was
anyone there?

Powell spoke. "Laarkamp's hyperventilating. We've got to
get him out of here." Klein looked back over his shoulder and
saw that Laarkamp was looking bad. Beneath his gas mask his
eyes were glazed and his face was white. His breath came raspy
and quick through the mask.

Berghaier spoke up. "I'll go." Before anyone could answer,
he was taking Laarkamp—who outweighed him by close to a
hundred pounds—out of the closet. Laarkamp was too heavy
to carry, so Berghaier led him down the steps. His voice
muffled by the gas mask, he shouted encouragement: "Keep
going! We'll make it!"

No shots came through the wall as Berghaier disappeared
out the doorway. The only sound was that of his combat boots
pounding on the hallway floorboards and down the stairs.

Downstairs Mulvihill and D'Ulisse were crouching behind a
radiator. They'd heard the gunfire and the muffled yelling
from the upstairs bedroom—and then, seconds later, the living

room had been filled with flying bullets and they had scrambled for cover. As Berghaier came down the stairs he saw that the wall behind D'Ulisse and Mulvihill had been destroyed by gunfire. He helped Laarkamp down the broken cellar steps and to the back door. Running at a trot, staying close to the houses, they made their way down the alley toward Cobbs Creek Parkway and the waiting ambulance.

Ed Connor stood in the bathroom of 6217, poking a long, slender object through the skylight above. It was a military periscope, and Connor was looking through it to see if there was any way they could mount an assault across the rooftops.

Through the periscope the bunker looked almost close enough to touch. It wasn't more than twenty feet away, and Connor could clearly see the heavy planking, the foot-square cutouts framed in rough lumber. It was a crude structure, almost juvenile—it looked almost like a treehouse built by a bunch of neighborhood kids.

But it was more sophisticated than it looked. Although Connor couldn't tell from his vantage point, the inside of the front bunker was lined with heavy steel decking stolen from road-repair sites around the city. Years ago people had said that Vince Leaphart could build anything out of a pile of sticks. This was undoubtedly his masterpiece.

Ed Connor shook his head and lowered the periscope. There would be no rooftop assault this day.

After some twenty minutes Powell and the others warily came out of the closet. The shooting had stopped.

His hands still shaking, Klein placed the third jet-tapper on the wall in the hallway. This one finally worked, blowing a rough eighteen-inch hole in the wall.

Mellor brought the pepper fogger over and shoved it into the hole. He pulled the cord, and the small gasoline engine roared to life. Then it quit—damaged, perhaps, in the gun battle or by the explosions.

By now they were simply improvising. They lobbed flash-bangs through the hole—to scare off anyone who might be nearby—followed by half a dozen tear gas grenades. Some of the tear gas went into the MOVE house—police in the posts around the house could see it coming out through the slats that covered the windows—but most of it came back into the hallway and filled the second floor of 6223. Giving up in disgust, Powell and the others went back downstairs.

In the relative safety of the kitchen Powell and his men listened as the barrage of gunfire outside went on and on. Klein checked his watch and was surprised to find that it was only nine o'clock in the morning. It felt like dinnertime to him. He hadn't slept a wink in more than twenty-four hours. Since the operation had begun, he'd been gassed, soaked, shot at, rained on by cockroaches, and thrown through the air by the blast of explosives. And still they weren't close to accomplishing their objective.

Powell radioed Marandola. He could barely hear him over the sound of the gunfire and the chopper that was hovering overhead. "What do we do now?" he yelled into the walkie-talkie.

Marandola radioed back. "Is there any way you can get tear gas into the house?" he asked.

Powell thought it over. He had one idea, he told Marandola. Perhaps they could place a shaped charge low on the living room wall. It would be designed to blow downward at an angle, creating an opening into MOVE's basement. Then they could toss tear gas grenades through the hole.

Marandola listened. "Wait a minute." He turned to Captain Kirchner and Commissioner Sambor, just behind him in the living room, and explained Powell's proposition.

"Ask him if it's high or low," Sambor told Marandola.

Marandola relayed the message. "Low," Powell answered.

Later Sambor would say that he had been asking whether the charge would be a high explosive or a low explosive. Powell would say that he had understood the question to be whether the charge would be placed high on the wall or low on the wall. Sambor told him to go ahead.

Some minutes later three more officers arrived at the back of the house with more explosives. Carefully they picked their way through the rubble of the basement and climbed up to the first floor.

Officer Raymond Graham and Klein built the shaped

charge. Using about a third of a pound of C-4, as well as det cord and deta sheet, they created a two-foot-square cardboard-backed charge. For reasons that are not clear, they placed it at about waist level on the wall.

By now Berghaier had returned with a ladder requisitioned from the fire fighters. Team A evacuated down the ladder and through the basement door. Klein set the fuse for five minutes and followed.

Five minutes passed. Second by second they waited—the insertion team in the alley against the back of the house, the brass in Post 1. Powell was just starting to wonder if they had another dud when the house shook and an air conditioner flew over his head.

Graham was the first one back in. He took a few steps into the house and stopped. He could see a two-foot hole in the MOVE house. Looking into the shadowy interior, he couldn't tell whether they'd succeeded in penetrating the basement.

Not that it mattered—the blast had destroyed the interior of 6223. As Klein had feared earlier, this explosion had dislodged the first-floor joists from the foundation. The floor lay in ruins, warped and twisted like a carnival funhouse. "Forget it," he shouted back to the others. "We can't go in there. It's about to collapse." The group retreated to the alley.

In the back Powell was now considering one last assault on the house. Team A kicked down the fence to prevent anyone from firing from behind it—an act that would later save Birdie Africa's life.

With the fence down, the back of the MOVE house was exposed. From here the cops could see the garage door, closed off by cinder blocks, and the small hatch fortified with timbers.

"Here, listen to this." Powell was standing next to a drain-pipe that led into the MOVE garage. Through the pipe he could hear the agitated sound of women's voices. And of crying children.

The cops looked at one another in disbelief. Despite all the planning, no one had ever told Powell or the others that they'd been unable to pick up the children before the siege had begun. None of them had known that the house that they'd assaulted all morning with guns, tear gas, and explosives had been full of children.

Someone suggested dropping tear gas grenades down the pipe.

"Are you crazy?" Powell asked. "You'll turn that thing into a pipe bomb!"

Just then the radio crackled. "Frank, you guys have to get out of there. Somebody's trying to point a rifle at you." Powell looked up and saw a gun barrel sticking out of an upstairs window. Quickly they evacuated down the alley.

It was a little after noon. The day was half over.

10
The Afternoon of May 13

WHAT IS SURPRISING ABOUT the interludes of war is that the birds continue to sing.

Even after the hours of gunfire, after all the explosions, the shouting, the sirens and smoke, the voices of birds were recorded on the police video that was shot behind the houses on the south side of Osage. They had not flown away. They stayed on—guarding their nestlings, perhaps—in the park and in the yards behind the surrounding houses.

Now that the shooting had stopped, the birds rioted, their calls high-pitched and agitated, rolling on and on and filling the trees with sound.

Shortly after Team A left the alley, Sambor summoned Powell for an impromptu meeting at the corner of Sixty-second and Osage.

"Well," he asked, "how many houses are we going to have to buy?" The explosions had destroyed at least three or four, Powell answered—and that didn't include others damaged by gunfire and water.

But Sambor had more on his mind than damaged real estate. All morning the stakeout officers in the surrounding posts had taken fire from the bunkers. Now Sambor wanted to know if Powell had any ideas for getting them off the roof. They'd thought about using a crane or a large drill, Sambor said, but there was no way to get one down the street. How about a rooftop assault?

Powell said he had to talk to Connor. They conferred briefly over the radio about what Connor had seen through the

periscope. Afterward Powell told Sambor that from what Ed
Connor could see through his periscope, going over the roofs
would be suicidal.

"Well," Sambor said, "talk to your people and see if they
can come up with anything."

After he left the commissioner, Powell sent one of his men
back to the police academy for more explosives. He figured
they might be needed.

Virtually all of General Leo Brooks's long and distinguished
army career had been spent in stateside offices, commanding
regiments of file clerks, secretaries, and deskbound procure-
ment officers. In fact, he'd never had a combat assignment
until he'd retired and gone to work for the city of Philadelphia.
Now, in the hot and crowded living room of Post 1, he found
himself on the front lines for the first time in his life.

Sambor had brought him, along with the fire commissioner
and others, into Post 1 so that they could see for themselves
what the police were up against. Peering over the sandbags,
Brooks could make out the debris littering the street in front of
the MOVE house, no more than fifty feet from where he stood.
In the shadows of the porch he could see the fortifications
exposed by Team B's explosions. The bunker on the porch was
built out of solid logs stacked on one another almost to ceiling
height.

They did not know what to do next. The first plan hadn't
worked, and they had no backup plan. Brooks looked at the
bunker again and then at Sambor. Now what? his eyes asked.

The waiting dragged on. In the middle of the afternoon
Ramona Africa, unarmed, stepped through the hole that Klein
had blown in the wall of 6223. Under the wary eyes of the
police sharpshooters, she spent several minutes on the buckled
first floor of the house, calmly surveying the wreckage. Finally
she turned around and disappeared again through the hole.

Berghaier and his friends had gone for lunch. Still wearing
their coveralls and battle gear, carrying their Uzis and gas
masks, their faces smeared with petroleum jelly and streaked
with dirt, they piled into an unmarked van and drove two miles

to City Line Avenue and the shops bordering the wealthy suburban neighborhoods of the Main Line.

On the way out of the area, they stopped at a police barricade where a young cop was making time with a girl. They blew the horn, but the guy wasn't about to be rushed.

Tommy Mellor had had a long day, and he wasn't in a mood to be kept waiting. Stretching his foot over from the passenger's seat, he stomped the gas pedal and the van lurched forward, sending the barricades flying.

"Hey!" the cop shouted after them. "That's my barricade!"

Mellor leaned out the window as the van drove away. "Fuck your barricade!" he shouted.

They found a Wendy's and pulled into the drive-through lane. Patiently they waited their turn behind the noontime shoppers and office workers. The girl at the window stared when they pulled up, but she asked no questions as she gave them their change. They had a good laugh over it on the way back to Osage Avenue.

As they approached the police perimeter, the same young cop was standing there. He'd set the barricade back into position. As the van stopped, he caught Mellor's eye and smiled. "Yeah, I know," he said. "Fuck my barricade." Berghaier gunned the motor, and as the van crashed through the barricade and drove away, they could see him standing in the middle of the street, his head thrown back in laughter.

At the Philadelphia Geriatric Center a makeshift cafeteria had been set up for the cops and fire fighters. Deputy Fire Chief Miller was eating lunch as he watched Sambor sitting with the police brass. He could see that Sambor was angry, though he couldn't make out exactly what he was talking about. Then he saw the police commissioner stand up, displaying something between his thumb and forefinger to the people in the room. It was the slug that had been retrieved from Connor's vest.

Now Miller was really furious. So Sambor was mad because one of his men had taken a hit? What about the fire fighters, who were out there dodging bullets with nothing to protect them but their raincoats?

Later that afternoon the state police helicopter lifted off from the geriatric center parking lot. Aboard were Licenses and Inspections Commissioner James White and Bill Hawthorne, superintendent of a heavy equipment contractor that often did work for the city. White had suggested to Sambor that a crane might be able to remove the rooftop bunkers. Though the idea had been discussed and dismissed days earlier, Sambor seemed not to remember—or at any rate, he never mentioned it to White.

As the copter circled, Hawthorne looked out at the roof of 6221 and made some mental notes. The water from the squirts had scattered debris across the rooftops and pushed much of it onto the streets below. But despite the gunfire and explosions earlier in the day, both the front and rear bunkers appeared to be intact.

Back on the ground White escorted Hawthorne into the rear of a house on Pine Street. Hawthorne looked at the bunkers, not saying much. He went back out into the street and methodically began pacing off various distances. He made some more calculations and turned to White.

"I'd need a 290-, 300-foot boom to do it," he told White.

"Do you have one?" the commissioner asked.

"We've got two. But one's up in Langhorne on a job, and the other's in south Jersey. We'd need at least two or three days to get it here. That's including the labor you'd need to disassemble it and time to get permits. These are big cranes—they need an escort."

They talked some more, but the crane option wasn't promising. Finally Hawthorne had to get back to work. "Let me know if you want it," he said.

He had driven only a few blocks when he heard them calling him on his truck radio. Could he come back again?

When he got back to the geriatric center, White had a few other people with him.

"What about if we came over from Sixty-second Street?"

Again Hawthorne paced off the distances. The reach from Sixty-second was even farther than from Pine Street.

Someone suggested knocking out the front of a house on Pine Street and actually bringing the crane *into* the house to reduce the distance that the crane would have to reach.

Someone else asked Hawthorne if he had a crane available that a police officer could operate.

"I've got a hydraulic crane that's mounted on a truck. I could teach someone the basics in half an hour. But it's only got a hundred-foot boom—you'd have to get within twenty or thirty feet of the house to reach the bunkers." They talked some more, but no one came up with a solution.

Later in the afternoon Hawthorne reviewed the options with Sambor. Sambor agreed that none of them looked feasible. As an afterthought he asked Hawthorne to leave a crane at the site. "We might have some need for it after all this is over," he said.

Someone was shaking Powell awake. "The commissioner wants to see you."

Powell sat up and rubbed his eyes. He'd been dozing in a car for an hour, maybe two. It was nearly 5:00 P.M. "What's going on?"

"I don't know. They said Sambor's looking for you."

A few minutes later Klein and Powell walked into the small office in the geriatric center that was serving as Sambor's headquarters. Whatever was going on, it must be important, Powell thought. Sambor had the fire commissioner and the managing director in the room with him. Brooks was speaking into the phone: "Yes, sir. They're here now. I'll let you know."

It seemed as if they'd walked into a meeting that had been going on for some time. Sambor dispensed with the introductions and got right to the point.

"How much plastic would it take to put a hole in the roof and blow the bunker off?"

Powell huddled with Klein. "I don't know. Two, two-and-a-half pounds."

"Can you use the helicopter to drop a charge onto the roof?"

Powell paused before he answered, looking at Klein. "Yeah, I think so."

Everyone, it seems, had learned from the events of the morning. This time they asked questions.

"What about the people in the house?"

"It would be a minimal charge. It shouldn't be dangerous to anyone inside the house."

"Even if they're on the second floor?"

"Even if they're on the second floor."

Brooks asked Powell for more details. "What exactly will the explosion do?"

Klein explained that it would stand the front bunker up on its end and drop it down on the sidewalk.

"What about the people inside the bunker?"

"Well, if they survive the fall, they won't be able to hear for a week, but they'll probably live. The blast itself won't kill them."

"Are you sure it'll get rid of the bunker?"

"If it doesn't, it will at least disable it," Powell answered.

Sambor asked Powell whether he would deliver the charge personally or appoint someone else to do it.

"I'll do it myself," Powell said.

Fire Commissioner Richmond had only one question. "What are the chances that this thing might cause a fire?"

"Practically none."

When there were no more questions, Brooks called the mayor. "Sambor doesn't have any other way that he can find to get that thing down from there," he explained. "He plans to take a helicopter and drop an explosive device right on the bunker and then go up to it and put water and tear gas in the hole."

In the mayor's office, Wilson Goode said nothing for a long time.

"Commissioner Sambor knows about this?"

"Yes, sir. It was his idea."

"Do you think it will work?"

"Yes, I think it will work."

Goode paused again. "Okay."

Brooks hung up the phone. "He says to do it." According to Klein, Brooks also said, "He wants them out of there before it gets dark"—a claim that Goode and Brooks both deny.

The meeting broke up quickly. On the way out Powell mentioned to Sambor that he'd pass on word of the plan to the cops in the post via Marandola.

"No," Sambor interjected. "Don't tell them." There was no need to get people all worked up and excited, Sambor reasoned; they might do something to screw up the plan. Besides, Powell and Klein had told them that the charge would pose no danger to the people in the house—therefore, it shouldn't hurt anyone in the posts.

What happened next depends on who is telling the story. Powell and Klein tell one version that, if it is true, says a great deal about the commissioner's state of mind and his intentions.

Powell says that after the meeting he approached the police commissioner with the news that they didn't have any C-4 at the site. He suggested that they use Tovex instead.

Sambor waved him off. "I already talked to Billy. Billy Klein knows what I want."

Confused, Powell walked over to where Klein was gathering his gear. "What did he mean, you know what he wants?"

Klein was distressed and perplexed. "He told me not to tell anybody—"

"What the hell are you talking about?"

"He says he wants plenty of frag."

Sambor, says Klein, had taken him aside as they walked toward the helicopter and told him, "Use frag and shrapnel if you have to, to get them motherfuckers out of there."

Frag—white-hot shards of metal that are thrown out of an explosion—was one of the first innovations of modern warfare. Also known as shrapnel, it magnifies the power of an explosion and can cause fires. To a soldier or demolitions expert, frag is understood to be an "antipersonnel" weapon. In plain English its purpose is to kill people.

The word itself is short for "fragmentation device"—a catchall that includes everything from pipe bombs and hand grenades up to large-caliber cannon shells. During the Vietnam War it took on an especially sinister meaning: the murder of unpopular officers by their troops, usually by hand grenade.

Powell asked Klein what the frag would do.

"Nothing to the bunker."

"Don't do it, then." He wasn't concerned so much about the MOVE people, who were protected by the house and the bunker. But he was worried about the guys in the posts. They'd be exposed.

Klein wondered whether he should argue with the police commissioner. "Don't worry about it," Powell said. "What he don't know won't hurt him."

(Sambor says these conversations with Powell and Klein never took place. In fact, he says, he didn't even know Klein— and hadn't even met him until after the charges were constructed. Further, he says, he wouldn't use the word *frag*. He would have used only the term *shrapnel*.)

Marandola's voice came over the radio, ordering all posts to evacuate their positions. "Bring your weapons with you, but leave your gear behind," he told them.

Despite Sambor's orders, Powell had warned Marandola about the plan. The cops in the posts around the house were in too much danger, he'd felt. Anything could happen, Powell figured—depending on where the charge landed, the bunker might get thrown right into Post 2 or Post 1. The charge might miss the roof altogether and land near one of the posts.

Klein met Graham at the explosives truck and explained what he needed. He put Graham to work making the fuses while he assembled the charges in the cab of the truck.

He used two long tubes of Tovex and added a block of C-4 as "detonator" to set it off. He could have used regular blasting caps but figured the C-4 was safer. He added the timer and packed it all into a canvas bag that had held tear gas grenades.

Next he made up another charge. They might need a spare in case Powell missed or the charge didn't work. He had no more long tubes of Tovex, so he used short ones; otherwise this charge was identical to the first. He stuffed it into a white bag and attached the fuse.

He was just finishing as Powell pulled up in his car. On the way to the geriatric center he explained that one of the bags was a backup.

The center was only a few blocks away. They arrived in less than a minute.

In the parking lot everyone's nerves were on edge. Sambor hurriedly introduced Powell to the state police pilot. The pilot looked like he would have preferred to be somewhere else.

Powell put on his headset and a harness attached to the frame of the copter. The pilot was already bringing the engine's speed up as Klein handed the two bags up to Powell.

"Use the gas bag first!" Klein shouted above the noise, pointing to the green tear gas bag. "Use the gas bag first!"

Powell nodded. As the chopper pulled away, Klein could see Powell in the open door, the green bag in his lap and the other one safely tucked between his feet.

The roar inside the helicopter shut out everything except the radio transmissions coming over the headset. The pilot made several quick practice passes over the MOVE house. They were ready to go in when Marandola's voice came over the radio.

"Wait," he said. "There's someone on the roof."

The chopper circled in a high, wide pattern for the next five minutes. Below, police spotters searched for the figure they'd seen. It did not reappear. Finally Marandola radioed Powell and the pilot. "Okay, the roof's clear."

The helicopter roared in from the east and slipped quickly into position. The pilot didn't want to be within the bunker's range any longer than absolutely necessary.

It hovered, its nose slightly down, the rotor clawing at the heavy, humid air. Powell checked his harness. Holding on to the airframe with one hand, he edged himself halfway out the hatch until his foot touched the skid.

Five stories beneath him was the bunker.

From here he could make out the debris that littered the roof, the heavy cross framing on the roof of the front bunker, the flat tar paper roofs of the houses on either side. The helicopter dipped and bobbed as the pilot fought to hold it in position. Powell pulled the fuse igniter; they had forty-five seconds to drop the charge and get out of the way. Still he lingered, waiting for the pilot to bring him into position.

Finally, satisfied, he let go of the bag. It dropped away,

headed exactly where he wanted—just behind the front bunker.

The pilot was watching, too. As soon as he saw the bag fall away, he gunned the engine and sliced away toward the geriatric center. As he did, the rotor threw a powerful blast of air straight down at the roof.

Powell watched in dismay as the downdraft gently picked up the bag and swept it across the roof to the opposite parapet.

11
The Evening of May 13

AS THE BOMB EXPLODED, a shock wave traveling nearly 24,500 miles per hour—approximately 35 times the speed of sound—spread across the roof. In less than one-thousandth of a second it picked up the gasoline can that sat in front of the rear bunker and hurled it against the parapet. It ruptured like an overripe tomato as the heat of the explosion instantly vaporized and ignited the gasoline inside.

The ball of flame did not ignite the rooftop materials or the bunkers; it mushroomed upward into the air. Perhaps a thousandth of a second later, lumber that had been hurled into the air and reduced to kindling by the blast fell back through the burning cloud of gasoline vapor that rose away from the rooftop. The burning wood landed in flames onto the tar-soaked roofing material.

In the area where the can had ruptured—a spot adjacent to the eastern parapet and just behind the front bunker—a small flame slowly began to grow.

About ten minutes after the helicopter landed—about 5:45 P.M.—Powell borrowed a camera and went back up in the helicopter to see what effect the charge had had. As the helicopter circled, he could see what appeared to be a hole in the roof next to the bunker and a small fire.

On the fire escape at the geriatric center Brooks could see the apparent hole and the fire as well. He heard an unidentified voice on the radio. "No fire—no fire," the voice said.

Brooks grabbed a radio from his bodyguard. "Yes, there is a fire," he said.

"What are we going to do about the fire?" Deputy Fire Chief Frank Scipione asked Commissioner Richmond. Richmond had just ordered another fire engine to the scene as backup.

They had walked up to the corner of Sixty-second and Pine to get a better view of the fire on the monitor of Channel 10's MAST camera. Operated by remote control, the MAST camera provided a view across the rooftops to the bunker.

A cop who was watching the video with obvious fascination turned to the commissioner. He pointed out that the fire had wrapped itself around the base of the bunker. If they were lucky, he said offhandedly, the fire would do what the bomb hadn't: take out the bunker. Richmond didn't answer; he just continued to watch the screen intently.

It was obvious from the color and volume of the smoke that the fire wasn't serious. It was a simple Class A fire, fueled by wooden debris. The squirts could have put it out in no more than a few minutes.

But Richmond hesitated to turn them on. He didn't know whether the mission was aborted or whether cops would be sweeping across the roof in the next few moments. If they did, the squirts could knock them right off the roof and kill them.

"Go find out what the police want to do about the fire."

Scipione headed down Sixty-second Street again, looking for the police commissioner. He didn't find Sambor, but he did find Inspector Tiers. "Who's in charge?" Scipione asked him.

"Commissioner Sambor," Tiers answered.

"Where is he?"

"I don't know."

"Well, can we turn the water on? I need to know what to do about this fire." There was a frantic edge to Scipione's voice.

"Leave the water off. The steam is blocking the view of the stakeout teams," Tiers answered.

Moments later, two weary fire fighters were half listening to the chatter on the fire radios when Scipione's voice on the radio caught their attention. He was talking to Richmond about the fire.

"The police say let it burn," Scipione said over the radio.

The fire fighters looked at one another in surprise. Years later both of them would be able to recall the radio transmission with almost perfect clarity. It was easy to remember; they had never heard an order like that before.

Minutes later Scipione, still looking for Sambor, encountered Tiers once again. "Can I turn on the water yet?" he asked.

Tiers pointed down the street to where Sambor and Richmond were walking toward one another. "My boss and your boss are going to have a meeting in two minutes to decide what to do."

The batteries had died on the MAST camera, and the camera boom came down as cameramen rushed to change the batteries. At 6:11 Richmond left the Channel 10 van and went looking for Sambor. He found him down at the corner of Osage Avenue.

Sambor explained his dilemma to Richmond: "We've got to get the high ground. We want to use the fire to neutralize the bunker." He looked at Richmond.

"If we let the bunker burn, can you control the fire?"

Richmond thought back to the last camera scene before the camera came down on its boom. The fire had not seemed that serious. Later he would learn that the camera angle had shown only the top of the flames and that the fire was actually much worse than he thought.

"Yes," he told Sambor. "We should be able to control the fire."

Sambor crossed over to where Scipione stood. Could he put water from the squirts on the houses on either side of the MOVE house to prevent the fire from spreading?

Scipione gave the order, but Sambor almost immediately rescinded it. The steam generated when the water hit the growing fire on the MOVE house obscured the vision of sharpshooters. Over the next half hour the water would go on and off several times.

Still at his vantage point on the ninth-story fire escape, Leo Brooks watched the fire burn and waited for the squirts to come on. When it became apparent that nothing was happening, he tried for long minutes to raise Sambor on the radio. By the time he finally reached him, the fire had engulfed the bunker.

Brooks asked Sambor why no water was being put on the bunker. Sambor explained that he was using the fire to "neutralize" the bunker.

"Well, you've accomplished your mission," Brooks shot back. "Why don't you put out the fire? What are you doing?"

"I want to let it burn a little longer and make sure the bunker's completely destroyed," Sambor radioed.

Brooks answered again that he wanted the fire out. Still Sambor resisted. Finally Brooks issued him a direct order.

"You've accomplished your mission," he told Sambor. "Put out the fire."

At 6:18 P.M., a fire department spotter observing the fire from a ladder shifted his weight from one foot to the other. As he did so, his vision of the rooftop was obscured for a few seconds by the chimney that his ladder leaned against. By the time he'd leaned to the left to look around the corner of the chimney, the bunker had disappeared, crashing through the flaming rooftop and into the interior of the house.

Just after 6:25, Goode's aides relayed a message that the mayor wanted to speak to Brooks. Brooks stepped back into the hallway of the geriatric center and picked up the pay phone. He dialed the mayor's number.

"I can see this fire on my television, and it looks bad," Goode said. "Why aren't you putting it out?"

"Mr. Mayor, I just gave the order."

It would later become apparent that the order had come a few critical minutes too late. The moment the bunker fell through the roof, the fire could not be fought externally. Once the interior of the house became involved, the only way the fire could have been extinguished successfully would have been for fire fighters to carry water lines into the building itself. Water from the squirts, in fact, would only make the fire worse; it would drive it down farther into the house. And when the fire reached the sun porch, as it inevitably would, the other houses would follow. The long line of glassed-in porches had no fire walls between them, only thin, easily combustible plywood. The long run of porches would act like a horizontal chimney as the fire raced outward, groping for fresh fuel and oxygen.

At 6:25 Leo Brooks could not know that this would happen. Wilson Goode could not know, nor could Gregore Sambor. But an experienced fire fighter—someone like Bill Richmond, for example—would know exactly what the collapse of the bunker meant.

After his brief conversation with Sambor, Richmond continued to walk down Sixty-second Street to get a better view of the front of the house. No more than ten minutes had passed since Sambor and he had agreed to let the bunker burn.

When he turned and saw the flames coming out the second-floor windows of the MOVE house, Richmond was shocked— first by the extent of the fire and almost immediately afterward by the realization that he was looking at a burning house full of men, women, and children, with no possible way to put out the fire.

If MOVE surrendered quickly, his crew could probably still contain the fire within the MOVE house and, possibly, the houses on either side. But if they remained in the house until the fire spread into the sun porches and across the roofs, the entire block was probably lost.

From 6:18, when the bunker fell through the roof, it took less than an hour for the fire to spread to nearly all the houses on the north side of Osage Avenue. Still unable to go down the street or the back alley, the fire fighters carried lines into the houses on Pine Street and the south side of Osage. They trained portable water cannons from each end of the street, and the squirts—still stationed on Pine Street—played water across the tops of the houses that were not yet burning, in an attempt to stop the flames from spreading.

But all that water power was nothing against the gathering fire storm. Fueled by the tar paper roofs and the dry old timbers of the houses, it burned with an unstoppable fury. Thick black smoke rose into the early evening sky, creating a cloud that could be seen from every part of Philadelphia and beyond. The fire burned with such intensity that the houses across the street simply burst into flame from the radiant heat.

As the flames rose into the sky, the stakeout cops moved back into position and waited. At any moment they expected to see people fleeing from the house.

Berghaier, Mellor, and Tursi took up a position at the west end of the alleyway, along a three-foot-wide elevated walkway that ran behind the houses on Cobbs Creek Parkway. As they looked down the alley, they could see the houses on Pine Street to the left, each with a small enclosed rear yard. Right in front of them, the walkway ran the length of the alley along the back of the Pine Street properties. There was a cast-iron fence on the right-hand side of the walkway, with a five-foot drop on the other side down to the driveway that went behind the Osage Avenue houses.

The smoke and flames quickly grew so bad that they could not see the far end of the alley, where more cops waited. They could barely see the fence they'd pulled down earlier in the day and the debris-filled driveway behind the MOVE house.

The three were good friends—almost as close as family— and it was strange how events had brought them all together now. Despite all of Mike Tursi's efforts, things were turning out worse now than his blackest fears. Berghaier and Mellor had barely escaped death inside 6223 Osage. Not a thing had worked in their favor on this day, almost as if an evil omen had descended on all of them.

Exhausted beyond anything they had ever known, now they could do nothing except wait. Their job wouldn't be done until the people were out of the house and in police custody. Anything could happen.

But as the fire continued to burn and burn and burn, they sensed that something was terribly wrong. At the MOVE house there was no sign of life. Why weren't the MOVE people coming out?

Mellor heard a crackling overhead and looked up. A transformer was burning. Directly below it, where the driveway dipped down, made an L, and headed out to the street, a two-foot-deep pool of water had collected from the action of the squirts.

They continued to wait, with the growing certainty that the people in the house must already be dead. Gradually they relaxed their vigilance. Berghaier bummed a cigarette.

From Pine Street a fireman came down the alley, hunched over as if he expected shooting to break out. Mellor nudged Berghaier. "Get a look at this guy," he said. "Maybe he knows something we don't."

The fireman wanted to bring water hoses up the alleyway and close to the MOVE house. No way, the three cops told him. MOVE members were still in the house and presumably armed.

One of them asked the fire fighter whether anyone could possibly be alive in the house.

"It's possible," he said, "if they've got enough oxygen." The heat from the fire would go upward, and if they were below it the critical factor would be the smoke, not the heat.

The fireman was right. Inside the house the family of MOVE had crowded down into its final refuge, the sealed-up garage in the basement of the house. For the children huddled in the darkened garage, time had no meaning that night. But thirteen-year-old Birdie Africa remembers the heat and the smoke that had already filled the room when all of the adults joined the children for the last time.

He has told his story to investigators a number of times, and it contains inconsistencies that one would expect from a confused and terrified child. He has, for example, sometimes included John Africa among the people who were with him at the end, although autopsy reports and eyewitness accounts suggest that he died earlier in the day; other times he has not.

Even so, he is the only survivor of the house who has told his story to authorities, and it is clear at least in its general outlines. As the heat and smoke intensified, Birdie has testified, the adults gathered to discuss the children. Someone—Birdie has said it was John Africa—decided that they would send the kids out. The kids, in tears, clung to the adults and pleaded to stay with them.

The only way out of the MOVE house was through the small hatch, no more than two feet by two feet, that led from the walled-up garage to the back alley. It had to be opened from the inside using a wrench, and only an adult could do it.

Birdie remembers that Conrad opened the hatch but does not recall whether he crawled through it or simply stayed by it. When it opened, he heard what he thought was rapid gunfire coming from outside. Conrad closed the door. No one said anything about the gunfire.

Then the adults began to shout: "The kids are coming out! The kids are coming out!" He remembers the kids crawling over each other to reach the hatch. As Birdie made his way to the hatch, he thought his mother, Rhonda, was right behind him.

When he got outside, it was as if he had stepped into hell. The garage had been hot and smoky, but it had not been on fire. Out in the alley, flaming branches and lumber fell out of the sky. The concrete driveway was already buried under a foot or more of burning debris. To the left, where the western fence had been, Birdie could see a wall of flames. To the right were more flames and smoke and a cinder block wall blocking his way.

Birdie had not eaten for nearly twenty-four hours. He had been in the garage, huddled under a wet blanket, for most of the last twelve hours. His lungs were seared by the hot, smoke-filled air. Still he struggled to make his way forward.

He could see Conrad in the driveway, and Ramona was on the elevated walkway that ran along the back of the alley. She was trying to help Tree and Phil onto the walkway. Phil's skin looked like it was melting.

"They're coming out!" The voice of Sergeant Don Griffiths crackled on the radio. Griffiths, stationed on the upper floor in Post 4, was no more than fifty feet from the back of the MOVE house. Though from his position inside the house he could not see into the alley itself, he heard banging and the people shouting, "We're coming out! Don't shoot!"

At the windows in Post 4, Officers Markus Barianna and William Trudel could see what Griffiths couldn't. Looking down into the smoke-filled alleyway, Barianna saw the shadowy figure of a boy making his way across the fiery driveway. It was Birdie, trying to reach the elevated walkway.

Next Barianna saw a younger boy and a woman in the driveway and then a man. The man was carrying a rifle.

The man with the rifle turned toward Barianna. He raised his rifle, aiming directly at Barianna's window. Barianna ducked.

As he did, he heard the crack of a rifle, followed by several more single shots. When he looked out the window again, the gunman had vanished in the smoke and flames.

Trudel, in a window off to one side, saw the man fire at Barianna's position. From where he stood, the man seemed to be crouching behind one of the children. Unable to get a clear shot at the man, Trudel held his fire.

At the west end of the alley, Berghaier, Mellor, and Tursi saw people moving in the alley just as Griffiths's voice came over the radio. They saw Ramona scale the fence onto the walkway and try to pull the children after her. They saw Birdie try to climb up and fall back onto the burning debris. And they saw the man with the rifle. He seemed to be holding a child under one arm and firing with his free hand. Tursi saw him fire toward the Pine Street houses and then turn and shoot toward them. Mellor saw a light-skinned man with dreadlocks peer over a mound of debris at them and then duck down out of sight.

Mulvihill, D'Ulisse, and Officer John Reiber had taken up positions near the west end of the alley, in the yards behind the Pine Street houses. From where they stood, it was difficult to make out what was happening behind the MOVE house.

As the MOVE members emerged from the house, Jim Berghaier's attention became fixed on young Birdie. It was his son's birthday, and this kid looked to be almost the same age.

He saw Birdie, dizzy from the smoke and heat, stumble through the wall of flame that spread across the alley.

"Come on, son! This way!" he shouted, waving his arms. The boy didn't seem to hear him.

Ramona was walking parallel to Birdie, up on the walkway.

She turned behind her and motioned with her arm, as if she expected the others to be coming behind her. She walked a few steps more, turned, and motioned again. When no one else emerged from the smoke, she stamped her foot in a gesture of frustration and impotence.

Berghaier watched as Birdie stumbled over toward Ramona. Once again she reached over the fence and down into the driveway. She tried to haul him up and over the fence, but he lost his footing and fell back. Berghaier could almost feel the thud of his skull against the concrete.

Birdie lay motionless on his back. "Here," Berghaier said, handing Mellor his shotgun. "I'm going to get the kid."

"Be careful," Mellor said. "It could be a trap. I'll cover you."

"It's only a kid, Tom," Berghaier answered. He jumped the fence and landed in the pool of water at the bottom of the driveway. Overhead the transformer still crackled dangerously.

Berghaier made his way up the alleyway, retracing his footsteps of that morning. Unbelievably, it had been only thirteen-and-a-half hours since the operation had begun.

As Birdie lay motionless on the concrete, Berghaier crouched in the shelter of the houses, trying to sort out what was happening and decide what course of action to take. He knew that if he went into the middle of the alley he would be a perfect target. But the boy needed help. Gingerly, hoping this step would not be his last, he started toward Birdie. He had not even taken a second one when he felt a hand on his shoulder.

He turned instinctively, not knowing what to expect. Thank God it was Mike Tursi. He'd followed Berghaier out into the alley to help him get Birdie.

In the next seconds, Birdie began to stir. With a relentless instinct for survival, he picked himself up once again and began to walk forward.

"Over here, son! Come over here! Come to us!" Berghaier and Tursi, trying to stay out of the line of fire, called and waved to Birdie, but he seemed not to hear them. At the end of the alley, Mellor stood exposed on the walkway, covering the other two cops.

Birdie staggered toward the water. The cops could see that he was stumbling, about to fall forward into the water. They could tell he wasn't going to make it to the end of the alley under his own power.

Berghaier turned to Tursi. "I'm getting the kid."

Tursi was thinking about the man he'd seen shooting down the alley. "Be careful, Jim—it's a trap."

"He's just a kid, Mike. I can't leave him there."

"Go," Tursi answered. "I've got you covered."

Berghaier dashed into the alley. He grabbed Birdie under the shoulders and dragged him through the water. The boy looked at him in fear and confusion. "Don't shoot me," he pleaded. "Don't shoot."

It seemed to take forever for them to wade through the water. All that time Berghaier's eyes were fixed on Tommy Mellor's face as he stood on the walkway above them. Mellor was watching them, and he was looking down the alley, watching for snipers. As long as he was still looking, Berghaier knew he was fine. The last thing he wanted to see was a change in Mellor's expression.

When they got to the end of the alley, Tommy Mellor was still looking. Holding Birdie with one hand and holding up his waterlogged pants with the other, Berghaier ran down the driveway and out into Osage Avenue. Still running, he and Birdie came out past the barricades and onto Cobbs Creek Parkway. A shout went up from the crowd: "They got one! A kid! The cop's got a kid!"

His adrenaline pumping, Berghaier turned Birdie over to juvenile aid officers and ran back down Osage Avenue toward the alley.

Ramona had made her way down to where the two walkways intersected. Mellor kept his Uzi pointed at her. "Just keep walking," he told her. Docile, she walked in front of him. Suddenly Mellor realized that he'd left Berghaier's shotgun standing against the fence. Ramona and he looked at it in the same instant. "Just keep walking," he repeated. She walked quietly on to the mouth of the alley, where detectives waited to take her into custody.

When Berghaier got back to the alley, the three of them waited to see if more people would come out.

Suddenly they heard someone shouting—not from the MOVE house, but from the house almost directly across the alley from them. A man stood at the kitchen doorway—an elderly white man. He was calling for help. He had been in his home all day, unseen, overlooked during the evacuation and apparently oblivious to the fighting. They watched as Reiber dashed from his position on the Pine Street side of the alley, ran across the alley, and carried the old man to safety.

The police officers do not know how many more minutes they remained there before Mellor, watching the still-burning transformer and the sparking live wires swinging above them, suggested that they leave. "Let's get out of here," he said, "before we all get electrocuted."

It was not long afterward that all of the posts were abandoned because of the heat. The fire itself burned at a temperature of more than two thousand degrees Fahrenheit—hot enough to melt the plastic eyeglass frames of one cop in Post 4.

Sergeant Griffiths and the others finally left Post 4 at around eight o'clock. Before they left, Griffiths and another officer went into the basement and opened the back door. Anyone who did manage to escape from the burning MOVE house could use the door to escape from the alley.

"The door is open! Come out this way!" Griffiths shouted into the rolling inferno. The noise from the fire was so loud he could barely hear himself.

At 9:30 that night the police declared the site safe for fire fighters, and they moved in to fight the fire for the first time. Already fifty houses were gone. Six alarms had been sounded, each bringing four engine companies, two ladder companies, and two battalion chiefs. The fire fighters battled with what one expert later called "superhuman effort." They saved all but another eleven houses. At 11:40 P.M. they declared the fire under control.

Leo Brooks was a man who rarely displayed anger, but when

he found Sambor on Pine Street during the evening he was visibly upset. "How could this have happened?" he wanted to know. "Why wasn't this fire put out sooner?"

Sambor looked at him. "I suggest you ask the fire commissioner about that," he said.

After midnight a clearly exhausted Leo Brooks tried to answer the same question, this time posed by a reporter: "How could this have happened?"

He explained that of course they'd had no intention of letting the fire burn out of control. "We felt it was appropriate," he told the reporter, "to let the fire burn to disable the bunker."

12
The Aftermath

WHEN DAWN CAME AGAIN to west Philadelphia, it seemed that even the skies mourned. The blue skies of May 13 had given way to dark, low clouds. The late spring warmth of the day before had turned thick and oppressive.

In the gray light of dawn, scattered fire fighters stood among the ruins, playing water across still-smoldering debris. Amid the rising steam and smoke, crumbling structures emerged from the darkness—the fire walls that had once separated the homes on this street. They were the only thing left standing above the rubble.

The 6200 block of Osage Avenue was gone.

Later in the day investigators would map the site of 6221 Osage like an archaeological dig and begin to sift through the debris. Over the next several days they would uncover the charred, twisted, and half-consumed remains of eleven people. Among them they would find the bodies of five children, most of them curled in fetal positions beneath blankets.

But just now, at sunup, the work at Osage had not yet begun. The block was strangely tranquil. The guns were silent; the loudspeakers that had taunted the police were buried. Now there was only the echo of unanswered questions.

By the time Jim Berghaier returned home in the early morning hours of May 14, he had been up for nearly two days. He lay down, but he couldn't sleep. The images of May 13 ran through his mind—the early morning assault down the gas-filled alleyway, the wall of the upstairs bedroom exploding in gunfire, the small dark figure making his way through the smoke and flames. Finally, toward dawn, he dressed quietly and went outside. He walked to a ball field near his house, lay down on his back, stared into the black sky, and cried.

No one had expected things to turn out the way they had, so it wasn't really anybody's fault that the cops hadn't been warned about what might happen to them afterward: that even the toughest among them would have their psyches scarred by the bullets and fire in ways they wouldn't even understand. Powell began to dream about the helicopter and the bomb. Bill Klein, who had taken only a handful of sick days during his entire career with the force, was out a few days that week with a violent case of the flu.

The sick exhaustion that plagued the front-line cops seemed, to greater or lesser degrees, to infect the city bureaucracy itself. On Osage Avenue, no one seemed to know what to do with a crime scene that was a block and a half wide and buried under six feet of hot debris.

Problems began almost immediately. The walls that still stood were so unstable that they swayed in the breeze, and a crane was used to knock them down as a safety precaution before any digging actually began. But instead of knocking the walls of 6221 into the adjoining properties, the crane operator brought them tumbling down on top of the remains of the MOVE house, adding another layer of scrap that investigators would have to sift through and potentially damaging any evidence that lay underneath.

Because of the heat, digging could not begin until the afternoon. By then four different offices had investigators on the scene, under the overall coordination of the Philadelphia fire marshal's office: fire investigators, homicide detectives, crime scene technicians from the police department, and agents from the Bureau of Alcohol, Tobacco and Firearms.

Conspicuously absent was the medical examiner. After two calls, Chief Medical Examiner Bernard Aronson told the fire marshal that no one from his office would come out until the first body was recovered.

At four in the afternoon, as the clamshell pulled away from

the debris, a shout went up to stop the crane. Dangling from the jaws of the crane's scoop was a charred and twisted human leg. The crane operator gently brought the scoop back down and opened the clamshell. Someone called the medical examiner's office as the investigators sifted through the site with shovels and rakes.

It took them twenty minutes to uncover the remains of what they thought was the first body. It was so badly burned and mangled that it was impossible to tell without a detailed autopsy that they'd actually discovered the remnants of two bodies.

The work continued in the area of the first body. A pathologist from the medical examiner's office arrived at 5:00 P.M. and supervised the digging. When night fell at 7:30, they had recovered a total of six bodies—all of them from the garage that Birdie and Ramona had escaped.

They had been found only inches from the concrete floor, with more than six feet of debris on top of them. Not one body was intact; many were simply fragments of bone and charred flesh.

The investigators found eleven bodies altogether. All of them lay within the walls of the foundation; none were found in the back alley.

Nine of the bodies lay in the area that had been the garage. All five of the children, some of them found beneath blankets, were there: Phil and Tree, whom Birdie had last seen outside in the fiery alley; Tree's sister Zanetta, Delitia, and Tomaso. Tomaso, the youngest, was approximately nine years old when he died; Tree, the oldest of the children, was about fifteen.

All but two of the adults were there, too. They had been among the most stalwart members of MOVE: Birdie's mother, Rhonda, who had braved the police blockade in Richmond; Raymond, the demolitions expert who had wired explosives in the Powelton house during the 1978 siege; pretty young Theresa, whose passionate letters to her family had defended and tried to explain John Africa's teachings; and Conrad— though temperamental and often violent with the neighbors, Birdie's favorite among the men—who had left the house with

Ramona and the children and in those final terrible moments had gone back inside to be with the others.

In the front of the house, investigators found two more bodies. Judging from the amount of debris under the bodies, Frank James apparently had been on the second floor or in the bunker when he died. It was not clear how or when he died; though no soot was found in his lungs, his body showed no evidence that he had died by gunshot wounds or explosions.

In the area of the front porch, investigators recovered the body of a muscular middle-aged man. The lungs were free of soot, and blood samples showed no evidence of carbon monoxide, suggesting that the man was already dead by the time the fire reached him. The heat of the fire had completely consumed the body's head, hands, and feet. Two forensic pathologists examined the body but could not definitively state a cause of death. Months later the pathologist hired by the MOVE Commission would use circumstantial evidence—including Birdie's testimony as to who was in the house that day—to identify the body as that of Vincent Leaphart.

Investigators sifting through the mess expected to find an arsenal of weapons even greater than they had recovered from the Powelton house in 1978. They did not. In all, they found two pistols, a shotgun, and a .22-caliber rifle.

The medical examiner's lack of interest on the morning of May 14 set a pattern that would persist throughout the investigation. Virtually every detail, from blood chemistry to the position in which the bodies were found, would be clouded by controversy over the handling of the evidence. Some of the bodies were not photographed until after they had been removed and placed on litters. The crane simply scooped up buckets of debris and deposited them onto Osage Avenue for investigators to sift through with rakes and shovels, making it impossible to establish precisely where much of the evidence had been found. The police, fire department, and medical examiner's office used three different labeling systems for the bodies, and the truckloads of debris that were hauled to the police auto pound for further sifting bore no identification to indicate from what part of the house they had come. Later, during the autopsies, delays in obtaining blood and tissue samples would compromise laboratory analysis.

The fire marshal's investigation was directed at discovering the cause and origin of the fire. Using videotapes and police surveillance photos as a guide, investigators sifted through tons of scrap, eventually recovering a charred and twisted gasoline can. It still bore the mark of impact where it had slammed against the parapet wall and a long ragged rupture where the gasoline had burst through in a fireball, igniting the splintered debris on the roof.

As the investigators began the long and difficult task of determining when and how the people in the house had died, the rumors had already begun to fly. That morning, a front-page story in the *Philadelphia Daily News* announced:

> 3 MOVErs Slain; 60 Homes Burn
> Three members of MOVE were shot to death in a gun battle with police stakeout units at the rear of the cult's headquarters, police sources told the Daily News early this morning. The sources said the bodies of the three were lying in the rubble at the rear of the home on 6221 Osage Avenue, west Philadelphia.

A follow-up story three days later would add more details: stakeout police had seen the first MOVE gunman "blown back" into the house by a barrage of bullets. "Everybody started shooting," one source said. "It became a 100 percent bona fide shootout."

With the publication of the *Daily News* report, a disturbing new wrinkle had been added to the emerging tale of incompetence on Osage Avenue. Was it possible that the other MOVE members who were trying to escape from the burning house along with Ramona and Birdie had been pinned down by police gunfire?

The cops who had been in the back alley read the *Daily News* stories with incredulity—and the first pangs of paranoia. None of them had fired in the back alley. And anyone who had seen the back of the MOVE house would know that there was no way someone could be "blown back" through the two-foot by two-foot hatch that was the only ground-floor entrance to the rear of the house. (Three-and-a-half years later, the reporter who broke the story revealed that it had come to him from three police officers, each of whom had heard it from someone else. None of them actually claimed to have seen the events they described, and one of them later changed his mind about what he believed had happened in the back alley that night.)

None of the cops who had actually been in the back alley had seen or heard police firing their weapons that evening in the alley. Each of them, in fact, had given independent statements to homicide detectives the same night. Cops who had been at far ends of the alley, and who hadn't spoken to one another that night, all had provided consistent accounts. Nobody could seriously believe that they had all gathered together that night and cooked up a story to cover up the murder of innocent children. And yet already the term *cover-up* was being heard.

If the cops had hoped that Sambor would dispel the rumors they were disappointed. Every time he rose to their defense, he seemed to leave them deeper in trouble.

On May 14, Sambor, Goode, Richmond, and Brooks were beyond asking what had gone wrong; they walked and spoke as if they had not yet fully awakened from a terrible collective nightmare. Goode held a brief news conference in which he pledged to rebuild the block but offered few details about what had gone wrong.

That first day, the four of them sat down with Goode's press secretary and made an initial attempt to sort through the events of May 13. They began to put together a chronology that would plague them throughout all the subsequent investigations. Based solely on their joint recollections and never completed, it placed Goode's and Richmond's order to put out the fire at six o'clock in the evening—just fifteen minutes after the fire first became apparent over the Channel 10 MAST camera.

The chronology suggested that Goode and Brooks had reacted relatively quickly to the fire, but at the same time it raised the question as to why that order was not put into effect until almost 6:30, nearly a half hour later—thus pointing an accusing finger at Richmond and Sambor.

Goode would cling tenaciously to this timetable, even after later evidence from police band radios and other sources almost certainly fixed the time of Goode's order at about 6:25. Unable or unwilling to explain why he watched a fire burn uncontrolled for more than half an hour without picking up the phone and ordering it to be put out, he became increasingly defensive about his handling of the entire affair. Though he said he accepted "full responsibility" for the tragedy, he nonetheless left the clear impression that he had acted properly and honorably by delegating most of the decision-making authority to his managing director and police commissioner.

Brooks came across as soft-spoken and sincere, but he seemed oddly distant. The plan had been conceived and the first phases of it put into place while he'd been in Virginia, and he seemed like a man who'd come back from vacation to find out that the office had gone to hell in his absence. He'd permitted himself one outburst of recriminations when he ran into Sambor on Pine Street the night before, but now he was focused on damage control.

As more attention began to focus on the police, Sambor was unrepentant. The outcome, of course, had been tragic, but it wasn't *his* fault. The bureaucratic instincts had emerged almost immediately: he began passing bucks as quickly as they came to him. He suggested that MOVE had set the fire, and if it had burned out of control, it was because the fire commissioner hadn't been willing to send his men in to fight it.

Of those whom the media would dub "the Big Four," Bill Richmond was the only one who seemed to be thinking more about the kids who'd died than about his own political neck. He did not try to sidestep reporters' questions. He explained how and why he and Sambor had decided to let the bunker burn. He tried to describe the fear and fatigue and concern for his men that had contributed to that decision, but he did not try to defend its wisdom.

Two days after the confrontation, he broke down at a memorial service honoring Philadelphia police officers and fire fighters who had died in the line of duty over the years. He was barely able to conclude his speech, which had been written before May 13 with a chilling prescience.

"Once again," he read, "sad evidence is shown that the dangers in our work as we operate from day to day—" He paused for a long moment, choking back tears. Finally he finished, his voice cracking over a phrase that in its irony seemed to sum up all that had gone wrong that day: "—in the routine performance of our duties."

At 9:30 A.M., on Friday, May 17, Goode and his subordinates held a press conference. It was a disaster.

The questions were obvious: Why was a bomb used on the house? Hadn't they foreseen a fire? And most important, why had the city permitted the fire to burn for almost an hour before trying to extinguish it?

Goode, Sambor, Richmond, and Brooks did not yet have any clear understanding of what had gone so terribly wrong the Monday before (some of them, in fact, never would), and the more they tried to explain themselves, the worse their claims sounded.

First, Sambor mistakenly confirmed the *Daily News* report about the mythical back-alley gunfight. Minutes later, Tiers and Marandola, who were watching on television, phoned the press room and asked to speak to Sambor. After talking with them briefly, Sambor returned to the microphones and announced that his earlier statement had been based on "unconfirmed reports." Police had *not* fired back at MOVE members in the back alley, he said.

Reporters asked whom he'd been speaking with on the phone. "None of your business," Sambor replied testily. When the questioning persisted, he exploded.

Interrupting Goode, he shouted, "Damn it—excuse me, Mr. Mayor—I've said once and for all that in the beginning I said there was gunfire returned. I did not say categorically or unequivocally that gunfire was returned, okay?"

A reporter tried to pose a question, but Sambor cut him off. "Will you let me finish, damn it? Now I said it twice—that it was unconfirmed. And now I've confirmed it that no gunfire was returned. I hope that that is clear now. Do you want me to say it in another language?"

Goode himself seemed as poorly informed as Sambor at the press conference. He told reporters that the fire had been permitted to burn because MOVE gunfire prevented fire fighters from getting close enough—despite the obvious fact that the remote-control squirts were available but never used; despite Brooks's explanation on the night of the fire that the fire had been used to disable the bunker; despite the fact that at the news conference itself Richmond gave the same explanation as Goode stood listening.

Richmond unwittingly added to the growing speculation about a gun battle. Describing where the bodies had been found, he correctly stated that all of the bodies were "in the rear of the dwelling of 6221." But in answer to a reporter's question, he added: "Yes, that's the rear alley."

Charges of police cover-up were now being made openly— and it was only four days after the fire.

Ever since the fire, Managing Director Leo Brooks had been quiet and reclusive. On May 23, he resigned. His departure, the mayor said, had nothing to do with the disaster of May 13—in fact, he said, Brooks had mentioned plans to retire several weeks before.

There *was* a cover-up going on in the police department, but it had nothing to do with the back alley. And so far, the press had no inkling of it.

The problem was the C-4. The bomb guys had used a lot of it on May 13. What would happen if people started asking where it had come from?

FBI agent Mike Macy had done them a favor when he'd brought them the C-4 "Christmas present" the winter before. Connor, Powell, and the others didn't know whether what he'd done was illegal, but it was certainly done outside official channels. Since the controls on procuring C-4 were strict, people would eventually start asking where the bomb squad had acquired so much and why it hadn't been documented properly. Sooner or later that trail would lead back to Mike Macy. That would mean a major embarrassment for the FBI, and the FBI did not look kindly upon agents who embarrassed the bureau.

The decision to cover up the use of C-4 actually began inside 6217 Osage Avenue on the morning of May 13. According to the grand jury's public report, after the early morning battle, as the insertion team waited for its next instructions, Connor had turned to Angelucci and Muldowney and asked, "What are we going to say about the C-4?"

"What do you mean?" one of them asked.

"We can't say we used C-4," Connor said. He'd been nervous, as if he'd just realized that there might be a problem. "We're not supposed to have any C-4." He proposed that if they were asked, they should say that the explosives used that morning had been HDP boosters, commercially available explosives that had similar detonation characteristics.

Angelucci and Muldowney looked at one another. It had been Connor's idea to use C-4 in the first place. Reluctantly, they agreed to go along with Connor, in part because they didn't want Macy to get jammed up, in part because they knew about the kind of problems a cop could face if he spoke out against a fellow officer, and in part because the deception seemed so minor—as Connor would later say, "A bomb is a bomb no matter what's in it."

Klein had used C-4 twice on May 13, once to construct the charge that had ended up destroying the interior of 6223 late in the morning and later when he constructed the charge that Powell had dropped on the MOVE house roof. Connor urged Klein to keep quiet about the C-4, too.

If Klein had had any doubts about going along with Connor, they were dissipated a few days later when Sambor, relying on information that Klein had provided to homicide detectives, publicly announced that the charge dropped on the roof had been made of Tovex. For Klein to come clean after that would have been a disaster; the department would crucify him.

Frank Powell says that he didn't know about the C-4 in the

charge he dropped from the helicopter until a few weeks after
the confrontation, when Graham—the bomb squad technician
who had constructed the timer for the charge—mentioned that
he thought there had been C-4 in it. Graham hadn't seen what
Klein had used, but from the sound of the explosion he
guessed it had been C-4. After Graham told him that, Powell
had a conversation with Klein. "Don't tell me what was in the
satchel," he told Klein. "I don't know what was in it, and I
don't want to know."

The cover-up was conceived hastily, and unfortunately, it
had three weaknesses. The first was that Connor and the
others had to give statements to homicide detectives. Once
they'd identified the explosives they'd used as HDP boosters,
there was no way they could change their story—it could cost
them their careers if they admitted that they'd provided false
information. The second problem was the fact that HDP
boosters looked like sticks of dynamite and bore no resem-
blance to the puttylike bricks of C-4. The stakeout cops who'd
been members of the insertion teams weren't in on the cover-
up, and, totally ignorant of explosives, they had innocently
given detailed descriptions of charges that could only have
been C-4.

The clincher came from the detective work of Eugene Dooley. Dooley was the captain of the homicide division, which
was conducting the police department's internal investigation
of the May 13 incident. Unflappable and methodical, he'd
overseen a series of tests at the police academy in which police
had tried to reconstruct the events that had created the rooftop
fire on May 13. Based on Klein's description of the charge and
information about the gasoline and other materials stored near
the bunker, they had been unable to start a fire short of
actually placing the explosives inside the gasoline can.

The test results reinforced Sambor's earlier belief that
MOVE members had set the rooftop fire themselves—as, in
fact, Ramona had threatened to do the night before. But
Dooley came to a different conclusion. As he played the tape of
the explosion and the tapes from the tests again and again,
Dooley felt something was wrong. He was no expert in explo-

sives, but when he played the tapes in slow motion it seemed clear that the size and pattern of the blasts just didn't match up.

He showed the tapes to Sambor and suggested that he interview Klein again. In August of 1985, Dooley brought Klein in and showed him the tapes. Didn't he agree that there was something odd about the two explosions? After intensive questioning, Klein admitted to Dooley that he had included C-4 in the charge, and the cover-up quickly began to unravel.

The press had covered the C-4 issue without really understanding what it was about. All they knew was that the cops had lied about what was contained in the bomb and that C-4 was a powerful military explosive, not the "commercial" explosive Tovex, as they had been told at first.

What reporters couldn't figure out—and what no one was telling them—was *why* the police had lied about the explosive. The obvious, though erroneous, conclusion was that someone—perhaps Klein or Sambor—had tried to conceal how powerful the bomb was. That, in turn, could only mean that the bomb might have been intended to do more than simply disable the bunker. Perhaps it had been designed to kill.

It was in this atmosphere that a remarkable series of hearings was broadcast in the fall of 1985: the hearings of the Philadelphia Special Investigation Commission—better known as the MOVE Commission. Goode, moving to deflect the rising tide of criticism, had announced the formation of the commission just two days after the fire.

It had been widely viewed as a clumsy political move on Goode's part. A group of people handpicked by the mayor could hardly do anything other than vindicate him. At the same time, they would forestall the internal police investigation, as well as a special investigation that was being considered by the city council.

Goode sought to blunt those criticisms by selecting commissioners whose reputations were beyond reproach. Within a week he had established a legal framework for the commission and recruited eleven commissioners who would represent a cross section of views and whose credentials would be above reproach. All of them served without pay.

To chair the commission, he chose William H. Brown III, one of the city's most prominent black attorneys and a former chairman of the U.S. Equal Employment Opportunity Commission. In consultation with Brown, he selected Henry S. Ruth, Jr., who had served as one of the chief Watergate prosecutors; Neil J. Welch, the former assistant director of the FBI who had helped develop the Abscam cases that netted fraud convictions against several congressmen; and Charisse Ranielle Lillie, a law professor at Villanova University just outside Philadelphia, who had been a trial lawyer for the Justice Department's civil rights division and a deputy director of Community Legal Services.

The commission also contained three ministers: Monsignor Edward P. Cullen, who had been trained as a social worker and headed Catholic Social Services in the city; Reverend Audrey F. Bronson of the Sanctuary Church of the Open Door in west Philadelphia; and Reverend Paul M. Washington, rector of the Episcopal Church of the Advocate in north Philadelphia. A well-known and respected civil rights activist, Washington had served as host of the 1970 Black Panthers convention and had attempted to mediate the 1978 MOVE standoff.

Representing widely diverse constituencies were two commissioners whose presence represented (at least symbolically) the conscience of the community: M. Todd Cooke, the chairman and chief executive officer of the Philadelphia Savings Fund Society—the region's oldest savings and loan association—and Julia M. Chinn, who was president of the Cobbs Creek Town Watch and lived near the site of the confrontation.

Rounding out the commission were two more lawyers. One was attorney Charles W. Bowser, a political ally of Goode's who had been the city's first black deputy mayor in the late 1960s and, as an unsuccessful candidate for mayor in 1975, had helped pave the way for Goode's election in 1983. Bowser was widely regarded as Goode's man on the commission, the one who would be most likely to come to the defense of the mayor and his administration if the going got tough.

The other was Bruce W. Kauffman, chairman of the city's most prominent law firm, member of the state Judicial Inquiry and Review Board, and a former Pennsylvania Supreme Court justice. Of all of the lawyers on the panel, only Kauffman had served as a judge and had had experience in sifting through tangled legal complexities and weighing the quality of evidence against the often baffling requirements of the law.

The commissioners kept a relatively low profile over the summer, but investigators had been busy conducting interviews and gathering evidence in preparation for the public hearings. They interviewed virtually every cop and fire fighter on the scene, as well as other key players, but the interviews themselves were neither recorded nor transcribed. Instead, investigators wrote summaries based on their notes. Some of those who were interviewed later said that investigators either misunderstood or misrepresented what they'd said.

To a great extent, these investigators were shooting in the dark. Though Klein had admitted using the C-4, the police still weren't saying where it had come from. During the summer, MOVE investigators paid a call to Frank Powell at the bomb squad headquarters, looking for C-4, and Powell had given them the runaround.

Then too, the attorneys hired by the police officers' union actively resisted the inquiry. Concerned that the MOVE Commission's mission and methods were too vague, they feared a witch-hunt that would place the blame on the cops. Rumors were still circulating about a gun battle in the back alley. The rank-and-file cops began to suspect they were being set up. The lawyers advised the cops to plead the Fifth Amendment—despite the fact that Goode had vowed to fire any city employee who didn't cooperate with the commission.

To the MOVE investigators—and, later, to most of the commissioners—the cops' lack of cooperation suggested that they were hiding something. In a criminal proceeding, of course, a court cannot infer guilt because a defendant invokes the Fifth Amendment. But the commission did not consider itself bound by the strict rules of evidence that would be applicable in a criminal court of law and at least informally seemed to regard the cops' refusal to testify as evidence of their guilt. In fact, in its final report the MOVE Commission recommended a disturbingly McCarthyistic course of action, urging the city to fire those police officers who had taken the Fifth Amendment.

Officer Tommy Mellor, who had been trapped in the closet with Powell and the others on May 13, would later say that as scared as he was that day, he was more scared by his interviews with the MOVE investigators. To him it seemed clear that something strange was going on.

The first round of interviews didn't concern him. He simply explained to the investigators what had happened. It all seemed straightforward.

During the second round he sat drinking a cup of coffee as the investigator reviewed his notes. Suddenly the investigator made a perplexing request: "Tell me again about the water charges."

The coffee cup paused halfway to Mellor's lips as alarm bells went off in his head.

"I didn't say anything about water charges," he answered. He didn't even know what a water charge was.

The investigator became upset. "Yes, you did—it's right here in black and white!" he shouted, waving his notes from the first interview.

"Let me see," Mellor answered, reaching for the notes. The investigator pulled them back out of his reach.

Mellor repeated that he didn't know anything about water charges. The investigator continued to insist that he did. Other statements came up that Mellor didn't recognize. By the time he left, he was confused and worried.

Angry, he left the interview room by the wrong door and found himself in a stairwell. As he made his way back, he overheard the investigator, still in the room, talking to someone in a loud voice. "They're all nothing but a bunch of liars," he was saying.

Outside, Mellor caught up with Berghaier, who was just finishing an equally hostile session with another investigator. He looked at Berghaier and said quietly, "We're dead."

Berghaier and Mellor weren't the only cops who sensed that they were victims of a witch-hunt. Frank Powell, for example, says that MOVE investigators attributed statements to him that he never made. In fact, he says, they reported an entire interview with him that never took place. The suspicions of the MOVE Commission ran deeply throughout the police department.

William B. Lytton III, who supervised the MOVE Commission investigations, later defended both the methods of the investigation and its personnel. The investigation team, he said, was made up of seasoned law enforcement professionals who, if anything, would be expected to be sympathetic to the cops' point of view. He stated that because of the number of interviews that were conducted over such a short time period, it is possible that some errors crept into the statements. And he acknowledges that as the investigations went on, there was a great deal of friction between the investigators and the police. But he lays responsibility for that with the attorneys who represented the cops. He believes it was their behavior and hostility, not the investigators, that contributed to the atmosphere of paranoia. There was no witch-hunt, he insists.

By the time the MOVE Commission public hearings began in October 1985, considerable code evidence seemed to point toward a police conspiracy: the two *Daily News* stories suggesting that police gunfire had driven MOVE members back into the house, Sambor's confusing confirmation and subsequent denial of a gun battle in the back alley, the police department's admission that the bomb had contained more powerful explosives than the department had first stated, and the lack of any valid explanation for the deception. Goode had told the people of Philadelphia that the fire had been permitted to burn because fire fighters had been shot at by MOVE members; his subordinates had said they had been trying to disable the bunker.

These points taken together, it is easy to see why the commission—and many other people—already believed that the cops had something to hide. The conclusion that there had been more than incompetence on Osage Avenue was nearly inescapable.

And now "cover-up" was not the only accusation echoing throughout the city. Starting to make the rounds in Philadelphia—sometimes whispered, sometimes shouted—was a new word: murder.

The public hearings did nothing to allay the growing suspicions. The attorneys for the police officers clashed openly with the commission, contending that the commission, with its relaxed procedural and evidentiary standards, did not provide adequate protection of their clients' Constitutional rights. They sought and obtained a court order that prohibited the commission from using the investigation reports to challenge or cross-examine witnesses. They repeatedly objected to the questions that were asked of their witnesses—objections that Brown usually overruled with ill-concealed anger. They filed a lawsuit challenging the validity of the commission's charter to conduct the investigation.

All of that, as well as the revelations of poor planning and execution, made for good television drama. The hearings, held in the studios of local PBS affiliate WHYY-TV, were broadcast live, six hours a day, four days a week, for five weeks. Every day the viewing audience included at least one million people in the Philadelphia area.

Jim Berghaier was one of the officers who chose to testify before the MOVE Commission. He had nothing to hide, and he wasn't about to take the Fifth Amendment.

Even so, he had been feeling the weight of the suspicions and speculations about what the police might have done in the back alley. By the time he testified he was a nervous wreck, and his composure deteriorated as he sat before the glare of the television lights.

Mellor and Tursi had been called to testify the same day, and the three of them appeared together. As Berghaier sat next to Mellor and told his story, he felt as though he would break down and cry, as he had so many times already over the summer. He curled his toes inside his shoes and counted the tiles on the ceiling to calm himself down. Somehow he got through his testimony.

The strain showed on his face as he testified. As Mellor spoke about the burning transformer that had threatened to

fall into the pool of water, one could see Berghaier's eyes
darting upward, searching for the transformer. While Mellor
spoke, Berghaier felt he was no longer in the studio; he was out
there in the alley again.

When it was over, Commissioner Bowser, who had been one
of the harshest critics of the operation, spoke of Berghaier.

"I've been sitting here listening for many days, and it's all
been depressing and discouraging—except for what I've heard
of Office Berghaier and heard from Officer Berghaier today.
And if there's any hope for this entire situation, it's from that
officer. And I want to thank him."

The other commissioners joined in commending Berghaier,
and over the next several days letters came to his home—from
an old schoolmate, from a stranger, and one from Birdie's
attorney, who thanked Berghaier on behalf of the boy's father
and stepmother.

But the praise did little to boost his spirits. In the weeks
after the confrontation he had waited for the black despair to
pass, for his life to settle back into the happy routine it had
been, but it did not. He was having trouble sleeping, and when
he did drift off he was haunted by one recurring dream: He
was in the alley, and he could see MOVE children running
around in circles in the flames, melting before his eyes. And off
to one side, untouched by the flames, he could see his daughter. "Daddy," she cried. "Do something!"

The horror of it all for Jim Berghaier was that no matter
what he'd done that day, no matter how many people had
praised his heroism, he felt as though he should have found a
way to save the other children. And yet when he went over that
day in his mind, he knew he'd responded with sure instincts;
he couldn't think of anything he could have done better.

That was the worst: he had done everything right, and yet
everything had turned out so wrong. Eleven people were dead,
and the newspapers were calling the cops murderers and liars.

Even the other cops seemed against him. There had always
been cops who'd said Berghaier was full of himself, a show-off
who looked down his nose at other cops. Now, in the aftermath
of May 13, it seemed that he was the only one who was going
to be painted a hero for saving the kid. Every time someone

called him a hero, he could feel the hot, angry eyes of the other good cops out there who'd been ignored or who were being treated as if they were murderers.

Of course there were plenty of cops who weren't going to shed a tear over the deaths of May 13—even the kids. There were cops who said Berghaier hadn't done them any favors by saving the kid; he'd just grow up and kill some other cop. There were, frankly, plenty of guys who didn't give a damn about a bunch of "crazy niggers" in west Philadelphia. And there were those who said that they couldn't do any "real police work" in the alley that night because Berghaier was there. Someone painted the words "nigger lover" on his locker.

For Jim Berghaier, the weeks passed and the nightmares did not go away. One more week, he would tell himself; one more week and I'll be fine. But he was not.

The thing he loved most about police work was that the job was so moral: it was the good guys against the bad guys. But now he couldn't tell which were the good guys and which were the bad.

One night Berghaier was working a stakeout operation on the elevated railway in west Philadelphia with his old partners Tommy Mellor and Jesse Freer. A group of muggers had been robbing people as they left the el stop late at night. Berghaier was the decoy; he would dress as an old man and walk down the dark and menacing stairwells from the el station. He put his pistol in its shoulder holster, slipped a sweatshirt over it, and pulled a jacket over the whole thing.

"Jim," Freer told him, "you'll never be able to get to your gun in time."

"Sure I will, Jesse. No problem," Berghaier told him.

The operation didn't come off; the muggers were scared off by a passing police car. Afterward, as he walked down the stairs to meet up with Mellor, Berghaier felt as if he were coming out of a daze. He looked down at his sweatshirt and realized that his partner had been right: there was no way he could have pulled out his gun.

And then an even more frightening realization hit him. He had done it on purpose.

He was shaking by the time Mellor reached him. "Tommy, I

can't get to my gun." Mellor looked at him quizzically. "I don't *want* to get to my gun," Berghaier went on.

Tommy Mellor said nothing for a long time. Then he laid his arm across Berghaier's shoulder. "That's it, Jimmy," he said quietly. "You're done."

It was Jim Berghaier's last stakeout operation.

At home there were fights, as his black moods spilled over into his relationship with his wife and kids. A cop's life is rough on families, as the divorce rates testify, but Berghaier had always had the kind of family life that other cops kidded him about. When they went out for drinks after work, he usually headed straight home.

To his wife and kids, he'd always been a tower of strength. Maybe he pushed his kids a little too hard, worried about them a little too much, but they knew he did it only because he wanted the best for them. Now he seemed so distracted that they weren't sure what he wanted. They did not know how to deal with his black moods and long silent spells. His marriage faltered, and his kids began to look at him the way one would look at a wounded animal—half pitying, half fearful. He'd always felt his life was built on solid bedrock. Now the ground was giving way beneath him, and he was falling, falling into darkness.

The highlight of the MOVE Commission's public hearings came at the end, with the testimony of the Big Four. Here, laid out in detail, was the story of Goode's delaying tactics and the final frantic planning that led to the confrontation. Here too were revealed the confusion and terror of May 13 and the stumbling series of decisions that led to the fire and then permitted it to burn.

Appearing before the MOVE Commission in his Idi Amin–style police commissioner's uniform, Sambor seemed angry and defiant, and his testimony was confused and contradictory. Brooks was earnest, but it was clear that he had chosen to stay on the sidelines that day. Richmond wept openly for the lives that had been lost.

Goode, who had at first accepted responsibility for the tragedy, hinted in his testimony before the MOVE Commission that he had not been kept informed about the course of events that day. He had not been told, he said, that the police would use a helicopter to drop the device, and he would not have approved the plan if he had known. He made the startling assertion that his order to fight the fire had been delayed because of poor television reception at City Hall: as he watched the news reports, he said, he had mistaken "snow" on the TV screen for water from fire hoses.

The public hearings came to a close toward the end of November, and the commissioners voted to reconvene after the first of the year to review the evidence and begin drawing up their final report.

On November 13, 1985, Police Commissioner Gregore Sambor resigned, six months to the day after the fire. Goode and Sambor both described the resignation as voluntary. Several weeks later, however, Sambor displayed his customary flair for making a bad situation even worse. He told a group of reporters that he had been "forced out" by Goode.

By the following February, a bloodied but unbowed Sambor was telling a police conference in Florida that he had been "given a choice . . . to retire or be fired." Goode had made him the scapegoat for the May 13 fiasco, he contended, because of the mayor's plans to run for reelection in 1987. He warned the cops attending the International Disaster Management Conference to "deal with political realities." He had not done so during the May 13 operation and, he said, had lost his job as a result. He also repeated his claim that MOVE members had set the fire themselves, despite clear evidence to the contrary. And unrepentant to the end, he said that he would take the same action again under similar circumstances.

Christmas of 1985 was a bleak one, especially for MOVE's former neighbors. For seven months they had lived scattered throughout the city, some in temporary housing supplied by the city, others with relatives. Goode had pledged to have them back in their rebuilt homes in time for Christmas, but the reconstruction was marked by delays and incompetence.

Goode had pledged to give the work to a black contractor, and he bypassed the usual competitive bidding process to award it to a man named Ernest Edwards. He did so despite the fact that the city's most prominent real estate developer, Willard Rouse, had offered to rebuild the houses at cost, and he also spurned an offer by a manufacturer to provide furnaces for the new homes free of charge.

When it became apparent that Edwards was having trouble obtaining credit, Goode had intervened, personally telephoning bankers about the loans. Despite his assurances, however, Edwards proved to be a bad credit risk. He used some of the money that the city advanced him on the project to pay off old loans, and soon it came to light that he had left a trail of bankruptcies and unfinished projects behind him.

The city fired Edwards, and a grand jury began an investigation of his finances and his handling of the Osage Avenue project. Meanwhile, a second contractor came in and soon ran into delays and cost overruns.

The cost of rebuilding the sixty-one houses, originally estimated at $4.9 million, eventually ran to more than $8.5 million. When other expenses were included, such as demolition costs and restoration of utilities, the cost to rebuild each house—each of which had a market value of perhaps $35,000 when they burned—totaled $154,673. And they were not finished until August 1986—eight months after the Christmas deadline.

When they finally moved back home, the neighbors were critical of the contractor's work. One neighbor pointed to the ten-year warranty that the builders had provided. "I have a feeling I'm going to need this," he said. He was right; with the first big snowfall of the following winter, several neighbors discovered that their brand-new roofs leaked.

While the neighbors were waiting for their houses to be rebuilt, the MOVE Commission reconvened and began wrapping up its work.

It took the commissioners all of January and most of February to slog through the transcripts and other evidence and hammer out a series of findings. Many of the factual issues were readily settled, as were the recommendations submitted for improvements in city policies and practices. But as the commission's work drew to a close, a number of issues proved to be thorny indeed.

Bruce Kauffman and Chairman William Brown had been at odds throughout the investigations and hearings. Kauffman had made no secret about the fact that he felt the cops on the line were getting a raw deal from the majority of the commission. Where others saw evidence of "unconscionable" police force—and perhaps even premeditated murder—Kauffman reminded them that, under the law, the police had been well within their rights to meet MOVE's resistance with deadly force. "You can beat up on the leadership all you want, but I won't go for beating up on the guy on the line. . . . Once an assault is under way and police are fired on, they have a right to fire back to kill," he argued in one discussion.

Nor could he fault them morally for their actions. He remained convinced that the commission's evidence of police shooting in the back alley was far too incomplete and circumstantial—a caveat that was nearly lost in the din at the time but that would prove to be prophetic. And Kauffman took profound exception to proposed wording that charged racism and that suggested the confrontation would have been handled differently in a "comparable white neighborhood." In the end, he broke with the rest of the commission on key findings and wrote a dissent.

The most difficult moment for the MOVE commissioners came on the very last day of deliberations, as the commissioners debated whether they should call for any resignations.

If Kauffman had been looking out for the cops, Bowser was watching out for the interests of Wilson Goode, and that became obvious as the commission came to the very brink of calling for Goode's and Richmond's resignations.

Bowser pressed for Richmond's resignation but adamantly opposed any suggestion of Goode's resignation. His justification was that Richmond, an appointee, was an appropriate target for the commission's recommendations to the mayor, but that Goode himself was answerable only to the people who had elected him. In addition, he argued that Richmond had played the key role in permitting the fire to burn; though Goode had "just walked away," his very detachment insulated him from responsibility. During the deliberations Bowser argued that "Mayor Goode cannot be held responsible for the dark tragedy of May 13th for the worst reason of all: he was not leading when it counted most."

During that meeting on the evening of February 24, 1986, the commission seesawed over the resignation issue. Todd Cooke, the savings and loan chairman, had drafted the original language, which stated simply that the MOVE Commission would not make any recommendations regarding the continued service of the mayor or top city officials. For the commission to do otherwise would "arrogate to itself the power which properly belongs to and should be exercised by the electorate," Cooke had written.

Bowser didn't buy it. "We can't tell people who to vote for or not vote for. . . . This commission needs to be careful to avoid any political scapegoating. But we must say something. I'd like to say that the mayor's decision to retain Richmond was ill advised, and he ought to rethink both that and his own position."

Kauffman wasn't crazy about the proposed language either, but for different reasons. To him it constituted an endorsement for Goode to stay in office.

Reverend Paul Washington searched for a middle ground. The commission could express its displeasure with the administration without openly calling for resignations: "Our findings are harsh. They speak loudly for themselves. And in light of these findings, the electorate can reach its own conclusions."

To Monsignor Cullen, the Catholic social worker, it looked as though Bowser were looking for a scapegoat that would get Goode off the hook. "If we say one should go, then all of them should go," he insisted.

The discussion continued into the night. Toward the end Brown suggested that the entire comment be taken out of the record. Bowser countered by calling for a poll of the commissioners. Cooke defended the original comment once again.

Bowser persisted, reading a new version he had jotted on his notepad: "The mayor has to consider the impact his performance on May 13, 1985, has on his continued performance in office. The mayor should also consider whether the fire commissioner should continue in office—"

"We're waltzing around the issue," Commissioner Welch interrupted. "At least the fire commissioner has to go."

Brown suggested that Richmond be given the opportunity to exit gracefully. But Cooke was now agreeing with Cullen: "Either we go all the way and tell them both to quit, or we say nothing."

Welch and Kauffman agreed. The report could simply speak for itself. A consensus seemed to be building, but Bowser saw an opening to go after Richmond once again: "We must make recommendations on each individual.

"We accuse the fire commissioner of homicide," he persisted. "We only accuse the mayor of cowardice and racism."

Cullen retorted, "If we say the fire commissioner must go, and don't say it about the mayor, we are definitely a mayor's commission."

After a few more minutes of debate, Brown took a straw poll. Cullen, Cooke, Kauffman, and Ruth insisted the mayor and Richmond would have to stand or fall together. Bowser, backed up by Washington, Chinn, Lillie, Bronson, and Welch, felt that the commission could recommend Richmond's resignation without demanding that the mayor step down. They weren't saying that the commission *should* make that recommendation, only that it need not link the two men.

The division was probably a fair reflection of public opinion in Philadelphia. But if the MOVE Commission was to have any meaning at all, it would achieve that by searching for and finding some common ground on this, the last and most important recommendation that it would make.

And so, once again, the weary commissioners groped toward compromise. Cooke offered an olive branch. He began to read from his notepad a new version of his original proposal. Once again, he embraced Washington's simple idea: let the report speak for itself. The final decision would lie with the voters.

Finally the consensus coalesced around this proposal. Bowser warned that the black community would be "outraged" if Richmond didn't go, but in the end he voted with the others to adopt Cooke's language.

In its published report, the commission concluded:

> Finally, in our democratic form of government, it is the voters who have the unique responsibility of choosing those who shall govern. The elected officials, in turn, select the key administrators to assist in the operations of government.
>
> The Commission considered at length whether it should make recommendations relative to the retention or termination of elected or appointed senior city officials who had grave responsibilities before and during the May 13, 1985 incident. The Commission has attempted in this report to state its findings fairly and fully. After thoughtful discussion, the Commission concluded that the Report speaks for itself.

If some saw in these words an attempt by the commission to duck the issues, no one could say the same about other conclusions in the report. The language was harsh and uncompromising—which was all the more shocking coming from a panel that had been appointed by the mayor himself:

"The Mayor abdicated his responsibilities as a leader when, after mid-day, he permitted a clearly failed operation to continue which posed great risk to life and property."

In the end, the most controversial part of the report was not the question of resignations that had so troubled the commissioners. Rather, it was an issue of fact that most of them—all but Kauffman—had seen as fairly well settled: police culpability for the shooting in the back alley.

The MOVE Commission had concluded that "police gunfire prevented some occupants of 6221 Osage Avenue from escaping from the burning house to the rear alley." The cornerstone of the MOVE Commission's evidence for this finding was young Birdie Africa's testimony. All of the commissioners but Kauffman had concluded that his testimony before the commission "so clearly supports [the commission's finding] that it is difficult to imagine any individual who saw this child testify or who has had the opportunity to read the transcript of his testimony could possibly reach any other conclusion."

Kauffman wrote a dissent challenging the commission's characterization of the police gunfire as "unconscionable" and its conclusions about the shooting in the back alley.

In light of MOVE's history of violence and the fortifications of the house, Kauffman did not agree that the police gunfire was "clearly excessive and unreasonable" or that "the failure of those responsible . . . to control or stop such an excessive amount of force was unconscionable." In his dissent he wrote:

> The life-threatening task of confronting this terrorist group did not fall to social workers or politicians or lawyers. This dangerous duty was assigned to the police. With the luxury of hindsight, contemplation, and analysis, and without a word of recognition for individual acts of police heroism, this Commission now presumes to second guess the actions taken under fire by those brave officers. This Commission criticizes both the caliber of the weapons the police carried and the number of bullets they fired. This, to me, is unconscionable.

Regarding the shooting in the back alley, he wrote:

> Michael Ward [Birdie Africa] testified that there were two escape attempts. During the first, Conrad Africa, carrying a child, allegedly was driven back in the house by police gunfire. Significantly, Michael did not actually see this surrender attempt. Rather, he remained inside 6221 and testified that he heard shots after Conrad attempted to leave. Moreover, Michael also testified that he had never heard gunshots before in his life and that he could not tell where the shots were coming from or who was firing them. (See testimony of Michael Ward, 10/31/85 at 323 *et seq.*)
>
> Most significantly, both the police and Michael agreed that when he surrendered, neither he nor the others leaving

the house with him were fired upon by anyone. (See testimony of Michael Ward, 10/31/85 at 365–66.) This critical fact strongly corroborates the police version of the events in the alley.

Finally, the record clearly confirms that Officer James Berghaier exposed himself to gunfire and risked his life to save Michael from drowning after he fled from 6221. (See testimony of Officers James Berghaier and Michael Tursi, 11/1/85 at 107 *et seq.*) This heroic act is totally inconsistent with any police attempt to fire on those MOVE members and children who tried to surrender.

One of the recommendations of the MOVE Commission report was that the Philadelphia district attorney convene a grand jury to investigate possible criminal charges arising out of the May 13 confrontation.

Later that year, DA Ron Castille petitioned the court to establish an investigating grand jury to examine the events that had occurred on Osage Avenue. In the summer of 1986, a jury of twenty-three regular jurors and seven alternates was selected by lot from a pool of three hundred Philadelphia voters. Shortly after Labor Day, they began hearing testimony.

Meanwhile, Berghaier continued his long dark plunge into despair. He was no longer living at home. Reassigned to the police pistol range, he was restless and unfocused. He already knew that he was finished as a cop, but the police department bureaucracy was fighting him over his eligibility for disability payments; it feared a flood of similar claims if it granted Berghaier disability pay for a service-related stress disorder.

In February 1987, with the disability issue still unresolved, he left the force. A friend gave him a bartending job. He had never been a heavy drinker, but now he was drinking himself into a fog virtually every night, just to blunt the pain.

At the age of thirty-seven, his career was over. The bills were piling up. His marriage was gone. His kids were probably better off without him. Jim Berghaier had always known where he stood in the world. He knew he'd made a difference to those in his life. Now it seemed he was just dragging them down. He began writing suicide notes.

What was left of his survivor's gut-trusting instinct that had helped him on the street now helped him hang on, to reach out for help.

He was admitted to Philadelphia Psychiatric Center for treatment. The staff put him on a suicide watch, taking away his belt and placing him under continuous observation. Slowly, over a period of weeks, he began to sift through the backlog of guilt and pain, piecing his life together a little at a time.

One evening he saw his picture in the paper, next to a story that reported his admission to the hospital. All of the old feelings came welling back—and along with them his shame at being locked away. It crashed over him as he lay on his bed sobbing.

A nurse came in. The nursing staff didn't know how patients had come to be admitted, but she stopped when she saw the paper with his picture in it.

"That's you, isn't it?" she asked, already knowing the answer. "I want to tell you something," she said to him. "God put you in that alley to save that child. There's a purpose to all of this. Read the Bible. It will all be clear."

Berghaier had never been especially religious, but he was ready to look anywhere for help in understanding what had happened to him. He did not find it in the Bible, but he continued to search.

On May 6, 1987, a Philadelphia grand jury returned indictments against Ernest Edwards, the contractor Goode had handpicked for the reconstruction of Osage Avenue. The report also sharply criticized the role of Goode's administration and the mayor personally in the awarding of the contract to Edwards and the bureaucratic bungling that followed. It charged Edwards, along with his former partner, with stealing more than $200,000 from the project. Edwards, who is black, called the indictments racially motivated. The city housing director, who had overseen the project, resigned abruptly in the wake of the report.

The report came in the midst of a heated primary battle in the mayoral race, and Goode branded the timing of the report "political" and "inflammatory." Running under the cloud of the county as well as a federal grand jury that was convened to look into potential civil rights violations, criticized by yet another grand jury that had investigated the rebuilding of the block, and lambasted by his own commission, Goode had seen his political career written off by many of the experts.

At the beginning of his first term, Goode had enormous political capital among his black constituency. His election as Philadelphia's first black mayor was a historic occasion in the city and a source of enormous pride to the black community. The question in 1987 was whether he would be able to hold on to that loyalty despite the MOVE incident.

The race was full of familiar faces. Goode's challenger in the Democratic primary was former district attorney Edward Rendell, who had himself played a key part in the events leading up to the confrontation. At first, Rendell said that he did not consider Goode's handling of MOVE a campaign issue, and he studiously avoided it. But the primary race turned brutally nasty toward the end. Behind in the polls, Rendell aired commercials showing the burning houses on Osage Avenue. "In the end," the voice-over announced, "Wilson Goode will be remembered for only one thing."

Both of the city's daily papers and *Philadelphia Magazine* endorsed Rendell, but the black vote stayed with Goode during the primary, and he easily defeated Rendell. In the fall he faced another familiar personality: former mayor Frank L. Rizzo.

Rizzo had run against Goode as a Democrat in the 1983 election and lost. Now he'd switched to the Republican party and had taken up the standard against Goode once again. Unlike Rendell, he didn't hesitate to bring up MOVE. He dubbed the mayor "Bomber Goode" and made the MOVE confrontation and the subsequent rebuilding project key campaign issues. He was quick to point out that his own administration's confrontation with MOVE in 1978 had had a very different ending from Goode's in 1985.

In November, Goode was reelected by 14,201 votes—a margin of only 2 percent.

In May of 1988, two years after the probe began and three

years after the fire itself, DA Ron Castille announced that the grand jury had concluded its work without bringing any indictments. The jurors found the decisions that had led to the dropping of the bomb "morally reprehensible" but not illegal. The actions of Goode, Brooks, Sambor, and Richmond may have been poorly thought out, but they did not constitute a crime under the law. An essential requirement—intent—was missing. In addition, the grand jury report specifically disputed the MOVE Commission's finding that police gunfire in the back alley had driven people back into the house.

During his testimony before the grand jury, which was made public in the report, Goode had been shown videotapes and radio transcripts that clearly established that he had given the order to put out the fire at approximately 6:25 P.M.—almost 45 minutes after the fire was first spotted and too late to save the house. He had conceded that there was an "absolute possibility" that the order had come as late as 6:25, but he could not explain why he'd waited so long, other than to say he had expected someone to put the fire out at any moment. The videotapes, which had been time-coded by the television station that supplied them to the grand jury, showed that the flames were rising half a dozen feet into the air before Goode became concerned enough to pick up the phone.

(It is a striking coincidence that his decision to call Brooks and Brooks's order to Sambor to put out the fire came at almost precisely the same moment—and that both came just minutes after the front bunker collapsed. The timing raises the question of whether Goode and Brooks both knew about the decision to let the bunker burn and, like Sambor, waited until the bunker was gone before ordering the fire put out. The grand jury found no witnesses or other evidence that would prove such a scenario, but it remains a possibility.)

The reaction to the grand jury report was loud, often predictable, and in many quarters harsh. The *Daily News* succinctly (and accurately) boiled down the 279 pages of legal and factual analysis into a five-word headline: "MOVE Jury: Stupidity No Crime."

The more staid sister paper of the *Daily News*, the *Inquirer*, approved the grand jury's decision in an editorial.

William B. Lytton III, the chief counsel for the MOVE Commission, angrily disputed the back-alley findings. Only gunfire, he said, could explain why "three ran back into an inferno with an estimated temperature of 2,000 degrees." David Shrager, Birdie's attorney, told a meeting sponsored by the American Friends Service Committee that "every single thing [Birdie] said before the commission, he said before the grand jury, and then some. . . . When you heard from the district attorney that there was no gunfire at any time in the back alley . . . that is utterly false." Shrager, who had been in the grand jury room with Birdie and his father, claimed that Birdie had testified that two children had been forced back into the house by gunfire after they had tried to climb up on the catwalk and onto a tree.

Despite Rendell's earlier campaign rhetoric, he praised the grand jury report. It had come to the same conclusion that he had when he'd first entertained the possibility of calling a grand jury in the summer of 1985. What had happened on May 13 was a result of tragic incompetence, but it was not criminal, he said.

But for the man on the street the grand jury report raised the issue: how was it possible for eleven people to die and a neighborhood to burn without a crime being committed?

The answer to that question requires a careful examination of the law—the grand jury report itself required 279 pages to cover all the issues—but it reveals a great deal about the philosophical underpinnings of the law.

The decision to drop the bomb may have been ill considered, but those involved in the decision understood it to have a limited purpose: their *intention* was to disable the bunker and blow a hole in the roof, not to burn down the house or harm the occupants. Whatever the wisdom of that decision, it was legally permissible for them to use such force to make arrests.

Under the law, it was the decision to let the fire burn that was the most significant from the standpoint of intent. That decision had been made by just two people: Sambor and Richmond. Again, their intent was not to set the house on fire or to drive the occupants out of the house with the fire.

The MOVE Commission suggested that the decision to let the fire burn was, at the very least, criminally reckless. The grand jury, however, concluded that neither Richmond's nor Sambor's conduct rose to the level of criminal recklessness. The report stated that " 'recklessness' has a specific definition under the law":

> A person acts recklessly with respect to a material element of an offense when he consciously disregards a substantial and unjustifiable risk that the material element exists or will result from his conduct. . . .

The key phrase in that tortuous legal definition is *consciously disregards*. Sambor did not "consciously disregard" the risk that the fire might spread if left to burn; in fact, he was concerned enough about it to seek the advice of an expert at the scene—namely, Richmond. And, as the report stated, "A reasonable person would reasonably rely on an expert's opinion."

That, finally, left William Richmond's acts at issue. Though Sambor raised the question, it was in the end his call as to whether to let the fire burn. Once again, it was clear that Richmond did not *intend* the consequences that occurred: the spread of the fire and the loss of life and property. Lacking evidence of intent, he could not be charged with murder or manslaughter. But did he act with recklessness?

Again, the legal question turned on whether Richmond had *consciously disregarded* the risks of letting the fire burn. Testimony from fire expert Charles King suggested that Richmond had been right when he told Sambor that he could control the small fire that burned on the roof at the time. What he didn't consider, however, was the possibility that the fire might burn down into the structure of the roof and weaken it so much that the bunker would fall through. By Richmond's own admission, he simply didn't think of it: "I did not factually follow that through," he told the grand jury. "It was a unique kind of thing. It was something I had never seen in twenty-seven years. I guess in retrospect I certainly could have pursued it with Mr. Sambor. . . . I just did not follow through with that logic. . . ."

King's testimony suggested how Richmond might have overlooked the risk that the fire might spread out of control. He said that Richmond's conclusion that the fire could burn the bunker and still be put out was a "fair call"; because fires generally burn upward, it would be reasonable to assume that the bunker would burn without involving the rooftop. His answer to Sambor's question, King said, was reasonable, though tragically mistaken.

Some legal analysts criticized the grand jury findings, saying that there is enough latitude in these statutory definitions to establish at least recklessness, if not actual intent. But academic dissections of legal prose ignore the terrible reality of the circumstances. It was Richmond himself who described those circumstances most vividly in the grand jury report:

> There is no way you can recreate Osage Avenue in this room. You cannot do it. When you looked up at that bunker, it was just the most awesome thing you ever saw in your life. To say you were scared—everyone was scared. There were bullets ricocheting over the streets, which was frightening, for a long, extended period of time. I did not make the decision I normally make. I have a good history in Philadelphia. If I didn't make those decisions on that day, I feel—maybe they cannot be excused, but they certainly should have taken some consideration to the environment that we were working in at the time.

The grand jury's findings on the decision to drop the bomb and let the fire burn turned on legal analysis—a judgment call—but the facts that the grand jury had found were essentially in agreement with those of the MOVE Commission. In its other major conclusion, however, the grand jury flatly contradicted the MOVE Commission's key factual finding: it found that police had not shot at MOVE members in the back alley.

In part that conclusion was based on testimony from cops

who had not appeared before the MOVE Commission, but the report also criticized the commission's interpretation of its own evidence. The commission, the report said, had jumped to conclusions that weren't warranted by the facts—just as Commissioner Kauffman had warned in his dissent.

The commission had based its finding about the back alley on a relative handful of evidence: statements by "earwitnesses" that they heard what sounded like automatic gunfire and .22-caliber shots in the back alley; the testimony of Detective Stephenson that Sergeant Griffiths had said he'd "dropped" a MOVE member in the back alley and its apparent corroboration by Battalion Chief Skarbeck of the fire department; and, most important, Birdie Africa's videotaped testimony.

The "earwitness" testimony was the vaguest of the three. By the time the MOVE members had left the house that evening, Osage Avenue was a cacophony of noise. There were all the sounds that accompany a fire that is burning out of control: windowpanes shattering from the heat, aerosol cans exploding, electrical wires crackling, and the roar of the flames themselves. But there were also countless rounds of ammunition left behind in the abandoned police posts and the houses that the insertion teams had entered, as well as whatever bullets, explosives, and fuels MOVE had stockpiled in 6221.

More important, according to Mark Gottlieb and the grand jury report, the grand jury considered the testimony of the "earwitnesses" according to their proximity to the alley itself. Not surprisingly, the recollections of those who were the farthest from the alley tended to be inconsistent and contradictory. Fewer of the witnesses who had been close to the alley thought that they had heard automatic gunfire. Among those who had a direct view of the alley itself—fire fighters as well as cops—not one testified that he had heard automatic gunfire—although many of them had heard the half dozen or so shots fired by the MOVE member with his .22 rifle.

Detective Stephenson's testimony that he thought he'd overheard Sergeant Griffiths say he "dropped" a MOVE member in the alley also proved to have a number of flaws. Stephenson wasn't sure he'd heard Griffiths correctly; he was standing next to the diesel engine of the crane, on Osage Avenue, and Griffiths was at least fifty feet away, on the walkway in the alley. Second, Stephenson could not produce the notes he claimed to have made at the time; the originals had disappeared from his cubbyhole at the office, and he had only a "copy" of them to refer to.

Griffiths, meanwhile, testified before the grand jury that he'd pointed out to investigators the spot where the male had "dropped" out of sight in the smoke.

Skarbeck, whose statements to the MOVE Commission had seemed to corroborate Stephenson's testimony, clarified his statements before the grand jury. He was sure that the man he had seen had not been Griffiths at all.

The grand jury also differed with the MOVE Commission's evaluation of Birdie's testimony. Birdie testified before the grand jury itself, but the report noted that the MOVE Commission's findings weren't even justified by what Birdie had told the commission, much less by what he testified to later.

Even assuming that Birdie's recollections were accurate (his testimony on other points was confused and inconsistent), the simple fact remains that he did *not* tell the MOVE Commission that police gunfire had prevented people in the house from escaping into the rear alley.

He said that when Conrad opened the hatch, the police started shooting. But from inside the garage, he could not see them shoot; he simply heard sounds that he assumed were police gunfire. He could not tell where they were coming from; it could have been the noise of the fire or exploding ammunition. It could have been MOVE members shooting at police from the upper floors. It could have been Conrad or another MOVE member shooting.

But whatever it was, it occurred at least several minutes *before* anyone left the house, not while they were in the back alley. Birdie did not testify that he witnessed any police gunfire *while he was in the alley*. He did not say that the other children returned to the house because they were being shot at; in fact, he didn't know what happened to the children after they were lost in the smoke.

According to the public report, his testimony before the grand jury offered even less support for the murder-in-the-back-alley theory. He testified that Conrad opened the door, heard gunfire, and shut the door again. It was only then, Birdie testified, that the adults began to yell that the kids were coming out. After the door was opened again and the people started to come out, Birdie testified, he neither saw nor heard police fire their guns.

The only witness who has refused to testify about the back alley is Ramona Africa. But her behavior that day also suggests that police did not fire. Numerous witnesses testified that she walked slowly along the fence, in full view of the cops. She stopped and looked back a number of times, at one point stamping her foot as if in frustration when the others did not follow her. Twice she bent over the fence and tried to help Birdie climb up. She never tried to take cover from the cops or to shield herself or Birdie. Earlier in the day, by contrast, people three and four blocks away could be seen diving under cars and behind porch steps when the gunfire erupted.

The one area where the grand jury could have brought indictments but chose not to, according to Mark Gottlieb, were perjury charges related to the cover-up. Both Klein and Connor lied in their testimony before the grand jury, denying or obscuring their use of C-4 and where they had obtained it. Connor later returned and admitted that he'd lied in order to protect FBI agent Macy. Klein was not recalled.

In the end, the decision not to issue indictments against Connor and Klein came down to a judgment call, taking into account both the nature of the deception and the motives behind it: "Ending this massive investigation by charging a few front-line officers would not serve any purpose . . . when it was the city's high and appointed officials who were at least morally responsible for this great tragedy."

Since 1987, Jim Berghaier has won a personal battle or two: he feels he is past the suicidal stage, and inch by inch he is creeping away from the edge of the abyss. But he will never be the man he was. His marriage is beyond repair. With his history of mental illness, he can no longer be a shopping mall guard, much less a cop.

His search for the meaning of what happened to him is not over. So far, it has yielded no flash of insight that would make him whole again. His victories have been small and hard-won, and the struggle is far from over.

He has come to understand—and is beginning to accept—the fact that he cannot control his world. It is not an easy thing to do, for it means that he must face the world without that inner confidence that carried him through those dark and dangerous nights on the Granny Squad.

Jim Berghaier was not the only cop whose life was shattered by the events of May 13. All of them who were out there that day have become casualties in some sense. Some have suffered more than others.

In November 1987 the Philadelphia Police Department granted 70 percent disability pensions to four officers: William Klein, described in a psychiatric report as suffering from nightmares, suicidal depression, and "thoughts of shooting the mayor and other city officials"; James Berghaier; Daniel Angelucci; and Sergeant Donald Griffiths. A panel of psychiatrists concluded that all of them suffered from posttraumatic stress disorder as a result of the May 13 siege. Griffiths took an extended sick leave and left the department in December 1987. Angelucci quit the force in October. Klein officially left in November.

Tommy Mellor is still a cop, still working on the Granny Squad. Of the people who were in the back alley that day, he seems the least affected—at least outwardly. Berghaier sees Mellor as the rock-solid foundation of his old team, the kind of guy who simply lets trouble roll off his back.

But Mellor says that he is not the same person that he was before May 13. When he was trapped in the closet by gunfire, he was convinced he would die there, and he made his peace. Since then, he says, he likes to be by himself more. He used to feel that he had too little time and too many obligations to do all the things he'd always wanted to do. Now he makes the time. In the summer of 1988 he got onto his motorcycle and took a trip out west, all by himself, just to have time to think.

What worries Berghaier are the walking wounded—the cops he's heard about who are still on the force and carrying their pain inside them. He was surprised, after he testified before the MOVE Commission, when a burly cop quietly told him, "Don't think I haven't cried a few nights about what happened out there." His friends who are still on the force say that there are cops who are ready to crack but won't seek help, either because they're too proud or because they fear it will ruin their careers. He's afraid that when they do crack, it will be with a badge on their chest and a gun in their hand, and they're going to hurt either themselves or someone else.

Several months after the grand jury issued its findings, the U.S. Justice Department tersely announced that a federal grand jury probe had concluded without bringing any indictments. Barring any unforeseen developments, the criminal investigations of the police action of May 13, 1985, are closed.

That does not mean, of course, that the story is over. Civil suits brought by relatives of those who died are still pending. In 1987, one of the displaced residents shot and nearly killed his lawyer, angered by the city's low settlement offer and the lawyer's hefty cut of it. An estimate in 1987 put the total price tag for the MOVE confrontation at nearly $18 million. And that did not include the costs of the three grand jury investigations or any money that the city may eventually have to pay in damages awarded in civil suits.

The city's handling of MOVE quickly became a political touchstone. Only five days after the tragedy, U.S. Attorney General Edwin Meese said that Goode's handling of MOVE was "a good example for all of us to take note of." (Later, his chief spokesman "clarified" that statement, saying that the attorney general had been referring to the mayor's candor in explaining things to the public.) A documentary produced by Philadelphia's PBS station saw racist overtones in the confrontation, suggesting that it was but the latest chapter in a long history of violence against black neighborhoods—and apparently ignoring the fact that a black mayor and black managing director had explicitly approved the dropping of the bomb as well as the entire police operation that day.

The confrontation even became the subject of ads. One ad proposed in 1985, before the rebuilding delays surfaced, was designed to promote the city to outside businesses and potential residents. Headlined "Home for Christmas," it praised the mayor's pledge to the displaced residents of Osage Avenue as an example of how Philadelphians look after their own. The ad never ran, but two years after the tragedy a fire insurance ad in the city subways showed a picture of Earl and Pearl Watkins of Osage Avenue. The copy read:

> "Thank God we had Hanover Mutual Fire Insurance!" Do you?
>
> By 10:30 on the night of the MOVE catastrophe, the roof of Earl and Pearl Watkins' home was in the basement. Like all victims of the MOVE disaster, they had lost everything. *Unlike* many of the others, the Watkinses received a check from Hanover Mutual Fire Insurance *2 days later.*

Today the scars of Philadelphia's long and bloody conflict with MOVE remain. In Powelton Village, wildflowers grow where the MOVE headquarters once stood. On Osage Avenue, a block of uncharacteristically modern row houses stands out among the older homes. In a suburb of Philadelphia, Michael Ward—formerly Birdie Africa—lives a quiet middle-class existence with his father, who has never been involved with MOVE. Ramona Africa is in prison. Vincent Leaphart and ten of his followers have been buried.

And at another house in west Philadelphia, people live without heat and electricity, wear their hair in dreadlocks, and eat raw food. They are living by the principles of their founder and leader, a man who, it is said, can never die: the Coordinator, John Africa.

13
MOVE Today

ON DECEMBER 5, 1985, construction workers rebuilding Osage Avenue stopped working as a group of some sixty mourners came to bear witness to what had happened on that spring day more than six months before. From Cobbs Creek, the mourners continued to Whitemarsh Memorial Park in Montgomery County where the remains of Vincent Leaphart and Frank James were finally laid to rest. Five other cemeteries had refused to accept the bodies.

Uncle and nephew were buried together, without coffins, wrapped in white sheets, in a seven- by seven-foot grave—as close in death as they had been in life. No prayers were recited. No hymns were sung.

But angry words were cast out upon the chill air. Among the pallbearers that day was the Reverend Jesse Jackson. "People have been murdered," he told the crowd of mourners and reporters. "We cannot be in a state of rest until justice has been done."

After Jackson left—and with him most of the reporters—family and friends surrounded the grave, weeping bitterly. Their voices raised in unison, they recited:

> In natural law we trust.
> All praise is to the order of life.
> The power of truth is final.
> Long live MOVE.
> Long live Revolution.
> · Long live John Africa.
> Long live John Africa.
> Long live John Africa.

And then Louise, looking toward the oaks and fir trees surrounding the gravesite, said of her younger brother and her only son, "They are close to nature."

The body of Rhonda Harris Ward Africa lies in St. Albans Cemetery in the West Oak Lane section of Philadelphia. Every Mother's Day Andino Ward brings his son to this place to talk to his mother. He stands away from the grave and lets Michael speak his private thoughts. And as Michael Moses Ward, his mother's Birdie, stands before her grave, his father says that "he does not cry. He does not show emotion."

He has a new life now, living in a suburb of Philadelphia with his father, stepmother, and half-sisters. Andino Ward thought he had lost his son forever when Rhonda divorced him and, later, joined MOVE. He had enlisted in the air force and had been sent overseas. In 1978, he says, he had come to the MOVE house looking for his son and had been driven away by threats against his life. He created a life for himself that did not include Rhonda or the child she had renamed Birdie. The fire reunited father and son. The first time Birdie saw him in the hospital, he instantly knew that his father had come for him. They have been together ever since.

A year after the fire, Michael had truly become a "life style" teenager. His hair was short, he went to school, he watched television, and the things he wanted were what so many other teenage boys want: new Nikes, a GT Performer bike, a skateboard. Just ordinary things.

Michael has had to testify many times about what happened on May 13—in William Brown's offices, before the grand jury, at the trial of Ramona Africa. Each time brings Michael nights filled with dreams of inescapable fires. He has had three operations to repair the scars left by the fire, and he will undergo at least six more. He also has before him a lawsuit filed on his behalf charging that the city of Philadelphia violated his civil rights.

Soon Michael will come of age. His father's greatest fear is that he will someday choose to return to MOVE. MOVE members such as Alberta Africa hope that he will come home to them: "He's said that he still loves MOVE—that he loves all of us—and we all love him. That's all that's needed or important."

The only other survivor of the fire, Ramona Africa, is serving seven years in Muncy State Correctional Institution on riot and conspiracy charges arising out of the confrontation. She has been eligible for parole since 1986, but only on the condition that she agree not to associate with other MOVE members. She has refused to accept those terms and so remains in prison.

She is angry about what has become of her "little brother" Birdie. "The system has given him schoolbooks, a bike, candy—and murdered his mother, to perpetuate the belief that MOVE is wrong and the system is right."

She is also angry, but not surprised, at the grand jury's decision not to indict. Like all followers of John Africa, she does not accept the legal analysis of the grand jury. She believes that the decision, like her conviction, was a foregone conclusion.

Though she would not testify before the grand jury, she refuses to accept any responsibility for the lack of indictments. In a rambling, single-spaced statement in response to the grand jury report, she wrote:

> People have the *gaul* to question *me*, try to blame *me* in some way for the grand jury's refusal to indict any officials because I wouldn't go along with this system's charade and testify before the grand jury, but I ain't acceptin that responsibility because it don't belong to me. If the District Attorney's office was *serious* about prosecutin officials and thought that testimony from me was *necessary, important* to getting indictments they would have *subpoenaed* me, *made* me come to court to testify, which would have been easy since I'm in their custody, but they *didn't* do that because they never had any intention of prosecutin officials for murderin MOVE members or anything else.

The DA's office has said that it did not subpoena Ramona

because she had made it clear that she did not wish to cooperate, and therefore any attempt to force her to cooperate would have been unproductive.

City officials say they have taken steps to be sure the tragedy of May 13 can never be repeated. As examples, they point to improved procedures and additional training for bomb squad personnel and an ongoing "dialogue" with the MOVE organization.

Others aren't so sure that the city isn't painting itself into the same corner once again by adopting a policy of appeasement and special treatment for MOVE supporters. In February 1988 news broke that the city had spent some $50,000 to tutor nine MOVE children at home. The school district had gone to court to force MOVE members to send their children to school, but the city intervened and offered to pay for private tutoring through its Department of Human Services (DHS). The revelation came at a time when DHS was severely underfunded and understaffed; news reports had revealed several children who had died of child abuse because caseworkers could not keep up with their caseloads. The tutoring program was unprecedented for healthy school-age children; tutoring had been reserved for students who were temporarily disabled or whose disabilities made travel to school impossible.

In the wake of the revelations, angry taxpayers and parents flooded the school superintendent's office with calls. City Councilman Brian O'Neill wrote to Goode that the tutoring deal was made "in the spirit of appeasement and fear which have predominated our experience with MOVE. . . . Special privileges for MOVE people must cease." The city's new managing director, James White, said that the tutoring program was economically pragmatic, because the alternatives—putting the MOVE children in foster care and sending them to special education classes at the schools—would be more expensive. He also said that home tutoring had helped to prevent further violent confrontations with MOVE. He added, however, that the city should be able to begin phasing out the tutoring soon. Mayor Goode declined to comment.

By May 1988, approximately forty civil suits had been filed against the city in connection with the events on Osage Avenue. At that time two suits had been dismissed, two withdrawn, one settled, and another partially settled. None had come to trial. Among the plaintiffs are Michael Moses Ward (formerly Birdie Africa), Ramona Africa, Louise James, numerous relatives of those who died in the fire, and the estate of Vincent Leaphart Africa.

Of the MOVE members still in jail, nine are serving terms of thirty to one hundred years for the killing of officer James Ramp. Consuella Dotson Africa was acquitted of Ramp's murder but is serving time on a conviction for conspiracy and aggravated assault arising out of the 1978 confrontation. Alphonso Robbins Africa, convicted just before the 1985 fire on charges of assault and making terroristic threats, is still in prison. At least six other MOVE members and sympathizers are in prison on an assortment of charges; MOVE reports that it has also recruited many new members among inmates. Of those still in prison, Consuella lost two daughters in the fire: Katricia and Zanetta; Janine lost her son Phil; Janet lost her daughter Delitia; and Sue Levino Africa lost her son Tomaso. City officials count approximately seventeen MOVE members and sympathizers who are known to be living in several houses in the city.

By an odd coincidence, Alberta Wicker Africa was released from the state prison for women in Muncy, Pennsylvania, on May 13, 1988—three years to the day after the fire. She served every day of her seven-year sentence that had resulted from the 1978 charges and had learned of the May 13 confrontation while she was in prison. She refused an early parole that would have required her not to associate with other MOVE members.

She was married, according to MOVE law, to Vincent Leaphart Africa and lived with him not only at the Powelton headquarters but also while he was in Rochester. Today she is considered by some to be his logical successor as leader of MOVE. She denies that she is MOVE's leader; the organization has no leaders, she says: "John Africa has always taught that you lead yourself."

Two months after she was released from prison, Alberta Africa agreed to meet with us to talk about MOVE today. She has not spoken to other journalists since her release.

We met her in a park in west Philadelphia on a stifling summer afternoon. Accompanied by Alphonso's wife Mary and MOVE supporter Beverly Williams and their children, she told us about MOVE's philosophy and what the future may hold for the organization.

She is a short woman with dreadlocks that reach to her waist. She is soft-spoken and quick to smile. At times her voice rises in anger, but she has an air of gentleness and patience about her. She would make a good schoolteacher.

How has the fire affected the MOVE organization? It has been a terrible blow, she acknowledges, but MOVE continues to fight for the good of life, for clean air, pure water, and healthy children.

There are fewer followers now, but she is confident that they will prevail in the end. "John Africa can take a handful of people and turn things around. John Africa teaches that a lie is weak but the truth is powerful. Look at the power of the sun— but the sun only numbers one."

Will there be confrontations? "That is not up to us." But she says that John Africa had predicted the two great confrontations and that MOVE would then enter a different phase in which its confrontations with the system would not be violent.

Today, she says, MOVE's role is still to teach. More immediately, however, it is to obtain the release of its jailed members, including those who were convicted of killing James Ramp in 1978. She still maintains the innocence of those convicted; that is the cause that the people on Osage Avenue died for, and it is the primary thrust of the organization's efforts.

MOVE is not recruiting new members right now, she said, because so much of the group's energy is concentrated on getting its family out of jail. Meanwhile, everyday life within the group goes on as it has before. It has been nearly twenty years since the principles of MOVE philosophy were first laid down. In that time, people have come and gone. Children have been born; families have been raised. In Alberta's view, the truths of MOVE have been translated into actual fact. They have raised their children without the benefit of diapers, letting them lie naked in the grass in summer. They have raised them without toys and most modern conveniences. Today the children of MOVE are healthy and strong, she said. They do not get sick. Their teeth are strong and free of cavities.

The family of MOVE is stronger than many know, she said. There is the core of members, those who are "committed to the death for life, our belief, John Africa." There are others, MOVE supporters, who are "working to become committed." And there are some who subscribe to MOVE's philosophy but keep a low profile. Some live "underground," disguised as life style people, holding down regular jobs. MOVE even has underground members in the Philadelphia Police Department, she said.

It is difficult for those who do not know of MOVE personally to possess a clear picture of the group, she claimed. The media is "working for the government," she said, and has consistently distorted their way of life, calling them filthy, calling them cultists. "MOVE is not a cult," she said, her dark eyes flashing with anger. "We're not involved in drugs and free sex. MOVE people are loyal. John Africa teach MOVE to be clean, to marry, to have one mate for life.

"MOVE is not a cult," she repeated. "I want it to be very clear that John Africa teach what is right. John Africa is no Jim Jones or Charles Manson. John Africa is a godly man, wise and clean."

We asked her about Jesse Jackson, about the fact that he had spoken at Vincent's funeral despite MOVE's demonstrations against him in the 1970s. She emphasized that the burial of Vincent and Frank was in the hands of Louise James, who is no longer a MOVE member and whom she brands a "traitor" to MOVE. As for Jackson, she said, "He's just a politician. He

knows we demonstrated against him. He was a pallbearer at
the funeral out of guilt, and he used it as a political move. But
aside from that, what else has he done for us? What's he done
to try and get our innocent people out of prison? Have you ever
heard his voice raised in MOVE's behalf since May 13 or
before it?"

She said that she is "satisfied" with the grand jury report,
"in the sense that it's what we expected. It makes things easier
for us, because it makes John Africa's point. We told people
there's no justice in this system, and now they can see it for
themselves.

"Obviously we would not oppose those people being indicted. They killed our family. But we have a belief that teach
if anybody violates life, they will pay for that violation. We
don't have to lift a finger against them. They'll do it to
themselves. Their own conscience will do it. Look at Geist, the
cop who beat Delbert on August 8—he was shot in the face and
killed by his own wife. Meanwhile Delbert is alive and well."

We asked Alberta a question that many have put to the
organization over the years. If civilization is so bad, why do
they live in the cities? Why doesn't MOVE just go off and live
on a mountain?

"Going off in the woods wouldn't solve anything. Eventually the same disease that afflicted these woods would follow us
there.

"We're here in the cities because we've got some serious
work to do, informing people of the serious wrong they're
inflicting on life. But we want to be left the fuck alone while
we're doing our work. That's the message we've been trying to
convey to these officials for years now: leave MOVE alone."

We suggested that that was precisely what Clifford Bond
said the neighbors on Osage Avenue wanted.

"Well, we didn't come into their living rooms," she countered. "We didn't prevent them from walking down their own
street. We didn't put them out of their homes. The city did.

"But we have an obligation to speak out. This system is
wrong for jailing innocent MOVE people, and anybody right,

fair-minded, wouldn't oppose us fighting for our family's freedom."

Alberta had once told a reporter that MOVE would cycle its own children rather than give them up to the system. But she now says that statement was a way of explaining MOVE's position about giving in to the system. "We won't allow them to enslave us or our children. We intend to be free. I was using the example of the Maccabees when they were fighting the Romans; rather than giving in to Rome's slavery, they jumped from a cliff with their children."

She had harsh words for Andino Ward. She believes that he is using his son to win a lot of money in lawsuits against the city. And yet MOVE has filed similar suits. Yes, she said, but those suits were filed "not because we want money, but because the system loves money. The MOVE organization is gonna use that money to put pressure on the system for being wrong, to push them to do right."

All that has happened to MOVE has a higher meaning, she believes. "Nothing happens to MOVE that ain't meant to happen.

"You know, we were told years ago that people might someday have to cycle for this revolution. We were told everything we'd be facing years before it happened. We were told some people would have to spend a lot of years in prison for John Africa. We were told that if we weren't able to handle it, we'd be given something else to do. We have chosen to do what we're doing, out of our commitment and loyalty to John Africa, life, this revolution.

"Long live John Africa!"

Epilogue
Reflections, Personal and Political

THIS STORY HAS NO tidy ending. Even now, some four years after the bomb was dropped, its effects reverberate in the lives it has touched.

Following a brief stint on the lecture circuit, Gregore Sambor retired and is now living in Delaware County outside of Philadelphia. Leo Brooks is reportedly living in Virginia; his occupation is unknown. William Richmond continued to serve as fire commissioner for three years; in 1988, a few months after the grand jury released its findings, he took an early retirement. He continues to live in northeast Philadelphia. Mayor Wilson Goode, reelected in 1987, will serve until 1991, when, under the rules of the city charter, he will be ineligible to run for a third consecutive term. He has said that his plans after that are uncertain; he would like to teach.

Berghaier, Klein, Griffiths, and Angelucci continue to receive disability payments for service-related stress disorders. Klein eventually received his broker's license and sells real estate in Delaware. Frank Powell is still with the force though not with the bomb squad; he has been reassigned several times since May 1985.

Sergeant Ed Connor retired in 1986 and now is chief of police in a small town in central Pennsylvania. In an interview with the *Philadelphia Inquirer*, he said, "I can't go back to Philadelphia without my stomach knotting up. I don't think a day goes by that I don't have some thoughts about it. Mostly I feel for the guys that were involved. They were all good people, and they did the best that they could."

Today, most of the original residents of the block have returned. It is easy to pick out the streets that were destroyed; the contrast in architecture with the surrounding blocks is jarring. But that, of course, is the least of the changes that have come to the neighborhood. Even now, years later, television cameras and news reporters are not an unusual sight on Osage Avenue, as new developments continue to emerge. Louise James no longer lives at 6221; after the city condemned the property, it refused to sell it back to her. Of the neighbors who remain, many are still angry. Most simply want to be left alone.

The house at 6221 Osage is indistinguishable from the others on the street. There is nothing about it today to suggest the terrible events that happened there. The alley in back is likewise new, though it follows the general contours of the old one.

It is probably possible to find bullet holes in the brick facades of some of the houses in surrounding blocks, and perhaps even some slugs buried in the woodwork. But those are details easily overlooked. Most of the time, the neighborhood of Cobbs Creek is quiet.

There are many questions about the events of May 13 that will always remain unanswered. There is, for example, the question of who was shooting at Powell and the others as they huddled in the upstairs closet. Powell is still convinced that MOVE was shooting through the walls. The others aren't so sure. There is a good chance that the bullets that ripped through the wall came from a .50-caliber machine gun that the police had set up in the upstairs window of Post 1—that the bullets passed through the front of the MOVE house and kept going right through the side. Another theory is that they actually came from the opposite direction, through the front windows of 6223, from the police post at the western end of Osage Avenue.

Another mystery remains at the very core of this story: what happened inside the house on May 13? Was anyone killed in those morning hours? Did MOVE map out a strategy that would result in its destruction?

Angelucci thought he saw a body in the debris on the front porch during the morning assault on the house. The next day, police officers found the headless body of Vincent Leaphart among the rubble of the porch. The amount of debris found above and below the body suggested that he had been on the first-floor level—not in the basement or on the second floor— when he died. Laboratory analysis of his lungs showed that he died from causes other than the fire.

But his body was so badly damaged that investigators could not establish precisely when or how he had died. And Birdie later testified that Vincent Leaphart was alive that evening— he says, in fact, that it was Vincent Leaphart who finally made the decision to send the kids out of the burning house.

What actually happened? It is possible—indeed, probable— that Birdie was mistaken. The garage was pitch-black that evening; Birdie was, by his own testimony, dizzy from smoke and lack of food; his account of other events that day is confused. Perhaps Vincent Leaphart had been in the garage earlier; perhaps Birdie mistook someone else's voice for his in the darkness.

If, in fact, Vincent Leaphart did die on that porch in the first hours after dawn, we can only guess at the effect his death might have had on the others in the house. But it may help to explain why most of the MOVE members chose to stay in the burning house that evening. For fifteen years, this man had guided his people through confrontations with the system again and again—and won. He'd taught them everything they knew about the world. Some of them, like Frank, he'd virtually raised since childhood.

Knowing that he was dead, would this house full of his most devoted followers give themselves up without a fight to everything John Africa hated? Would they give the police a double victory—their own surrender and the knowledge that the police had destroyed the heart and soul of MOVE? Would they now emerge into the glaring lights of the television cameras like whipped dogs—their leader gone and their resistance shattered? It is only speculation, but it is easy to imagine the adults gathering together during one of the lulls that morning and vowing in the name of John Africa that they would remain in that house and fight until every man, woman, and child among them was dead.

And it is possible to imagine that resolve faltering in the final moments—to envision the last desperate attempt to get the children out of the house; to see Conrad in the back alley, perhaps thinking that the cops had opened fire on the kids, perhaps believing that he had to provide cover fire so they could escape; and to envision their final confused retreat back into the house as tons of fiery debris collapsed at last through the basement ceiling.

Prosecutor Mark Gottlieb, who directed the two-year grand jury inquiry, wrestled with the legal and factual questions of the MOVE case. When we interviewed him six months after the grand jury report was issued, Gottlieb said that he was "absolutely comfortable" with the decision not to return indictments. Police and city officials did many things wrong that day, he says, but they did not commit a crime.

Gottlieb has worked under three Philadelphia district attorneys since 1976. As head of the rape unit and then the homicide unit, he has investigated and prosecuted some of the ugliest crimes in the city. Still, he says, this case terrified him.

When he first began reviewing the evidence, making out charts showing where each witness had been that day, reviewing the testimony and evidence gathered by the MOVE Commission, the statements and opinions and theories that clouded the events of May 13, he did not know where it all would lead. What scared him was the thought of finding out that cops had cold-bloodedly murdered the men, women, and children of MOVE as they tried to escape the burning house that evening. "That was the bleakest, most sinister thing that could have been lurking here," he says. "I was afraid that I would find an act of utter evil at the bottom of this case."

For more than two years, he searched for evidence of that evil. He did not find it, he says, because it wasn't there to find.

The tragedy of May 13, he says, is not that those in charge were evil. It was that they were trying to do the right thing but, in an act of collective misjudgment, brought disaster instead.

From the standpoint of criminal liability, says Gottlieb, the essence of the case was not the fire, or even the deaths. It was the decision to let the fire burn and the intent behind that decision. That is why, Gottlieb says, one of the key questions in the investigation was Sambor's state of mind. For Gottlieb, the crucial question was *why* Sambor wanted to let the fire burn. If he was trying to neutralize the bunker, he was guilty of a tragic misjudgment. If, on the other hand, Sambor was using the fire to try to drive the people out of the house—if he was using the fire against the people rather than the bunker— then, Gottlieb says, "I would have charged him with murder."

That, he says, is why Sambor's precise whereabouts during those thirty minutes between 6:00 P.M. and 6:30 are so important. The first fragmentary evidence seemed to suggest that Sambor spent all of that time in Post 1—that he deliberately waited until *after* the bunker had collapsed through the roof and the second floor was in flames before he went looking for Richmond.

Later evidence, however, changed that picture. The multitude of witnesses who saw Sambor during that time could not have known why Gottlieb and the other investigators were so interested in Sambor's whereabouts. Nor did they know what other witnesses had said. But a consistent picture emerged from their testimony. Sambor was in and out of Post 1 during that half hour. At some point before the burning bunker collapsed into the second floor, he sought out Richmond.

It is Richmond's testimony, Gottlieb says, that provides the most convincing evidence of Sambor's state of mind. Had the initial theory been correct, Sambor would have borne sole responsibility for the tragedy that followed. Richmond would have walked away with his reputation and his career intact. Instead, he risked his job, his reputation, and perhaps even his freedom by acknowledging that he had shared in the decision to let the fire burn.

As for evidence of malice on the part of Sambor or the others, Gottlieb says that there is "absolutely none. We were considering every charge up to and including murder. We were looking high and low for malice. And we couldn't find it.

"Remember that the whole world was watching. If you're going to murder somebody, you don't do it on national TV."

When the grand jury report was issued, it was criticized harshly by many. Gottlieb maintains that those criticisms stem from a misunderstanding of the facts or the applicability of the law and that people's perception of the intentions of those involved have been colored by the results of their actions.

He is angered by suggestions that the grand jury was railroaded into its decision by the district attorney's office. "It ignores the responsibilities that a prosecutor has. We have a legal canon of ethics that we are sworn to abide by. You don't go into a grand jury and present an unfair or biased case. You work with a grand jury, in good faith, and you try to reflect the consensus that you perceive from them.

"If we had simply wanted to make a clear-cut case, with no shades of gray, it would have been easy to do. We could have channeled the evidence to get a desired result. But we didn't. We presented over 150 witnesses and every piece of evidence we could uncover. We didn't hold anything back."

He points, for example, to the issue of charging Connor or Klein with perjury. It would have been easy, he says, for the DA's office to have swept that issue under the rug and avoid the controversy that he knew would follow it. "But we brought it all before the grand jury. We didn't try to cover it up."

If, as some of his critics say, the cops killed the people in the back alley and then conspired to cover up the murder, it would have been a conspiracy so vast, and so perfect, that it involved not only all of the cops, but also fire fighters and civilians. To attribute such a conspiracy to the same bureaucracy that bungled the C-4 cover-up so badly is virtually incredible, he says.

Beyond that, he says, the physical evidence is incontrovertible: "Birdie wasn't injured by gunfire. Ramona was not shot. There were no bodies found in the back alley—whatever you can say about the quality of the crime scene processing, there's no question that all the bodies in the back were found huddled together within the walls of the house. They couldn't have been thrown back inside the house—the hatch was too small, and the alley was too hot. And by the next day the whole scene was buried under six feet of smoking rubble."

Gottlieb also gave great weight to the testimony of Pete Kane and another reporter at the scene, neither of whom heard automatic gunfire during the evening hours of May 13. Finally, he says, the evidence is clear that *police* were fired on in the back alley—and that they therefore had a legal right to return fire. Why, then, would officers perjure themselves to cover up acts that were not criminal?

The failure to bring indictments, Gottlieb says, does not diminish the fact that terrible wrongs were committed on May 13, 1985. "We spent two years examining what happened that day. You can't do that and not feel how tragic that day was. You can't help but feel the outrage over what was permitted to happen.

"But outrage isn't enough to convict someone of a crime. As a prosecutor, you can't act out of emotion. It is the function of the prosecutor to apply the law to the facts."

Wouldn't prosecuting the officers for perjury have provided a public airing of the incident?

"It would have provided a public airing," Gottlieb agrees, "but to the detriment of the commonwealth. The defense would argue that it was unfair to prosecute the front-line officers when the people who made the decisions got off scot-free."

Is there a lesson to be learned from the tragedy of May 13? Gottlieb sees two. "First, you can't let any organization hold a city hostage. You can't let them control the situation the way MOVE controlled this situation. The moment that there is a violation of law, you take action."

The second lesson? It is a simple one, though often over-looked. "Think before you act. You can't act out of haste. You can't act out of anger. You can't make these deadly decisions in thirty seconds.

"It's almost impossible to imagine what it was like out there that day. You had a police commissioner under the gun, a neighborhood evacuated, a mayor who abdicated responsibility, and everyone wanting to get it over with before the evening news came on. They should have said 'Let's pull back and consider the options.' But the pressure was enormous, and they didn't."

Clifford Bond has also looked for the lessons of that day. He has long pondered the meaning of this story. Why, he wonders, did it happen to him?

What is wrong, he asks, with a world in which the rules do not work, in which a government will not safeguard its innocent citizens from hate, harassment, and violence?

For him, the events of May 13 have destroyed his faith in justice. "People sense there's no justice anymore," he says. "I see total chaos coming. People will take the law into their own hands."

Bond, a religious man, looks for answers in the Bible. "I've been let down by human beings," he says. "I believe in God. I believe the Lord is gonna come through all of this shining like a large sheet of armor."

Jim Berghaier continues to search for the meaning of what has happened to him.

He came to my house one day last summer to talk about May 13 and what it's done to his life. He arrived one evening after umpiring a softball game, running through the first spatters of rain.

He talked about how those events have destroyed his career, his marriage, his sanity. He talked about his stay in the psychiatric hospital and the suicide notes; about the worried looks of his children when they see him cry. He talked about the burden of being called a hero when there were others that day who would have done the same, but who were instead called murderers. He cried for the people who did not make it out of the house and for the guilt he feels that he did not see and could not save the other children who escaped from the house and then went back inside.

We talked—mostly he talked—for more than five hours. As he talked, the storm outside grew and grew. Through the windows we saw the lightning flash. The rain—the first good rain Philadelphia had had in weeks—drove straight against the windowpanes like an animal trying to get in.

As he talked, you could see the storms that raged in Jim Berghaier's soul—his struggle to survive, to be the father and the husband that he once had been, to find the meaning to his life that he'd once found catching bad guys on the dark streets of Philadelphia.

He believes that he is past the worst of it. He is struggling now, a step at a time, to rebuild his shattered life. For the first time in many years, he is hopeful. But still he does not know why fate chose him to carry this burden.

Of all the people whose lives have been touched by the events of May 13, he feels a bond with one person in particular. His kinship, he says, is with Ramona Africa.

He has seen her once since that day, when he was still on the force, in City Hall. She was there for her trial on riot and conspiracy charges stemming from the confrontation, and he'd been assigned, by sheer chance, to a security detail. She stood in the hallway, eyes downcast, surrounded by cops. He doesn't know if she recognized him, but he kept moving into her line of sight, bending his head down, trying to catch her eye.

His fellow cops thought he was crazy. But he thought if he could only see her eyes, he might find something there that was reflected in his own. Would she understand what he'd gone through—that awful responsibility of having been *chosen* for something, against his will and seemingly at random? It made no sense, but he felt as though he and Ramona had been touched by the fire in a way that others could not share and would never understand.

He thinks about her often. He suspects that when she is alone, away from the cameras and tape recorders and the boilerplate rhetoric of MOVE, when she is in her cell late at night, she might share his pain. He knows that she must anguish over the people who died in the house and in her most private moments must ask herself whether she might have done something to save them.

We told him that we had spoken with Alberta Africa. We

had asked her whether she believed, in light of MOVE's principles, that Birdie would have been better off if he'd cycled in the fire. Tears had come to her eyes, and she had said softly, "Oh, no. I could never say that. I love Birdie."

Now, as we told Jim this, tears came to his eyes as well. "I didn't know that," he said. "Thank you for telling me that."

By the time we finished talking, it was one in the morning. The storm had passed, and the night air was cool and clean. Jim paused at the front door, and he turned to us with all the earnestness of a child.

"If you talk to Ramona," he said, "tell her I said hello."

How does a society respond to an organization such as MOVE? How can it protect itself from those who share none of its values and beliefs and would destroy them to the roots? How can civilization withstand the awesome combination of an idea and an automatic rifle?

Certainly Goode waited too long to act against a group that was building a gun bunker in a residential neighborhood, but ultimately he was right when he told the neighbors that arrests on misdemeanor charges and zoning violations wouldn't solve their problem for good. MOVE was able to defy the city for more than a decade because it did not play by the rules that others do. What is the threat of a jail term to someone who is willing to barricade himself inside a house and die for his cause? How does one negotiate with people whose aim is the annihilation of modern civilization?

I have thought about that question often, and I do not have an answer. The closest I can come is to suggest that we must somehow look at *why* a John Africa can inspire people to die for a cause. In himself and in others, he was able to tap wells of anger so profound that they offered no room for compromise. Where does this anger come from?

It is not poverty alone—many of MOVE's members came from stable middle-class and working-class backgrounds. Nor is it simply the perspective of an oppressed black minority, though that is certainly a large part of it.

The root of MOVE's appeal, I think, is that there is an

undeniable truth to much of what the group says. Clifford Bond says that he still agrees with MOVE's message, though not with its methods. Berghaier, who spent long hours listening to MOVE rhetoric when he was assigned to the siege in Powelton in 1978, remembers telling other cops that a lot of what these people were saying made sense. Indeed it does: pollution is strangling the earth, the system serves the rich and powerful and grinds down the poor and weak, politicians lie and cheat. The world of mankind is not a just one. And if someone believes that, then shouldn't he strive with his entire being to change it?

We live in a world that is overrun with John Africas—angry voices that advocate violence in the service of Higher Truth. They are rampant in the Middle East, in Northern Ireland, among the right-wing hate groups of middle America and the militants of the radical left. With the power of modern technology at their disposal, they can blow planes out of the sky and sink cruise ships on the high seas. None of us are secure from their anger.

If we wish to diminish the power of these prophets of destruction, it seems to me that we must somehow teach our children and ourselves that the world is not split neatly into the forces of good and evil. We must teach them to tolerate—no, celebrate—life's ambiguities and contradictions. We must teach them that questions do not always have answers. And somehow we must teach them to look beyond simple truths and discover wisdom.

We are so fond of simple explanations. We hear them from politicians, columnists, editorial writers, the guys at the corner bar. But if there is a moral to this story, it is that simple explanations do not exist.

For example, it would be easy to lay the events of May 13 entirely at Wilson Goode's feet—and yet it is not clear that he could have avoided the confrontation in the end. Gregore Sambor is perhaps the most enticing candidate for scapegoat— but which of us can say what we would have done in his place that day? One can feel the withering heat of Louise James's bitterness—but we must remember that she had begged the police to help her save her son, only to watch him die in the flames of Osage Avenue.

One can call MOVE a band of lunatic cop-killers—but its members are sincere, committed, and absolutely convinced that they have been the victims of an official policy of murder. And one can look at the life of Vincent Leaphart, the man known as John Africa, and still see the wounded, motherless child who grew up among the bleak streets of the city and dreamed of forests full of rich black soil and tall green trees, and animals and children, forever running, running free.

What makes a leader out of a man? What was it about John Africa that inspired the devotion of his followers? Those closest to him lived for years with the knowledge that he was leading them toward their own death—and still they followed. In the last hours of their lives, their loyalty overpowered every human instinct to flee a house that was burning down around them.

John Africa's ability to lead seems to have little to do with his beliefs about the evils of technology. Rather, it seems to have come from his ability to give his followers something they were desperately searching for. He couldn't give them money or prestige. But he could give them a sense of meaning, a sense that their lives made a difference, a sense, ultimately, of power.

What makes a leader? Four men—Goode, Brooks, Sambor, and Richmond—each had the power and authority to put out the fire that raged on the rooftop of 6221 Osage Avenue on the evening of May 13. In that moment of crisis, four men who had spent their lives as leaders simply stood aside. Why?

Today, not one of them can offer a satisfying explanation; in fact, they often seem as perplexed by their behavior as anyone else. There are people—most of whom have sifted through the facts until they found a few they like—who have ready explanations. Some say it was malice. Others say it was simply incompetence—which was clearly in abundance on that day.

But even so, there seems to be something more involved in this story. One is haunted by a sense of inevitability. The irony is that the leaders of the city, all on their own, created the tragedy that they were so desperately trying to avoid.

Finally, I am left to wonder about my own small part in all of this. I voted in favor of the grand jury's decision not to bring criminal charges. I believed that I was doing the right thing, and I continue to believe that.

There is an old adage among lawyers and judges: "Hard cases make bad law." This is a hard case. It goes to the very heart of the question of what constitutes a crime. Behind all the obscure legal jargon of "intent" and "mens rea," there is, I believe, a useful notion. A crime must be more than incompetence. We must acknowledge that in the area of criminal law, good intentions *do* count. The criminal code must punish wickedness, not mistakes. To do otherwise would be to call us all criminals.

And yet I do not believe that justice has been served. The mistakes in this case were so grievous, and their consequences so profound, that they cry for atonement.

There is nothing that can undo the events of May 13. There is nothing that can make the world whole once again. There is no grand jury, no court, no commission that can restore those children to life.

The night we spoke with Jim Berghaier, I had a dream that he and I were lifeguards and that someone had run to us with the news that a man had drowned. Swiftly we put a boat in the water and began to search for the victim. Minutes passed, and then more. After twenty minutes we knew the man must be dead, but still we went on searching. We knew it was hopeless, but we could not bring ourselves to stop. We could not give up. The man was dead, but still we had to try to save him. We told ourselves there must be something we could do. Again and again we probed the icy waters with long poles. We were still searching when the alarm woke me up.

Notes

Chapter 1: The primary source of material for this and other chapters related to the events of May 13, 1985, was the evidence collected by the Philadelphia Special Investigating Commission (the MOVE Commission), now maintained by the Urban Archives Department at Temple University, Philadelphia. Additional material was collected from the news reports, videotapes, and interviews.

Chapter 2: Information on the history of Cobbs Creek came from historical sources and interviews with current and former residents of the neighborhood. Information about Louise James and Frank James came from news reports and Mrs. James's testimony before the MOVE Commission.

Chapter 3: A key source of material on the origins of MOVE and the background of Vincent Leaphart was an article appearing in the *Philadelphia Inquirer*'s Sunday supplement in 1986, entitled "Who Was John Africa?" It was supplemented by additional material from news reports and interviews of MOVE members and former residents of Powelton Avenue.

Chapters 4 and 5: Sources included testimony given to the MOVE Commission, law enforcement files provided to the MOVE Commission, eyewitnesses to the confrontation, and news reports.

Chapters 6 through 8: Most of the material in these chapters came from MOVE Commission files and testimony, as well as interviews with police officers, neighbors, and MOVE members.

Chapters 9 through 11: Again, the MOVE Commission files and testimony were the primary sources of material; additional sources included news reports (where noted) and interviews.

Chapters 12 and 13: Sources included the MOVE Commission files, news reports and interviews, and an interview with Emerson Moran, who served as the communications officer of the commission, attended the deliberations, and wrote an article on them for *Philadelphia Magazine*.

Appendix A
Final Report of the Philadelphia Special Investigation Commission

FINDINGS AND CONCLUSIONS

1 BY THE EARLY 1980s MOVE HAD EVOLVED INTO AN AUTHORITARIAN, VIOLENCE-THREATENING CULT.

John Africa and his followers in the 1980s came to reject and to place themselves above the laws, customs and social contracts of society. They threatened violence to anyone who would attempt to enforce normal societal rules. They believed that only the laws of John Africa need be obeyed.

The members of MOVE saw themselves as the targets of persistent harassment by regulatory agencies, unjust treatment by the courts, and periodic violent attempts to be suppressed by the police.

John Africa and his followers believed that a catastrophic confrontation with "the system" was necessary, if not inevitable, because of the campaign by "the system" to force MOVE to conform to society's rules.

MOVE's last campaign for confrontation began in the fall of 1983, and was predicated on (1) the unconditional demand that all imprisoned MOVE members be released; and (2) that harassment of MOVE by city officials cease. The stridency and extremism of individual MOVE members escalated during the first years of the Goode Administration.

2 THE RESIDENTS OF 6221 OSAGE AVE. WERE ARMED AND DANGEROUS, AND USED THREATS, ABUSE AND INTIMIDATION TO TERRIFY THEIR NEIGHBORS AND TO BRING ABOUT CONFRONTATION WITH CITY GOVERNMENT.

The death of Officer Ramp and the wounding of many police and firefighters in the 1978 clash confirmed that MOVE members would use deadly force when confronted.

On Osage Avenue, the occupants of 6221 Osage Ave. committed violent acts against their own neighbors and threatened violence against public officials and private citizens in a manner which was intended to shock and intimidate both the general population and the city's officials.

MOVE's deliberate use of terror included the intentional violation of the basic rights of those living in the Osage Avenue neighborhood. This was achieved by:

- Both verbal and physical assaults upon targeted individuals living in the neighborhood.
- The periodic broadcast over outdoor loudspeakers of profane harangues against the government and threats of violence against public officials.
- The public acclaiming by MOVE of the 1978 death of Officer Ramp, and the repeated threat that, if the police come to 6221 Osage Ave., "we'll put a bullet in your motherfucking heads."
- The prominent fortification of an ordinary row house.
- The aggressive display of a weapon by a hooded man at midday in a normally peaceful neighborhood.
- The compelling domination of the neighborhood by MOVE's rooftop bunker, which, by itself, became a commanding public notice of imminent confrontation.

Through this use of terror, MOVE, in some respects, held Osage Avenue "hostage" for nearly two years. During that period, the city's leadership chose not to secure the neighborhood's release, and, instead, drifted toward the confrontation that MOVE had declared was preordained.

3 MAYOR GOODE'S POLICY TOWARD MOVE WAS ONE OF APPEASEMENT, NON-CONFRONTATION AND AVOIDANCE.

The Goode Administration assumed that any attempt to enforce the law would end in violence. MOVE-related issues thus became "too hot to handle," and the Administration pursued a do-nothing and say-nothing policy. Avoidance of the problem was so pervasive that city officials did not even discuss the issue among themselves.

The Mayor attempted to mollify neighbors with claims that a proper legal basis for action was being sought, and with superficial actions that were designed to diffuse neighborhood frustrations without addressing the crux of the problem.

With this policy of benign avoidance, the Mayor hoped that the problem might dissipate on its own, particularly, that MOVE would weary of unanswered challenges, modulate their confrontational behavior and/or relocate. To a great extent, then, MOVE effectively paralyzed the normal functioning of city government, as it applied to MOVE and to the Osage neighborhood.

4 THE MANAGING DIRECTOR AND THE CITY'S DEPARTMENT HEADS FAILED TO TAKE ANY EFFECTIVE ACTION ON THEIR OWN AND, IN FACT, ORDERED THEIR SUBORDINATES TO REFRAIN FROM TAKING ACTION TO DEAL MEANINGFULLY WITH THE PROBLEM ON OSAGE AVENUE.

As early as March, 1984, the Mayor treated the problem on Osage Avenue as a "police matter."

The Mayor assigned the responsibility of monitoring the problem to the Managing Director who was to be his "eyes on things out there through the police department."

In May of 1984, Managing Director Brooks instructed his task force (established to coordinate and focus the city's programs related to neighborhood problems) that "MOVE is not an issue for this group, it is a police matter."

The Osage Avenue situation was never raised prior to May 13th in any of the weekly commissioner meetings during the Goode Administration. The Commissioners of Licenses and Inspections, Human Services, Water and Health each adopted, without question, this "hands off" attitude. Not a single city commissioner ever questioned the Mayor or the Managing Director about the rationale for this policy.

5 THE CITY ADMINISTRATION DISCOUNTED NEGOTIATION AS A METHOD OF RESOLVING THE PROBLEM. ANY ATTEMPTED NEGOTIATIONS WERE HAPHAZARD AND UNCOORDINATED.

The city's experience with MOVE in 1978, and MOVE's insistence on making release of its members from jail the sole basis for negotiation in 1985, promoted a view that rational discussion and compromise were impossible. Because the situation was believed to be inherently volatile, with no hope of acceptable compromise, it was thought that active negotiation would accelerate rather than postpone an ultimate confrontation.

All occasions on which the Mayor met with MOVE were instigated by MOVE members or sympathizers and were held for the sole purpose of airing MOVE's grievances. The Mayor's posture was to listen, but not act.

Formal and informal city groups chartered to deal with these kinds of problems were rebuffed and discouraged by the Administration from mediating or otherwise offering their services.

Into this vacuum stepped a number of community mediators with no active mandate from the city administration.

6 IN THE FIRST SEVERAL MONTHS OF HIS ADMINISTRATION, THE MAYOR WAS PRESENTED WITH COMPELLING EVIDENCE THAT HIS POLICY OF APPEASEMENT, NON-CONFRONTATION AND AVOIDANCE WAS DOOMED TO FAIL.

In March of 1984, the Mayor and the Managing Director were briefed thoroughly by the Police Commissioner and told the following:

- That, since late summer, 1983, the alley behind the MOVE house was blocked by fencing.
- That MOVE was barricading its house, including putting slats on all the windows.
- That a bullhorn had been affixed to the front of the home and was being used to harangue and threaten the neighbors.
- That construction material was visible on the roof.
- That, since Christmas, 1983, MOVE had been in a self-proclaimed confrontation with the city.

In May, 1984, a hooded MOVE member appeared on the roof of 6221 Osage Ave. brandishing a shotgun.

On Memorial Day and the Fourth of July, 1984, the Mayor met with Osage neighbors who gave him a detailed and emotional report of the difficulties of living on Osage Avenue and told him the city's response was inadequate.

In the summer of 1984, the Mayor met with Louise James and learned that John Africa and Frank James had become increasingly violent and intransigent. She told the Mayor that the failures of MOVE to obtain the release from prison of its members had provoked a sense of desperation in the MOVE leadership.

7 IN THE SUMMER OF 1984, THE MAYOR WAS TOLD
THAT THE LEGAL BASIS EXISTED AT THAT TIME TO
ACT AGAINST CERTAIN MOVE MEMBERS. YET, THE
MAYOR HELD BACK, AND CONTINUED TO FOLLOW HIS
POLICY OF AVOIDANCE AND NON-CONFRONTATION.

The Mayor requested and was provided in July, 1984, with a
detailed analysis of the possible legal grounds for taking action
against some of the occupants of 6221 Osage Ave.

The Mayor was also informed that delay in acting would cause the
problem to grow worse, providing MOVE with the opportunity to
become better fortified, attracting media attention to the area and
provoking greater tension among the neighbors.

The Mayor and the police believed that MOVE would provoke a
violent confrontation on August 8, 1984. The police, at the Mayor's
direction, were prepared that day to execute a "reactive" plan
designed to remove the occupants of 6221 Osage Ave. from the
house, thereby eliminating MOVE's presence in the community.

The confrontation never took place, and the Mayor believed the
threat posed by MOVE had eased. He took no further action, nor was
any recommended to him by either the Police Commissioner or the
District Attorney, until April, 1985.

8 FROM THE FALL OF 1984, TO THE SPRING OF 1985,
THE CITY'S POLICY OF APPEASEMENT CONCEDED TO
THE RESIDENTS OF 6221 OSAGE AVE. THE CONTINUED
RIGHT TO EXIST ABOVE THE LAW.

The construction of the rooftop bunker in October, 1984, was
unchallenged by the Department of Licenses and Inspections, despite the obvious violation of city building codes. By permitting the
fortification of the rooftop, the city granted to the occupants of 6221
Osage Ave. a critical tactical advantage over the 6200 block of Osage
Avenue and over the police.

Other areas of deliberate, selective non-enforcement of the law by
government included:

- The alley behind the 6200 block of Osage Avenue remained
  blockaded by fencing erected by MOVE. Neither Licenses
  and Inspections nor the Streets Department ever accepted
  jurisdiction over the obstructing of this public alleyway.
- Unpaid water, gas and electric bills were allowed to accumu-
  late without service being interrupted as police refused to

provide assistance to meter readers and revenue collectors.
- The children of MOVE adults remained out of school in flagrant violation of truancy laws.
- The Health Department refused to act on continuing complaints from the neighborhood of insects, rats, open garbage and animals running loose at 6221 Osage Ave.

The policy of appeasement produced a rule of silence in City Hall, where information on the Osage Avenue situation was not disseminated and where city officials knowledgeable about the problems chose not to speak of them.

9 MORE THAN ANY OTHER FACTOR, INTENSIFIED PRESSURE FROM THE RESIDENTS OF OSAGE AVENUE FORCED THE MAYOR TO ABANDON HIS POLICY OF NON-CONFRONTATION AND AVOIDANCE, AND TO DEVISE A STRATEGY FOR RESOLVING THE PROBLEM QUICKLY.

By the end of April, 1985, the Osage Avenue neighbors were so intimidated by MOVE's increasing belligerence and so frustrated by the city's inaction that they sought help from outside, appealing to the Governor and expressing their grievances to the media.

The Mayor and the police responded to this new pressure, and, in the first week of May, began to design a strategy of action. This strategy relied on the same legal basis that existed in June, 1984, but which had not been acted upon.

This strategy, formulated by the Mayor, had three components: a) To arrest as many MOVE members as possible on minor criminal charges, some pre-existing, some new. b) To remove, during the arrest process, all the inhabitants from 6221 Osage Ave., including non-criminal violators and children. c) To prevent MOVE members from reoccupying the house.

The City Solicitor and her Deputy suspected that outright seizure of the MOVE house after the arrests were made would be illegal. As a result, the City Solicitor was prepared for the city to be sued if this action was carried out.

The Mayor held little hope that MOVE would vacate the house voluntarily or even permit a court-ordered search of the premises. The Mayor's strategy, accordingly, presupposed the use of police force. During the week preceding the confrontation, the Mayor, in meetings with top officials, discussed the fact that bloodshed, and even death, was likely.

10 THE MAYOR INSTRUCTED THE POLICE
COMMISSIONER TO PREPARE AND EXECUTE A
TACTICAL PLAN, UNDER THE SUPERVISION OF THE
MANAGING DIRECTOR. THE MANAGING DIRECTOR
FAILED IN THAT RESPONSIBILITY, AND THE MAYOR
ALLOWED THE POLICE COMMISSIONER TO PROCEED
ON HIS OWN.

On Tuesday, May 7, 1985, the Mayor, in a meeting with the city's
highest legal and law enforcement officials, directed the Police
Commissioner to prepare and carry out a tactical police operation
against 6221 Osage Ave.

At that meeting the Mayor explicitly gave the Managing Director
supervisory responsibility for the development of the police plan. He
was ordered to keep informed of the planning process, to evaluate the
plan's viability and to report to the Mayor.

The Managing Director, however, did nothing. He was not in his
office on May 8th, and left town on personal business on May 9th.
He did not return to the city until the night of Sunday, May 12, at
which time the Osage neighborhood had been evacuated, in anticipation of the next morning's action.

The Police Commissioner neither sought out the absent Managing
Director, nor did he believe he was required to do so. In the
meantime, he proceeded through the final stages of preparation with
complete independence, though he twice advised the Mayor of his
department's progress during that weekend.

11 THE POLICE COMMISSIONER CHOSE AS HIS
PLANNERS THE HEAD OF THE BOMB DISPOSAL UNIT,
A SERGEANT FROM THE PISTOL RANGE AND A
UNIFORMED PATROLMAN. IN SO DOING, HE
EXCLUDED FROM THE FORMULATION OF THE PLAN
THE ENTIRE POLICE DEPARTMENT COMMAND
STRUCTURE AND OTHER AVAILABLE EXPERTISE.

The decision to entrust an undertaking of this magnitude and
delicacy to first line operation supervisors and uniform patrolmen
was irresponsible. As a result, the operation was deprived of a
breadth of practical knowledge and technical expertise at a critical
stage of the planning process.

The planners designated by the Police Commissioner lacked sufficient knowledge and technical background to evaluate properly
various alternatives to the operation. The central role played by the
head of the bomb squad invited the operation's reliance on explosives.

No serious effort was made by the Police Commissioner or his planners to explore alternative solutions or tactics with outside agencies or experts. Contacts with the FBI and the U.S. Treasury Department were cursory; no official attempt was made to draw on the resources of these agencies.

Other city agencies possessing specialized knowledge of MOVE and 6221 Osage Ave. were not consulted by the planners, nor were their views sought.

12 AS A RESULT OF THE POLICE COMMISSIONER'S ORDERS, THE THREE OFFICERS RESPONSIBLE FOR DEVELOPING THE TACTICAL PLAN DID SO HASTILY AND WITHOUT SUFFICIENT INFORMATION OR ADEQUATE INTELLIGENCE. THE MAYOR, THE MANAGING DIRECTOR AND THE POLICE COMMISSIONER NEITHER SOUGHT NOR RECEIVED FROM THESE MEN A WRITTEN TACTICAL PLAN.

A critique of the 1978 confrontation, which had been prepared by the Police Department's highest ranking officers, was never reviewed by the 1985 planners.

Despite the city's experience with MOVE in 1978, and despite the resurgence of MOVE on Osage Avenue in the early 1980s, the police did nothing to establish the means for the systematic collection, analysis and dissemination of intelligence information regarding MOVE and its members.

Much of the intelligence which was acted upon by the planners was insufficient, inaccurate or misleading. For example:

- The extent of the house's interior fortification was underestimated.
- Police believed MOVE was prepared to escape through tunnels carved out under the neighborhood. None existed.
- Gasoline was known to the Mayor and some officers to be stored on the roof of 6221 Osage Ave. The planners did not know this.

Though a 24-hour surveillance on the MOVE house was warranted by April 30, 1985, none began until late on the afternoon of May 9th.

The Police Commissioner never passed on to the planners the Mayor's direction to him to "take his time" in devising the tactical plan. Instead, the planners operated on a crash basis.

Months after the assault, the pistol range sergeant produced a two-page undated document he claimed was the written tactical plan. He said it was available to his superiors prior to May 13th. The police commanders, up to and including the Commissioner, as well as the Mayor and the Managing Director, said they never received such a written plan, nor did they ask for one. There is no evidence to corroborate the sergeant's statement that a written plan existed before May 13th.

13 THE MAYOR, THE MANAGING DIRECTOR AND THE POLICE COMMISSIONER SPECIFICALLY APPROVED THE USE OF EXPLOSIVES TO BLOW 3-INCH HOLES IN THE PARTY WALLS OF 6221 OSAGE AVE. TO ALLOW THE INSERTION OF TEAR GAS TO INDUCE THE EVACUATION OF THE HOUSE. THIS PLAN WAS INADEQUATE BECAUSE OF THE FLAWED INTELLIGENCE ON WHICH IT WAS BASED AND THE HASTE WITH WHICH IT WAS DESIGNED.

The Mayor was told in advance by the Managing Director and by the Police Commissioner that the walls would be breached by explosives.

The unanticipated fortification inside the first floor of 6221 Osage Ave. gave the house's occupants a protected firebase. Fire from this position forced "B" Team to concentrate on neutralizing the interior bunker instead of forcing tear gas into the house. This diversion in itself made the police plan inoperative.

The plan also relied on water from the Fire Department's "Squrt guns" to dislodge the rooftop bunker, despite warnings by fire officials that the "Squrts" were incapable of performing that task.

No alternative method of removing the bunker was seriously considered by the planners. The use of a crane was dismissed by the head of the bomb squad, whose decision was accepted without question by the Police Commissioner.

Police and fire mobile communications systems were incompatible, yet no consideration was given to coordinating the communication between police and firefighters during this complicated and life-threatening operation.

The plan failed to utilize the police department's professional negotiating expertise available and trained for barricaded persons and hostage situations.

There was no back-up plan if the explosives and tear gas failed to

drive the occupants from the house. The police planned no alternative to the assault's failure.

14 DIRECTIVES TO REMOVE THE CHILDREN FROM 6221 OSAGE AVE. WERE UNCLEAR, POORLY COMMUNICATED AND WERE NOT CARRIED OUT.

The Mayor should not have permitted the planning to go forward
when, on May 9th, he knew that the Managing Director was out of
town.

The Managing Director was instructed by the Mayor on May 7,
1985, to coordinate the efforts of the Police Department, the Department of Human Services and the Law Department to ensure that the
children were removed from the house prior to the implementation of
the plan. He took no action whatsoever toward achieving this, and
left town the next day without even advising his staff on how to
proceed.

The Human Services Commissioner first learned of the city's
interest in protecting the children four days prior to the confrontation. She responded with little interest or vigor and did not demand
any information from the police regarding the protection of the
children.

On the evening of May 9th, the City Solicitor's office gave the
Police Commissioner specific instructions to take the children from
6221 Osage Ave. into protective custody at the first opportunity.
Nevertheless, the City Solicitor's office did not attempt to secure the
legal authority to remove and detain the children until the morning
of the confrontation, when it was too late.

Police personnel responsible for carrying out the directive had
conflicting impressions about when they were to detain the children,
where the children could safely be retrieved, and which children
were subject to the directive.

15 THE MAYOR'S FAILURE TO CALL A HALT TO THE OPERATION ON MAY 12TH, WHEN HE KNEW THAT CHILDREN WERE IN THE HOUSE, WAS GROSSLY NEGLIGENT AND CLEARLY RISKED THE LIVES OF THOSE CHILDREN.

On Saturday, May 11, and Sunday, May 12, the Mayor was briefed
on the plan by the Police Commissioner and was aware that children
were known to be inside the MOVE residence. Nonetheless, he
authorized the commencement of the operation.

No children were taken into protective custody. At least two children, who were passengers in a car, were allowed to pass through a police barricade on the day before the evacuation of the neighborhood, with no attempt made to detain them.

16 THE MANAGING DIRECTOR AND THE POLICE COMMISSIONER WERE GROSSLY NEGLIGENT AND CLEARLY RISKED THE LIVES OF THE CHILDREN BY FAILING TO TAKE EFFECTIVE STEPS TO DETAIN THEM AND BY NOT FORCEFULLY RECOMMENDING TO THE MAYOR THAT THE OPERATION BE HALTED WHEN THEY KNEW, THE EVENING OF MAY 12TH, THAT THE CHILDREN WERE IN THE RESIDENCE.

The Managing Director and Police Commissioner knew, the evening of May 12th, that the Mayor's order to secure the safety of the children had not and could not be accomplished before the start of the operation. These men were obligated either to tell the Mayor that the plan should not proceed, or to order a halt to the operation themselves.

17 THE MAYOR FAILED TO PERFORM HIS RESPONSIBILITY AS THE CITY'S CHIEF EXECUTIVE BY NOT ACTIVELY PARTICIPATING IN THE PREPARATION, REVIEW AND OVERSIGHT OF THE PLAN.

At a meeting on May 7th, the Mayor rebuffed a suggestion that he be fully briefed on the plan, preferring instead to isolate himself by leaving that level of detail to his experts.

The Mayor's statement that he was reluctant to "meddle" in the affairs of his subordinates in this instance represents a striking departure from his self-proclaimed hands-on method of city management.

18 THE FIRING OF OVER 10,000 ROUNDS OF AMMUNITION IN UNDER 90 MINUTES AT A ROW HOUSE CONTAINING CHILDREN WAS CLEARLY EXCESSIVE AND UNREASONABLE. THE FAILURE OF THOSE RESPONSIBLE FOR THE FIRING TO CONTROL OR STOP SUCH AN EXCESSIVE AMOUNT OF FORCE WAS UNCONSCIONABLE.*

---

*Commissioner Kauffman dissents from this finding.

So great was the latitude given the police planners that they were allowed to augment the department's arsenal with military weapons and explosives not normally available to municipal police departments.

In a period of about 90 minutes during the morning hours, the police fired at least 10,000 rounds at 6221 Osage Ave.

Thirty-two police officers admitted to firing their weapons. One shooter acknowledged that, from his post within 50 feet of the house, he fired 1,000 rounds from his M-16 semi-automatic rifle.

Other weapons fired included M-16's, a Browning Automatic Rifle, a Thompson submachine gun, 30.06 and .22-250 sharpshooter rifles, two M-60 machine guns, Uzis, shotguns and a silenced .22 caliber rifle.

Found in the ruins of the MOVE house were two pistols, a shotgun and a .22 caliber rifle.

The excessive gunfire was inappropriate to the force generated by MOVE, and needlessly jeopardized the lives of the children in the house. It also placed in serious danger the lives of police officers in Posts 1, 2, 3, and 4, and Insertion Teams "A" and "B" immediately adjacent to the MOVE residence, as well as the several hundred police and civilians who were on the Osage perimeter.

19 THE MEMBERS OF THE BOMB DISPOSAL UNIT WERE NOT TRAINED FOR THEIR TACTICAL ASSIGNMENT. THEIR ACTIONS ON THE MORNING OF MAY 13TH POSED A HIGH RISK OF DEATH FOR BOTH THE POLICE AND THE OCCUPANTS OF 6221 OSAGE AVE.

The members of the Bomb Disposal Unit were not experienced, trained or proficient in the tactical use of explosives.

The Police Commissioner compounded the BDU's incompetence by allowing the unit to operate without adequate command or control. The unit's commander was permitted to plan and mount the assault without oversight or accountability. Through the default of his superiors, the lieutenant assumed unrestricted discretion in selecting and employing explosives which were excessive under the circumstances.

The Bomb Disposal Unit violated acceptable safety standards and imperiled human life by enhancing and misapplying explosives of such force that the results were completely different than those contemplated by the assault plan.

The misuse of the explosives in the morning virtually destroyed the front of four row houses. Once the MOVE house was laid open by this blasting, tear gas could have been introduced into the house without blowing a hole in the roof.

20 EXPLOSIVES WERE USED AGAINST THE MOVE HOUSE ON THE MORNING OF MAY 13, 1985, WHICH WERE EXCESSIVE AND LIFE THREATENING.

The pre-shaped charges detonated on the row house's interior party walls by "A" Team were misapplied, unacceptably dangerous, and caused destruction far in excess of what the police planners said they intended.

The Bomb Disposal Unit improvised their own powerful "flash-bangs" which were similar to fragmentation grenades, and were capable of causing serious injury to anyone nearby when they detonated.

The high explosive boosters used by "B" Team were designed as highly potent explosives and are not acceptable as tactical weapons for police.

Flashbang grenades and high explosive boosters were unsuitable for use by police positioned close to their intended targets, and put both user and target at high risk.

21 AT LEAST ONE AGENT OF THE PHILADELPHIA OFFICE OF THE FBI MADE AVAILABLE TO THE PHILADELPHIA POLICE DEPARTMENT, WITHOUT PROPER RECORDATION BY EITHER AGENCY, SUBSTANTIAL QUANTITIES OF C-4, SOME OF WHICH MAY HAVE BEEN INCORPORATED IN THE EXPLOSIVE DEVICES USED ON MAY 13, 1985.

In January, 1985, an agent of the FBI delivered nearly 38 pounds of C-4, a powerful military plastic explosive, to the Philadelphia Police bomb squad. Delivery of this amount of C-4 to any local police force without restrictions as to its use is inappropriate.

Neither agency kept any records of the transaction. The FBI agent told the Commission that he "never had to keep any kind of records or anything" regarding C-4. Nor did the bomb squad keep any record of delivery, inventory or use of the C-4, or any other explosives under their control.

Subsequent to May 13, 1985, at least one FBI agent deliberately withheld from his own superiors information concerning the unauthorized cache of the C-4. (This agent later said he was "in fear of losing my job" because of his delivery of the C-4.) As a result, officials of the FBI unwittingly furnished the Commission with inaccurate and untruthful accounts of that agency's involvement in events related to May 13, 1985. Because of the absence of record keeping by the FBI and the Philadelphia Police Department, all the facts of the use of C-4 on May 13th may never be known.

22 THE MAYOR ABDICATED HIS RESPONSIBILITIES AS A LEADER WHEN, AFTER MID-DAY, HE PERMITTED A CLEARLY FAILED OPERATION TO CONTINUE WHICH POSED GREAT RISK TO LIFE AND PROPERTY.

By 1 P.M., the Police Commissioner and the Managing Director, the Mayor's commanders in the field, knew that neither water, gas, smoke, gunfire nor explosives would force the evacuation of 6221 Osage Ave. Yet, the Managing Director and the Police Commissioner clung to the goal of forcing the people out of the house.

No one had requested or devised any contingency plan.

By 4 P.M., the only direction which the Mayor appears to have provided was revealed in an afternoon press conference when he said he was prepared "to seize control of the house . . . by any means necessary."

23 ON MAY 13TH, THE KEY DECISION MAKERS WERE PREVENTED FROM EASILY AND DIRECTLY CONTACTING EACH OTHER BECAUSE OF AN INADEQUATE COMMUNICATIONS SYSTEM.

The key officials at the scene could only contact each other by relaying messages along police and fire radio networks which were incompatible with one another.

The Police Commissioner and Fire Commissioner could be contacted only over short-range frequencies which were not accessible to the Managing Director.

The Mayor, at City Hall, could not directly reach any of his top officials person-to-person at the scene by radio or telephone. The Mayor could only reach the Managing Director, his top representative, by radio relays or a beeper system. Delays of several minutes were common in making contact.

The Mayor testified that at times the only information he could get from the scene came from television news reports.

24 THE PLAN TO BOMB THE MOVE HOUSE WAS

RECKLESS, ILL-CONCEIVED AND HASTILY APPROVED.
DROPPING A BOMB ON AN OCCUPIED ROW HOUSE WAS
UNCONSCIONABLE AND SHOULD HAVE BEEN REJECTED
OUT-OF-HAND BY THE MAYOR, THE MANAGING
DIRECTOR, THE POLICE COMMISSIONER AND THE FIRE
COMMISSIONER.

The only credible reason offered for dropping the bomb was to
destroy the bunker.

The Mayor, the Managing Director, the Police Commissioner and
the Fire Commissioner accepted the suggestion of an aerial attack on
a Philadelphia row house known by each of them to be occupied by a
large number of adults and children. By approving the bombing,
each of these individuals exhibited a reckless disregard for life and
property.

The absence of a final warning to surrender coupled with a lack of
knowledge of where the children were located in the house, under-
scores the recklessness of this act.

The preparation and execution of the bomb attack was entrusted to
the same lieutenant whose incompetence had contributed to the
miscarriage of the original plan. The plan to attack from the air was
doomed to fail, as well, because neither the explosives used nor the
method of delivery was capable of destroying the bunker.

The Managing Director told the Mayor, in a conversation overheard by two other people, that the police would drop the explosives
from a helicopter.

The Mayor was aware of reports of gasoline being stored on the
roof and of reports of explosives being stored in the MOVE house.

Although the Mayor conceded that there existed no compelling
reason to conclude the confrontation that day, he nevertheless approved a course of action which posed extreme risk to citizens, police
and firefighters.

The Mayor paused only 30 seconds before approving the dropping
of explosives. Had he taken more time before making such a critical
decision, he may have considered the presence of the children, the
possibility that gas was on the roof, and the possibility that explosives
were stored in the MOVE house.

25 THE FIRE WHICH DESTROYED THE OSAGE
NEIGHBORHOOD WAS CAUSED BY THE BOMB WHICH
EXPLODED ON THE ROOF OF THE MOVE HOUSE. THE
FIRE BEGAN A MILLISECOND AFTER THE BOMB BLAST
WHEN FRICTION-HEATED METAL FRAGMENTS

PENETRATED A GAS CAN ON THE ROOF AND IGNITED
GASOLINE VAPORS.

The bomb, an improvised combination of Tovex and C-4, was
dropped in an uncontrolled manner from a helicopter at 5:27 P.M.,
and detonated 45 seconds later.

According to the Commission's explosives expert, the bomb contained substantially more C-4 than was reported by the officer who
constructed it. As a result, the bomb's ability to fragment wood,
brick and metal present at the point of detonation was greatly
enhanced.

The high-energy mix of Tovex and C-4 generated blast tempera-
tures up to 7,200 degrees which, according to expert testimony, were
hot enough to evaporate water and ignite a fire even if flammable
liquids had not been present on the roof.

26 EVEN AFTER THE BOMB EXPLODED AND IGNITED
THE FIRE, LIFE AND PROPERTY COULD HAVE BEEN
SAVED WITHOUT ENDANGERING ANY OF THE POLICE
OFFICERS OR FIREFIGHTERS BY USING THE "SQURTS"
TO EXTINGUISH THE FIRE ON THE ROOF WHILE THE
FIRE WAS IN ITS INCIPIENT STAGE.

Two Fire Department "Squrts"—high pressure water guns
mounted atop movable booms—were positioned on Pine Street, the
street paralleling Osage Avenue. Each "Squrt" could pump up to
1,000 gallons of water a minute over the Pine Street houses onto the
MOVE rooftop. Throughout the day, the "Squrts" were used to
provide cover for police operations and to neutralize the effects of
possible gunfire from the bunker. From 5:20 to 5:25 P.M. the
"Squrts" were turned on to protect the helicopter which was preparing to drop the bomb.

After the bomb detonated at 5:27 P.M., until shortly after 6:00 P.M.,
the fire on the roof was in its incipient stage, i.e., it was just
beginning to appear and was considered small by firefighter criteria,
and was not spreading beyond or below the roof's surface. It was still
possible to save both the building and its occupants.

At any time until shortly after 6:00 P.M., the Fire Department
"Squrts" could have extinguished a fire without exposing police or
firefighters to any possible danger.

27 THE HASTY, RECKLESS AND IRRESPONSIBLE
DECISION BY THE POLICE COMMISSIONER AND THE
FIRE COMMISSIONER TO USE THE FIRE AS A TACTICAL

WEAPON WAS UNCONSCIONABLE.

The decision made by the Police Commissioner and the Fire Commissioner between 6:08 and 6:12 P.M. to let the fire burn constituted the use of fire as a tactical weapon.

The Fire Commissioner advised the Police Commissioner that firefighters could let the bunker burn and still contain the fire at a later time. Even if this were true, the decision to let the fire burn was reckless and irresponsible.

Allowing the fire to burn should have been rejected out-of-hand. That it was not rejected cannot be justified under any circumstances.

28 POLICE GUNFIRE PREVENTED SOME OCCUPANTS OF 6221 OSAGE AVE. FROM ESCAPING FROM THE BURNING HOUSE TO THE REAR ALLEY.*

At least two adults and four children attempted to escape the house after it caught fire.

First, a man and a boy tried to exit, but returned to the house as a result of police gunfire.

Next, a woman, three other children and the same man fled the house. At one point all were completely free of the building. Only the woman and one child survived. The bodies of the others were found later in rubble within the foundation line of the house.

The majority of police officers who were positioned within the alley, at either end of the alley, or overlooking the alley's interior, said they heard gunfire in the alley between 7:00 and 7:30 P.M.

But these officers denied firing their weapons during this period. However, fire personnel and other police, including an Inspector, who were outside the alley on the Osage Avenue perimeter, said they heard .22 caliber fire, as well as one or two bursts of either automatic or semi-automatic fire of a heavier caliber.

In this same period, several officers with a view of the rear of 6221 Osage Ave. observed a man emerge from the building clutching a child and carrying a .22 caliber rifle. Three officers testified they saw this man fire the rifle in the direction of police officers.

Those police in a position to shoot said no police returned the man's fire.

Police observed the man climb a fence in the alleyway, and then "he fell back down," and was lost to view. One officer said he saw the child crawling back toward the MOVE house.

---

*Commissioner Kauffman dissents from this finding.

29 FIVE CHILDREN WERE KILLED DURING THE CONFRONTATION ON MAY 13, 1985. THEIR DEATHS APPEAR TO BE UNJUSTIFIED HOMICIDES WHICH SHOULD BE INVESTIGATED BY A GRAND JURY.

The deaths of the five children were caused by one or more of a variety of injuries sustained during the May 13, 1985, confrontation.

These deaths could have been caused by carbon monoxide poisoning, burns, effects of explosions and wounds from firearms ammunition.

The body of one child found in the basement contained metal fragments which the FBI laboratory and the Commission's pathology expert said were consistent with 00 buckshot pellets.

30 SIX ADULTS ALSO DIED AS A RESULT OF THE MAY 13TH CONFRONTATION.

Frank James Africa, Theresa Brooks Africa and Conrad Hampton Africa, all of whom died as a result of the confrontation, had arrest warrants outstanding against them. This fact was announced to them by the Police Commissioner in the morning and they had a legal obligation to surrender to the police at that time.

Ramona Johnson Africa, who escaped from the MOVE residence, was also named in an arrest warrant and had a legal obligation to surrender to the police.

The remaining three adults, Raymond Foster Africa, Rhonda Ward Africa and Vincent Leaphart (a/k/a John Africa), for whom there were no warrants, also died as a result of the confrontation.

The Police Commissioner did not announce that he had a search warrant for the 6221 Osage Ave. residence.

Two of the adult bodies contained metal fragments which the FBI laboratory and the Commission's pathology expert said were consistent with buckshot pellets or the cores of jacketed or semi-jacketed bullets.

Three other adult bodies contained other types of metal fragments thrust into them by explosions set off during the encounter.

31 THE PERFORMANCE OF THE MEDICAL EXAMINER'S OFFICE WAS UNPROFESSIONAL AND VIOLATED GENERALLY ACCEPTED PRACTICES FOR PATHOLOGISTS.

After the fire, representatives of the Medical Examiner's Office on Osage Avenue violated standard procedures for body recovery and identification and the gathering of evidence at a disaster scene:

- Though it was obvious that bodies were in the rubble of 6221 Osage Ave., the Medical Examiner refused to be present until after the first body was discovered.
- Even after going to Osage Avenue, the pathologists in charge of the investigation failed to coordinate and control the actions of the various agencies which simultaneously were engaged in their own searches for evidence and victims.
- The pathologists did not follow a systematic procedure for uncovering and recording the position of each body. For example, locator stakes were not placed where each body was found; bodies were not numbered or tagged at the scene; no sequential photographic or descriptive record was made of the recovery process. As a result, there was no proper control or custody of the physical remains.

The procedures used, including allowing a crane with a bucket to dig up debris and bodies, resulted in dismemberment, commingling of body parts, and the destruction of important physical and medical evidence.

In the laboratory, the pathologists from the Medical Examiner's Office violated generally accepted practices in the storage, examination and analysis of bodies:

- The facility itself was unclean, and not conducive to disciplined, scientific examination.
- Animals bones were mixed with human remains.
- The bodies were improperly stored at a temperature of 56 degrees, causing accelerated deterioration and the growth of fungus and mold. Recommended storage temperature is 34 to 36 degrees.
- Tissue samples for toxicology tests were not taken until long after the fire, rendering them practically useless in determining the cause of death in most of the cases.
- The pathologists did not take lateral x-rays of the remains, although the equipment and expertise to do so was present. As a result, the pathologists failed to discover metallic fragments, including firearms ammunition, in six of the bodies.

The Medical Examiner's Office failed to identify five bodies, and incorrectly stated the number of dead adults and children.

RECOMMENDATIONS

These recommendations are grouped in six categories:

A) Operation of City Government
B) Operation of the Police Department
C) Police and Fire Department Coordination
D) Local Government Response to Crisis Situations
E) Laws and Regulations
F) Disciplinary Action and Further Investigation

A) Operation of City Government

1 Need for Strategic Planning Process: In anticipation of possible crisis situations, such as MOVE's apparent preparation for a violent confrontation, the Mayor should institute a strategic planning process involving all relevant city agencies. A single high ranking official, reporting directly to the Mayor, should have responsibility for initiating and monitoring strategic planning and adapting it to various threatening situations. The strategic plan should seek in every way to avoid violence and should include guidelines for any tactical or operational plan which may be prepared in response to a threatening, violent incident. (See also Recommendation 24.)

2 Departmental Participation in Strategic Planning and Police Determination: Members of the Mayor's cabinet and commissioners of city departments should participate actively in major policy deliberations and in strategic planning. This participation should be encouraged through regular scheduling of meetings, advance distribution of agenda, preparation of post-discussion policy papers and other devices.

3 Information Collection and Analysis: The City should promptly establish an integrated system for the collection, analysis and appropriate dissemination of relevant information relating to crises which affect public health, safety and welfare. The City Solicitor should have an advisory role in such a system to ensure that civil liberties and rights are respected. Interdepartmental communication should be strengthened to improve operational coordination.

4 Oversight of Police Department: The Mayor, as the city's chief law enforcement officer, and the Managing Director, as his deputy, must provide closer scrutiny of the Police Department. Particularly in police operations requiring major involvement of other city departments, the Mayor must act to ensure compliance with the Mayor's objectives and necessary interdepartmental coordination. A top staff aide of the Mayor should be assigned as full-time liaison with the Police Department.

5 Counsel for Police and Fire Departments: Both the Police and Fire Department require increased legal assistance to guide their operations and their interactions with the public. The Police Department should be assigned legal counsel on a full time basis. Similar legal assistance, at least on a part time basis, should also be made available to the Fire Department.

6 Public Information: The City should develop a program to ensure timely release to the media and the public of accurate information on the city's response during major incidents.

7 Possible Charter Revision: Careful consideration should be given to revision of the City Charter, now 35 years old, directing particular attention to the role of the Managing Director and the practicality of the ten department span of control now mandated by the charter. The reporting relationships of the public safety (Police and Fire) departments should also be carefully evaluated.

8 Medical Examiner's Office: The Commissioner of Health should undertake an immediate review of the Medical Examiner's Office to determine what steps should be taken to enhance the professionalism of the office and to bring its administration and operation into accord with generally accepted practices for pathologists.

B) Operation of the Police Department

9 Public Safety Board: Careful consideration should be given to the appointment by the Mayor of a Public Safety Board composed of city officials, including the Mayor, Managing Director or appropriate Deputy Mayor, President of City Council, City Solicitor, District Attorney and perhaps one or two additional high ranking city officials without direct public safety responsibilities. Such a board could regularly review key policies of the Police and Fire Departments and of other departments with ancillary public safety responsibilities, directing particular attention to tactical plans for crisis situations and the balancing of public safety and civil liberty considerations.

10 Comprehensive Review of the Police Department: The

appointment of a new Police Commissioner provides a timely opportunity for a comprehensive review, utilizing outside experts, of the overall operations of the Philadelphia Police Department, with particular reference to coordination with other city departments, command structure, training, specialized units such as the "bomb squad," professional relationships with other governmental public safety agencies, and relationships with the public.

11 Discretionary Appointments: The Police Commissioner should be permitted to appoint six to ten ranking officers without reference to Civil Service or residency requirements. Officers so appointed should, however, be required to conform to the existing city requirement that they become Philadelphia residents within six months of their appointment.

12 Review of Commissioners' Salaries: The current salary levels of the Police Commissioner, Fire Commissioner and of other commissioners and members of the Mayor's cabinet, should be reviewed to determine whether they are commensurate with the responsibilities and competitive with salaries paid by other major cities.

13 Police Intelligence: Correlated with the city's overall strategy (see Recommendation #1), the Police Department should develop procedures to collect, analyze and disseminate to appropriate city officials, (except where prohibited by law) intelligence and information covertly obtained relative to threatened crisis incidents. The City Solicitor should have, with respect to this activity, the same oversight responsibility outlined in Recommendation #3 to ensure that civil liberties are fully respected in connection with all information or intelligence collection activity.

14 Specialized Training: Energetic and continuing efforts should be mounted to improve the training, particularly specialized technical and sensitivity training, provided officers of the Police Department. Training, on an initial and periodic refresher basis, should be required for police officers who may be engaged in crisis incidents including those requiring specialized knowledge of firearms, intelligence gathering techniques, cultist or terrorist behavior and psychology, barricade or hostage situations. Such training should utilize not only departmental capabilities but the resources, where available, of the FBI and other appropriate governmental agencies.

15 Weapons Control: The Police Department should develop, document and maintain policies and procedures for the selection, use and assignment to police officers of weapons and ammunition in crisis situations. These policies and procedures should provide explicit controls for use of any unusual police weaponry, for example .50 caliber rifles, and should annually be submitted to the Mayor for his review and approval.

16 Use of Explosives: The Police Department should develop, for approval by the Mayor, a comprehensive policy statement outlining the limited circumstances under which use of explosives would be considered. This statement should prohibit offensive use of explosives except in extraordinary circumstances and unless expressly approved in writing by the Mayor based on a written Police Department recommendation.

17 Post Incident Accountability: Complementing Recommendation #15, the Police Department should develop policies and procedures for post-incident audit of use of firearms and of ammunition.

18 Explosives Control: Procedures should be formulated for establishing and maintaining, under high level Police Department supervision, a detailed register of purchase, storage, use and disposition of explosives by type. These procedures should prohibit informal and unauthorized acquisition of explosives and should be enforced through regular and unannounced inspections.

19 Expert Resources on Explosives: The Police Department should maintain a list of agencies and individuals knowledgeable in the use of explosives to permit ready access to expert views in case of need.

20 Assignment of Minority Officers: Since crisis incidents may involve minorities, the Police Department should ensure appropriate assignment of minority police officers to the Department's specialized units and their presence at the scene of incidents.

C) Police and Fire Department Coordination

21 Interdepartmental Coordinating Group: The Mayor, in consultation with the Police and Fire Commissioners, should consider forming an interdepartmental group to review and coordinate the two departments' tactical plans for responding to emergency or crisis incidents which might involve both departments.

22 Fire Hazards: The Fire Department should review and, as necessary, improve its intelligence capabilities to ensure it is fully informed regarding the possibility of fire developing during a crisis situation. All such intelligence should be promptly communicated to the Police Department. Further, the Fire Department should position itself to respond expertly and instantly to any public request regarding existence of possible fire hazards in properties in which the police are considering the use of explosives or other unusual offensive tactics.

23 Communications: As part of an improved government-wide communications capability (see Recommendation #26), the Police and Fire Departments should ensure that they have the ability to communicate, at appropriate command levels, during a crisis.

D) Local Government Response to Crisis Situations

24 Police Tactical Planning: Within the framework of the city's crisis intervention strategy (see Recommendations #1 and #2), the Police Department should prepare tactical plans for application in crisis incidents. Such tactical plans dealing, for example, with hostage or barricade situations, should be formulated through police command channels, should be documented in writing and should be regularly reviewed and updated. All tactical plans should include contingency options. The Mayor should assure himself both with respect to tactical and strategic plans that all means of avoiding use of force have been considered.

25 Consultation with Other Experts: In preparing and monitoring its tactical plans, the Police Department should utilize fully the capabilities and experience of other police departments, federal and state agencies and non-governmental experts.

26 Communications Network: The City should promptly establish a "fail safe" communications system to link key officials at the site of an incident with a nearby command post or posts and with appropriate city officials, including the Mayor, at their City Hall or other offices.

27 Fire Commissioner Responsibility: The Fire Commissioner should be made to understand clearly that it is his and his department's responsibility to fight promptly and extinguish all fires where this can be done without unduly endangering the lives of firefighters. The Mayor should explicitly instruct the Fire Commissioner that no circumstances exist which justify permitting a fire to burn where it can be fought without undue danger to firefighters.

28 Expert Panel: The City should maintain and periodically update a list of experts who could be consulted on short notice in situations involving hostages, cult groups, terrorist organizations, threatened use of explosives or other crisis situations. Appropriate city officials should maintain contact with these experts to insure their ready availability in time of need.

29 Command Responsibility: In any crisis situation, the Mayor should clearly assign to one ranking official responsibility for direction of the entire operation.

E) Laws and Regulations

30 City Solicitor and Court Orders: The City Solicitor should promptly seek court orders for appropriate relief, when necessary, to respond to a violation of a statute, or ordinance or regulation presenting risk to the health and safety of any citizen.

31 Determination of Legal Basis: The City Solicitor in consultation with the Mayor, and other city officials as directed by the Mayor, should develop the legal basis of handling crisis situations so that further legal and operating steps can be taken promptly and on a consistent basis.

32 Protection of Children: The relevant statutes should be amended to require the Department of Health and Human Services, with the assistance of the Police Department, to take into custody any children immediately threatened by a pending police action. The laws should direct the return of the child to his or her natural situation within a reasonable period, unless this clearly presents a danger to the child's safety.

33 Streamlining of Administrative Response to Crisis Situations: The building and zoning codes, health, truancy, and similar regulations should be carefully reviewed and modified, as appropriate, to permit, through use of citations and court powers, effective enforcement without endangering City personnel. For example, provisions should be framed to prevent carrying into a structure materials which clearly will be used to create or aggravate an illegal condition, such as modification of a building without appropriate license.

F) Disciplinary Action and Further Investigation

34 Internal investigations: Internal investigations by the police and other departments, which were started and then suspended, should now be promptly resumed. These investigations should focus

not only on the occurrences of May 13, 1985, but on events com-
mencing January 1, 1984, leading to this incident and on events
during the weeks immediately thereafter. These investigations
should be directed at diagnosing operational shortcomings, institut-
ing corrective actions, assessing individual responsibility and initiating appropriate disciplinary action through standing procedures.

35 Task Force Review: Those city departments which played a role
in the MOVE crisis and which had not already started an investigation should undertake an evaluation of the respective department's
planning or lack of planning and action or inaction related to the May
13, 1985, incident. Again, the objective should be to evaluate operations, determine shortcomings and initiate corrective action.

36 Assessment and Coordination of Reviews: The reports of
the various investigations and reviews covered in the two preceding
recommendations should be forwarded to the Managing Director for
correlation and review prior to submittal to the Mayor for his
analysis and as a basis for personnel actions, organizational restruc-
turing or other actions, as the Chief Executive Officer deems appropriate.

37 Police Officers and the Fifth Amendment: The Mayor and
the Police Commissioner directed all police officers to cooperate with
the Philadelphia Special Investigation Commission by providing
testimony concerning the performance of their assigned duties in
connection with the May 13 incident. Public officials, including
police officers, have a responsibility to describe the performance of
their official duties when so ordered by their superiors. Failure to
comply should be subject to discipline. If appropriate disciplinary
proceedings find that adequate basis exists, the few police officers
who refused to testify before the Commission and represented that
they would invoke their Fifth Amendment privileges should be
dismissed.

38 Law Enforcement Investigations: The ongoing investigations
of the District Attorney and of the United States Department of
Justice should proceed and should include the taking of testimony.
Immunity should be used as appropriate to resolve any open factual
questions, such as the full facts in the choosing, constructing, and
using a bomb, and the full facts as to the nighttime events in the alley
behind 6221 Osage Ave. The taking of testimony is also necessary to
resolve any issues that may arise as to possible perjurious testimony
before the Commission and before any grand jury. The Commission's files will be fully available to law enforcement investigators.

Appendix B
Philadelphia Special Investigation Commission

Dissenting Statement of
Commissioner Bruce W. Kauffman
March 6, 1986

I. The Police Use of Deadly Force

A majority of this Commission has concluded that the police gunfire on the MOVE house on May 13, 1985, was "clearly excessive and unreasonable," and that "[t]he failure of those responsible for the firing to control or stop such an excessive amount of force was unconscionable." (Finding #18). I strongly dissent.

No reasonable analysis of the police use of force on May 13 is possible without first considering the history of the MOVE organization and the circumstances that provoked the City to order 568 police officers to the scene at 6221 Osage Avenue on that day. This Commission has unanimously found:

> That MOVE was an "authoritarian, violence-threatening cult . . . (whose members place[d] themselves above the laws . . . of society . . . [and] threatened violence to anyone who would attempt to enforce normal societal rules." (Finding #1 and Commentary).
>
> That MOVE was an "armed and dangerous" group whose members "used threats, abuse and intimidation to terrify their neighbors and to bring about confrontation with City Government." (Finding #2).
>
> That "[t]he death of Officer Ramp and the wounding of many police and fire fighters in the 1978 clash confirmed

that MOVE members would use deadly force when confronted." (Commentary to Finding #2).

That MOVE publicly acclaimed its 1978 murder of Police Officer James Ramp and made "the repeated threat
that, if the police come to 6221 Osage Ave., 'we'll put a
bullet in your motherfucking heads.' " (Commentary to
Finding #2).

That MOVE "committed violent acts against [its] own
neighbors and threatened violence against public officials
and private citizens." (Commentary to Finding #2).

That MOVE terrorized its neighbors by an "aggressive
display of a weapon." (Commentary to Finding #2).

That MOVE gave "public notice of imminent confronta-
tion" by its construction of a rooftop bunker which gave
MOVE "compelling domination of the neighborhood."
(Commentary to Finding #2).

That MOVE plainly showed that the Mayor's "policy of
appeasement, non-confrontation, and avoidance was
doomed to fail" when MOVE began "barricading its house,
including putting slats on all the windows." (Finding #6
and Commentary).

That MOVE members John Africa and Frank James
"had become increasingly violent and intransigent" and
that there was a "sense of desperation in the MOVE leadership." (Commentary to Finding #6).

That MOVE made its deadly intentions unmistakable
when "[i]n May 1984, a hooded MOVE member appeared
on the roof of 6221 Osage Ave. brandishing a shotgun."
(Commentary to Finding #6).

That "the fortification of the rooftop . . . granted to the
occupants of 6221 Osage Ave. a critical tactical advantage
over the 6200 block of Osage Avenue and over the police."
(Commentary to Finding #8).

That "[d]uring the week preceding the confrontation,
the Mayor, in meetings with top officials, discussed the fact
that bloodshed, and even death, was likely." (Commentary
to Finding #9).

The life-threatening task of confronting this terrorist group
did not fall to social workers or politicians or lawyers. This
dangerous duty was assigned to the police. With the luxury of
hindsight, contemplation and analysis, and without a word of

recognition for individual acts of police heroism, this Commission now presumes to second guess the actions taken under fire by those brave officers. This Commission criticizes both the caliber of the weapons the police carried and the number of bullets they fired. This, to me, is unconscionable.

The police did not precipitate this tragic confrontation. Nor did they make the decision to proceed despite the presence of innocent children in the house. They, at the risk of their very lives, simply acted under orders to enforce the law. The circumstances in which the police may use deadly force are clearly defined:

> (1) A peace officer, or any person whom he has summoned or directed to assist him, need not retreat or desist from efforts to make a lawful arrest because of resistance or threatened resistance to the arrest. He is justified in the use of any force which he believes to be necessary to effect the arrest and of any force which he believes to be necessary to defend himself or another from bodily harm while making the arrest. However, he is justified in using deadly force only when he believes that such force is necessary to prevent death or serious bodily injury to himself or such other person, or when he believes both that:
>
> (i) such force is necessary to prevent the arrest from being defeated by resistance or escape; and
>
> (ii) the person to be arrested has committed or attempted a forcible felony or is attempting to escape and possesses a deadly weapon, or otherwise indicates that he will endanger human life or inflict serious bodily injury unless arrested without delay.
>
> 18 Pa. C.S.A. §508(a)(1).

That the police were entitled to use deadly force on May 13 is manifest. They were attempting to serve lawfully executed warrants upon persons this Commission has found to be armed, dangerous, terroristic, and dedicated to provoking a violent confrontation with authority. When the police approached 6221 Osage, MOVE members announced over a loudspeaker that they would resist arrest with deadly force, that they would kill those who sought to enforce the law, and that they would not come out of the house. Immediately after smoke and gas shells were fired into 6221 Osage, MOVE opened fire on the police. There is no credible evidence that any adult MOVE member was prevented from leaving the house voluntarily. I believe that all those who thus resisted the police on May 13 were guilty of numerous crimes, including aggravated assault (18 Pa. C.S.A. §2702), attempted murder (§§901 *et seq.*, 2502 *et seq.*), riot (§5501), criminal conspiracy (§§903 *et seq.*), terroristic threats (§2706), resisting arrest (§5104), hindering apprehension (§5105), and a variety of weapons offenses (e.g., §§907, 908). Use of deadly force in these circumstances was lawful and appropriate.

The law makes clear that once ordered to serve the warrants, the police were under no obligation to retreat from resisting MOVE members. Any conclusion to the contrary would render law enforcement totally ineffective and invite similar terroristic acts in the future. Given the shots MOVE fired at police, its repeated threats of murdering police, and its prior violent history, no one can seriously question that the police had a reasonable and compelling need to defend themselves.

The legal question aside, this Commission's criticism is unwarranted for other reasons. The police learned a bitter and costly lesson in 1978, when MOVE murdered one officer and injured eight other police and fire personnel. Once the Mayor ordered police again to confront this armed and deadly terrorist organization in 1985, it would have been irresponsible not to take every reasonable precaution to ensure that the tragedy of 1978 was not repeated. As a result, the police rightfully sought to reduce their exposure to death or serious bodily injury. With their concentrated return of MOVE gunfire, the police successfully held the attention of those armed individuals firing from inside the heavily fortified house while other officers attempted to carry out their orders to dislodge MOVE from its fortress through the use of water and tear gas. That this plan was poorly conceived was *not* the fault of the rank and file police officers, virtually none of whom played any role in its formulation.[1] The police simply tried to make the best of

---

1. Of the 568 police officers assigned to 6221 Osage on May 13, only Sergeant Albert Revel and Officer Michael Tursi were at all involved in the plan's formulation.

this impossible situation imposed upon them by the City Administration, and this Commission has unjustly condemned them for that heroic effort.

Moreover, it is apparent that the police gunfire did not result in anyone's death, but, rather, prevented any police or fire personnel from getting killed. The City's Medical Examiner found that those who died were not killed by gunfire, but by smoke inhalation. This Commission's medical expert has testified that he cannot determine the causes of death with certainty, and, therefore, has not offered conclusive proof contradicting the Medical Examiner. Furthermore, Michael Ward testified that all the occupants of the house were alive when the bomb was dropped on the roof of 6221 at approximately 5:27 P.M. (N.T. 10/31/85 at 322). It is undisputed that virtually all police shooting took place long before that time.

I emphasize that this Commission has *not* found that the police were unjustified in the use of *any* deadly force. The majority simply concludes that 10,000 rounds were too many. While assuming the role of critic, the majority does not state how many rounds or what type of weapons would have been appropriate in the battlefield conditions MOVE had created. Would they have approved 5,000 rounds? 2,000? 500? Where would they, through hindsight, draw that arbitrary line? I refuse to join this criticism which is grossly unfair and unwarranted.

II. The Events in the Alley at 7:30 P.M.

The majority of this Commission has found that "[p]olice gunfire prevented some occupants of 6221 Osage Ave. from escaping from the burning house to the rear alley." (Finding #28). I disagree that the evidence supports such a conclusion.

Two sources supplied the Commission with first hand testimony regarding what transpired in the alley: the police in the alley, and Michael Ward. The police have testified consistently that after the bomb was dropped, they fired no shots in the alley, nor did they see or hear other people fire their weapons. Although they heard .22 caliber weapons fire, they believed these shots were fired by MOVE members. (See, e.g., testimony of Officer Louis Mount, Walter Washington, James

Berghaier). Significantly, the noise from the raging fire was so great that some police officers said that they could not hear any shots. (See, e.g., testimony of Officers Terrence Mulvihill and Lawrence D'Ulisse, 10/31/85 at 30-47).

The police also testified consistently regarding surrender attempts of those inside the house. According to the police, there was only one such attempt. Although the officers' versions vary slightly, it appears that at approximately 7:30 P.M., they saw three children and an adult woman leaving the house. Closely following this group was an adult male with a rifle. He fired several shots at the police who did not return fire because of his proximity to the woman and children. (See testimony of Sergeants Donald Griffiths and William Trudel and Officer Markus Barianna, 10/31/85 at 145-65). The evidence to the contrary is far from sufficient to convince me to disbelieve the police.[2]

Michael Ward testified that there were two escape attempts. During the first, Conrad Africa, carrying a child, allegedly was driven back in the house by police gunfire. Significantly, Michael did not actually see this surrender attempt. Rather, he remained inside 6221 and testified that he heard shots after Conrad attempted to leave. Moreover, Michael also testified that he had never heard gunshots before in his life and that he could not tell where the shots were coming from or who was firing them. (See testimony of Michael Ward, 10/31/85 at 323 *et seq.*).

Most significantly, both the police and Michael agreed that when he surrendered, neither he nor the others leaving the house with him were fired upon by anyone. (See testimony of Michael Ward, 10/31/85 at 365-66). This critical fact strongly corroborates the police version of the events in the alley.

Finally, the record clearly confirms that Officer James Berghaier exposed himself to gunfire and risked his life to save Michael from drowning after he fled from 6221. (See testi-

---

2. The Commission correctly notes that some police and fire personnel who were not actually in the alley testified that they thought they might have heard noises that sounded like automatic weapons fire coming from the alley. I do not find this testimony to be persuasive, especially since the fire itself created noises that sounded like gunshots.

mony of Officers James Berghaier and Michael Tursi, 11/1/85 at 107 *et seq.*). This heroic act is totally inconsistent with any police attempt to fire on those MOVE members and children who tried to surrender.

III. Alleged Racism in Decision Making

Without a scintilla of factual support, the majority of this Commission has accused the Mayor, the former Managing Director, the former Police Commissioner, and the Fire Commissioner of racism. I fear that this unfounded accusation will prove needlessly divisive and will profoundly undermine the Commission's credibility.

I have joined with the majority in virtually all of their factual findings, abundantly supported by the evidence, relating to failures of leadership and errors of judgment. Although I deeply respect the sincerity of their beliefs, I cannot join the majority in this exceptionally inflammatory accusation based on nothing but surmise, conjecture, speculation, and suspicion. Mayor Goode may have his shortcomings, but I simply do not believe that he is a racist. Nor do I believe that race was a factor in any of the decisions that he made on or leading up to May 13. The same is true of former Managing Director Brooks, former Police Commissioner Sambor and Fire Commissioner Richmond.

On May 13, 1985, a black Mayor and a black Managing Director were responsible for the City's operation against a black terrorist group holding a black neighborhood hostage. The tragic events of that day were caused, purely and simply, by incompetence, bad judgment, and other errors. These inadequacies know no racial boundaries and, unfortunately, would have resulted in the same tragedy wherever the site of resistance may have been located.[3] Any conclusion that the decisions of that day were racially motivated is offensive, and I will have no part of it. This is particularly true when not a shred of evidence has been produced to substantiate any such extreme conclusion. Indeed, Councilman Lucien Blackwell,

---

3. Indeed, the site of the MOVE confrontation in 1978 was Powelton Village, a racially integrated neighborhood.

who represents the District in which 6221 Osage Avenue is located, testified before this Commission that he did not believe that the tragedy had racial overtones.

> Q. [By Commissioner Kauffman] Councilman Blackwell, you made a statement that I think is very important to the entire perspective of our inquiry, and that is although you originally had a different belief you, at a point in time, came to the view that the problem with MOVE was not a racial problem.
> Are you still of that view, sir?
> A. [By Councilman Blackwell] Yes, sir.
> Q. Thank you, sir.
>   (N.T. 10/22/85 at 112).

I have joined with the majority in condemning the decisions to allow the bunker to be built, to permit the dropping of the bomb, and to let the fire burn. I deplore racism in any form, and would also join with the majority's conclusion on that subject if it were supported by the evidence presented to this Commission. But there is *no* such evidence. The words "racism" and "bigotry" are too easily used today. The mere fact that a decision may adversely affect one ethnic group more than another does not, *per se*, mean the decision maker is a racist or a bigot. Yet, it is plain that the majority's conclusion that the decisions of the Mayor and his top aides were affected by race is based on nothing more than the fact that the MOVE confrontation tragically affected a black neighborhood. Accordingly, I feel compelled to express my emphatic disapproval of the majority's unsupported conclusion that these decisions would not have been made in the same way if the confrontation had occurred in a comparable white neighborhood.

Appendix C
Statement by Ramona Africa, 1988, on the Final Report of the Philadelphia County Special Investigating Grand Jury

ONA MOVE!
ONE OF THE MOST OBVIOUSLY PREJUDICED ASPECTS OF THE
MAY 13 CONFRONTATION IS THE FACT THAT I WAS ARRESTED
IMMEDIATELY, NO QUESTIONS ASKED, NO INVESTIGATION,
NO *NOTHIN*, AND THIS CAN NOT BE CASUALLY EXPLAINED
AWAY BY SAYIN THE POLICE HAD A WARRANT FOR ME
BECAUSE I WAS CHARGED WITH CRIMINAL VIOLATIONS
STEMMIN FROM THE EVENTS OF *MAY 13*, NOT JUST
CHARGES LISTED IN THE WARRANT, POLICE *CLAIM* THEY
CAME TO ARREST ME ON. ON THE OTHER HAND, *NOT ONE*
SINGLE OFFICIAL HAS BEEN ARRESTED FOR *MURDERIN* MY
FAMILY. IF I CAN BE ARRESTED WITHOUT AN
INVESTIGATION WHY CAN'T *OFFICIALS*. WHAT *REALLY*
MAKES US SO BITTER IS THAT *NINE INNOCENT* MOVE
PEOPLE ARE IN PRISON FOR *100* YEARS *EACH* FOR A MURDER
THAT *NOBODY* SAW EM COMMITT, A MURDER THAT NOBODY
CAN *PROVE* THEY COMMITTED, CAUSE THEY DID *NOT*
COMMITT IT. AT THE SAME TIME, THE *WHOLE WORLD* SAW
SYSTEM OFFICIALS DROP THAT *BOMB* ON US, KILLING
ELEVEN INNOCENT MOVE PEOPLE AND THESE OFFICIALS IS
STILL WALKIN THE STREET, STILL EMPLOYED BY THIS

SYSTEM, AND STILL BEIN PAYED WITH TAX DOLLARS TO
KEEP ON MURDERIN MONEY-POOR, UNOFFICIAL POOR
FOLKS. ON TOP OF THIS CRIMINAL ARROGANCE THESE
OFFICIALS HAVE THE NERVE TO SAY THAT MOVE THINK *WE*
ARE "ABOVE THE LAW" BUT IT'S THESE *OFFICIAL*
GANGSTERS WHO IMPOSE LEGALITY ON POOR FOLKS, THEN
IGNORE IT, ARROGANTLY THUMB THEIR NOSE AT LEGALITY
WHEN *THEY* ARE INDICTED BY IT. THESE POLITICAL THUGS
AIN'T GOT NO JUSTIFICATION FOR LOCKIN UP *NOBODY* FOR
MURDER LIKE THEY'RE *AGAINST* MURDER, LIKE THEY'RE
OFFENDED BY MURDER, WHEN *THEIR* HANDS ARE
DRENCHED WITH MOVE PEOPLE'S BLOOD. EVERY POOR
PERSON IN PRISON FOR MURDER SHOULD BE OUT*RAGED*,
SHOULD BE *SCREAMIN* AT THE TOP OF THEIR LUNGS ABOUT
BEIN IN PRISON FOR MURDER WHILE OFFICIALS THAT PUT
THEM IN PRISON FOR MURDER HAVE *THEMSELVES*
COMMITTED *MASS MURDER*. WITNESSED BY THE *WHOLE*
WORLD, AND ARE WALKING THE STREETS LIKE THEY AIN'T
DONE *NOTHIN*, TELLIN POOR FOLKS, "AIN'T *NOBODY* ABOVE
THE LAW, *EVERYBODY* IS SUBJECT TO THE LAW", AND
LOCKIN POOR FOLKS UP DAILY BASED ON THIS FRAUD. ON
MAY 13, POLICE COMMISSIONER SAMBOR CAME OUT TO OUR
HOUSE TALKIN ABOUT, "ATTENTION MOVE, THIS IS
AMERICA," AND FOLLOWED THAT COMMENT UP WITH
SOME RHETORIC ABOUT HOW WE *HAVE TO* ACCEPT AND
OBEY THE LAWS OF AMERICA. SAMBOR IS SO FULL OF HATE
AND *PREJUDICE* THAT HE COULDN'T REALIZE WHAT HE WAS
SAYIN, BECAUSE WHILE HE WAS TALKIN ABOUT, "THIS IS
AMERICA" HE DIDN'T REALIZE THAT ACCORDIN TO *HIS*
BELIEF, AMERICA WAS DEVELOPED BY *REBELS, RESISTERS*,
THAT *REFUSED* TO ACCEPT THE LEGAL LAWS OF THAT TIME
BECAUSE THEY INTERPRETED THOSE LAWS AS *OPPRESSIVE,*
UNJUST, WRONG. THOSE RESISTERS WENT TO *WAR* WITH
THE GOVERNMENT AND SHOT DOWN A WHOLE LOT OF

POLICE CALLED "REDCOATS" (ENGLISH SOLDIERS), BUT
SAMBOR-AND MANY OTHERS-CELEBRATE THOSE REBELS AS
HEROS, FREEDOM FIGHTERS WHILE *CONDEMIN* MOVE AS
TERRORIST, CRIMINALS. WHAT MAKES GEORGE WASHINGTON
A HERO FOR RESISTIN *LEGAL IN*JUSTICE AND MOVE PEOPLE
CRIMINALS FOR RESISTIN *LEGAL IN*JUSTICE. DO YOU KNOW
WHAT WOULD HAVE HAPPENED IF SAMBOR LIVED IN 1775
AS A POLICEMAN, AN ENGLISH SOLDIER, AND HE
APPROACHED NATHAN HALE OR PATRICK HENRY'S HOUSE
LIKE HE DID OUR HOUSE, TALKIN ABOUT, "ATTENTION
PATRICK, THIS IS AN ENGLISH COLONY, YOU *HAVE TO*
ACCEPT AND OBEY THE LAWS OF ENGLAND," SAMBOR
WOULD HAVE GOTTEN A BULLET IN HIS HEAD, *QUICK*, AND
THE REBEL THAT PUT THE BULLET IN HIS WORTHLESS
HEAD WOULD BE CELEBRATED TODAY AS AN *AMERICAN
HERO*. THIS IS THE PROFOUND WISDOM OF MOVE'S LOVED
FOUNDER, *JOHN AFRICA THE COORDINATOR. LONG LIVE THE
COORDINATOR JOHN AFRICA!!!* THESE OFFICIAL HOODLUMS
ARE THE MASTERS OF DECEPTION AND JUDGE STILES IS A
CRYSTALLIZED EXAMPLE OF THIS. ON APRIL 14, 1986 I WAS
FORMALLY SENTENCED, I SAY *FORMALLY* SENTENCED
BECAUSE THAT'S ALL IT WAS, A *FORMALITY*. *JOHN AFRICA*
HAS EQUIPPED ME WITH THE UNDERSTANDIN TO SEE THAT
I WAS *TRIED, CONVICTED*, AND SENTENCED (TO DIE) ON MAY
13. *NOTHIN* JUDGE STILES COULD IMPOSE ON ME COULD
COMPARE TO WHAT WAS IMPOSED ON ME MAY 13. SOME
PEOPLE *HALLUCINATED* THAT JUDGE STILES IS *FAIR* BECAUSE
OF HIS DECEPTIVE MANNER BUT THANKS TO *JOHN AFRICA*,
I WAS NOT FOOLED ONE BIT BY STILES, HIS POSITION WAS
CLEAR TO ME FROM THE VERY BEGINNIN-*LONG LIVE JOHN
AFRICA THE COORDINATOR!* I KNEW THAT STILES COULD
HAVE, WAS *LEGALLY OBLIGATED* TO DISMISS *ALL* THE
CHARGES AGAINST ME DURING THE PRETRIAL PERIOD
WHEN STILES *ONLY* DISMISSED THE CHARGES LISTED IN

THE WARRANT THE POLICE *CLAIMED* TO HAVE COME OUT
TO ARREST ME ON-WHICH MEANS THE POLICE HAD *NO*
REASON TO BE ARRESTIN ME IN THE FIRST PLACE,
ACCORDING TO STILES RULIN. THE POINT BEING MADE IS
THAT *ALL* THE CHARGES AGAINST ME WERE *IN*VALID AND
SHOULD HAVE BEEN DISMISSED, NOT JUST THE CHARGES
LISTED IN THE INITIAL WARRANT, AND IF STILES IS FAIR
INSTEAD OF *POLITICAL*, HE *WOULD* HAVE DISMISSED *ALL*
THE CHARGES. JUDGE STILES HAD PLENTY OF
OPPORTUNITIES TO DISMISS THOSE OUTRAGEOUS CHARGES,
NOT AS A *FAVOR* TO ME, NOT TO *APPEASE* ANYBODY AND
NOT AS A *MORAL* OBLIGATION, BUT AS HIS *LEGAL
OBLIGATION*, HOWEVER STILES DIDN'T DISMISS *ALL* THE
CHARGES, HE *REFUSED* TO DO IT, BECAUSE HE AIN'T *RITE*,
HE AIN'T *FAIR*, HE'S *POLITICAL*. JUDGE STILES AND ALL
THOSE THAT WANT TO PROTECT HIM AND CONTINUE
BELIEVIN IN THIS FILTHY SYSTEM MITE *TRY* TO ARGUE
THAT I AM IN PRISON BECAUSE THE JURY CONVICTED ME OF
TWO CHARGES AND *NOT* BECAUSE OF *STILES* BUT THAT'S A
LIE. *DISPITE* THE JURY'S VERDICT JUDGE STILES DID *NOT*
HAVE TO KEEP ME IN PRISON, HE COULD HAVE GIVEN ME
TIME SERVED OR A *SUSPENDED SENTENCE*. IN FACT IF
JUDGE STILES IS *FAIR* THE CASE NEVER WOULD HAVE
GOTTEN TO THE JURY DELIBERATION, BECAUSE STILES
COULD HAVE DISMISSED THOSE CHARGES AT THE *PRE*-TRIAL
STAGE, AT THE DEMURER STAGE WHEN THE PROSECUTOR
FINISHED PRESENTIN HIS CASE, AT THE END OF MY
DEFENSE OR JUDGE STILES COULD HAVE ACQUITTED ME
HISSELF BY *DIRECTED* VERDICT WITHOUT THE JURY HAVIN
TO DELIBERATE AT ALL AS JUDGE STANLEY KUBACKI DID
IN THE CASE OF THE 3 COPS WHO TRIED TO BEAT MY
BROTHER DELBERT AFRICA TO DEATH ON AUGUST 8, 1978.
EVEN *AFTER* I WAS *UN*JUSTLY CONVICTED OF RIOT AND
CONSPIRACY TO RIOT JUDGE STILES COULD HAVE

OVERTURNED THE CONVICTIONS BY WHAT'S CALLED AN
"ARREST OF JUDGEMENT," BUT STILES DIDN'T DO ANY OF
THIS BECAUSE HE HAD NO INTENTION OF *BEIN RITE, BEIN
FAIR*. THE *ONLY* THING JUDGE STILES INTENDED TO DO
WAS KEEP ME IN PRISON, AND THIS IS CLEAR BY THE
DRAMATICALLY HIGH BAIL HE KEPT ON ME AND
PARTICULARLY BY THE SENTENCE HE IMPOSED. STILES
SENTENCED ME TO 16 MOS.-7 YRS. AS A DECEPTIVE
MANEUVER TO BOTH PACIFY THOSE THAT ARE OUTRAGED
ABOUT THE BLATENT MURDER OF MOVE PEOPLE AND
DEMANDING MY RELEASE AS WELL AS *OFFICIALS* THAT
WANT ME IN PRISON BECAUSE OF *POLITICS*. PRIOR TO MY
FORMAL SENTENCIN, THE NEWS MEDIA REPEATEDLY
ADVERTISED MY POSSIBLE SENTENCE AS UP TO 7-14 YRS.,
EVEN THO' I WAS REALLY FACING 3 1/2-7 YEARS BECAUSE
LEGALLY I COULD ONLY BE SENTENCED ON THE RIOT
CHARGE SINCE THE *LEGAL* DEFINITION OF RIOT *INCLUDES*
THE CONCEPT OF CONSPIRACY, *THE* CHARGE OF *CONSPIRACY
TO RIOT* MERGED WITH THE RIOT CHARGE. THE POINT IS
THAT SINCE THE MEDIA MADE PEOPLE BELIEVE THAT I WAS
FACIN *MORE* TIME THAN I REALLY WAS, PEOPLE
INTERPRETED THE 16 MOS TO 7 YRS. AS A "LITE
SENTENCE", ESPECIALLY SINCE I HAD *11* MOS. ALREADY
SERVED BY THE TIME I WAS SENTENCED, ALONG WITH THE
FACT THAT PEOPLE WERE DELIBERATELY GIVEN THE
IMPRESSION THAT I WOULD BE HOME IN A FEW MONTHS.
IT'S A VERY OLD CON GAME THAT THIS SYSTEM WORKED
THRU THE MEDIA, PEOPLE WILL *THINK* THEY GOT A
"BARGAIN" BY PAYIN *"ONLY"* $5.00 FOR SOMETHIN THAT WAS
ADVERTISED AS SELLIN FOR $10.00 JUST BECAUSE THEY
BELIEVE THE OBJECT TO BE SELLIN FOR *MORE* THAN THEY
PAID FOR IT, BUT WHEN THEY REALIZE THE OBJECT THEY
BELIEVED WAS WORTH $10.00 AND PAID *$5.00* FOR AIN'T
EVEN WORTH *ONE* DOLLAR, THEN PEOPLE KNOW THEY

DIDN'T GOT NO *BARGAIN*, THEY GOT *RIPPED OFF.* I *KNOW* I'M COMPLETELY *INNOCENT*, I *KNOW* I DON'T BELONG IN PRISON *AT ALL*, SO I KNOW I'M NOT GETTIN NO *BARGAIN.* NO "LITE" SENTENCE-THANKS ONLY TO THE WISDOM OF *THE COORDINATOR* I'M NOT FALLIN VICTIM TO THAT DEVIOUS CON GAME BEIN RUN BY THE PROFESSIONAL CON ARTISTS IN *CITY HALL, HARRISBURG, THE WHITE HOUSE-LONG LIVE THE COORDINATOR!* PEOPLE ARE *DIVERTED*, BY THAT 16 MONTH MINIMUM SENTENCE, AND THEY'RE IGNORIN THAT 7 YEARS MAXIMUM THAT FOLLOWS IT-IT'S NOT THERE FOR *NOTHIN.* COMPLETIN A *MINIMUM* SENTENCE DOES *NOT* GUARANTEE PAROLE THAT'S WHY YOU HAVE A *MAXIMUM* SENTENCE. *MINIMUM* SENTENCES DON'T MEAN A THING, *ESPECIALLY* WITH *MOVE* PEOPLE, THAT THEM POLITICIANS DON'T WANT *ALIVE*, NOT TO MENTION *ON THE STREET.* MY SISTER, SUE AFRICA, WAS SENTENCED TO 6-12 YRS. AND SHE'S BEEN IN PRISON A TOTAL OF 7 YEARS. MY SISTER ALBERTA AFRICA WAS SENTENCED TO 22 MOS.-7 YRS. AND SHE'S BEEN IN PRISON 6 1/2 YEARS ALREADY, SO OBVIOUSLY MINIMUM SENTENCES DON'T MEAN ANYTHIN WHEN IT COMES TO MOVE. WHEN THIS SYSTEM'S OFFICIALS COME AT MOVE PEOPLE WITH PRISON SENTENCES OR ANYTHING ELSE THEY ARE THINKIN OF ONE THING, *STOPPIN* THE MOVE ORGANIZATION, *STOPPIN JOHN AFRICA*, BUT THEY WILL *NEVER* STOP *JOHN AFRICA.*

Index